MOVING FORWARD AND MAKING A DIFFERENCE

MOVING FORWARD AND MAKING A DIFFERENCE

7 Keys to Unleashing Positive & Progressive Principles to Fulfill Your Purpose in Life

ARTHUR L. MACKEY JR.

Moving Forward and Making a Difference: 7 Keys to Unleashing Positive & Progressive Principles to Fulfill Your Purpose in Life
by Arthur L. Mackey Jr.

Cover Design by Atinad Designs.

© Copyright 2014, Arthur L. Mackey, Jr.

SAINT PAUL PRESS, DALLAS, TEXAS

First Printing, 2014

All rights reserved. No part of this publication may be reproduced, stored in a retrieval system, or transmitted in any form or by any means, electronic, mechanical, photocopying, recording, or otherwise, without the prior permission of the copyright owner, except for brief quotations included in a review of the book.

Unless otherwise noted, Scripture quotations are from the King James Version of the Bible. All rights reserved worldwide.

ISBN-10: 0991585666
ISBN-13: 978-0991585663

Printed in the U.S.A.

Dedication

I dedicate this book to my wife of more than twenty one years, my baby, Brenda.

Contents

Introduction   17
    Moving Forward After Hurricane Sandy

PART I
MOVING FORWARD WITH THE PLAN

CHAPTER ONE   25
    Moving Forward—
    Tapping Into the Year of Influence

CHAPTER TWO   37
    Moved With the Fear of God—
    Noah Made a Major Difference

CHAPTER THREE   47
    Go Forward—God's Exit Strategy

CHAPTER FOUR   67
    Moving Forward In Inter-generational Ministry—
    "We Will Go"

CHAPTER FIVE   83
    Moved at the Presence of God—
    When God Marches Through the Wilderness

CHAPTER SIX   99
    Making A Difference by Setting Forward & Raising the
    Standard—What Flag Are You Marching Under?

CHAPTER SEVEN   115
    Leaders, Learners, and Levites—Go After It

PART II
MOVING FORWARD THROUGH THE PAIN

CHAPTER EIGHT   129
   Moving Forward from Prostitution to Proclamation—
   The Scarlet Thread of Redemption

CHAPTER NINE   141
   Moving Forward In the Power of Friendship—
   The True Test of Friendship

CHAPTER TEN   167
   Moving Forward In a Backwards World—
   Life on the Left Hand of God

CHAPTER ELEVEN   179
   Moving Forward in Praise Inspite of Pain—
   The Mandate of the Palm Tree Christian

PART III
MOVING FORWARD WITH THE PRINCE OF PEACE

CHAPTER TWELVE   195
   Moving Forward With Meaning—
   The Impact of the Forward Dream

CHAPTER THIRTEEN   203
   Moving Forward With the Conviction of Communion—
   The 7 Principles of Communion

CHAPTER FOURTEEN   219
   Moving Forward and Making a Difference—
   The Ministry of Compassion

CHAPTER FIFTEEN   241
   Moving Forward In Worship—
   The Woman, The Water, and The Well

PART IV
MOVING FORWARD WITH PRACTICAL TEACHING

CHAPTER SIXTEEN   259
    Moving Forward With You-Ward Grace—
    Shout-out for the Shutout

CHAPTER SEVENTEEN   267
    Moving Forward for This Cause—
    Bear Witness To The Truth

CHAPTER EIGHTEEN   291
    Moving Forward With Love—
    Prove the Sincerity of Your Love

CHAPTER NINETEEN   303
    Moving Forward for the Health of the Church—
    Overcoming Spiritual Illnesses, Injuries,
    Instabilities, & Impairments

PART V
MOVING FORWARD WITH PASSION

CHAPTER TWENTY   325
    Making A Difference By How We Walk, Stand, and Sit—
    Moving Forward In spite of Negativity

CHAPTER TWENTY-ONE   343
    Moving Forward In Operation Evangelism—
    Equipping The Church to Carry Out Christ's Commission

CHAPTER TWENTY-TWO   353
    The Forward Journey—Learning From the Elder, the
    Encourager, the Ego Maniac, and the Excellent Example

PART VI
MOVING FORWARD WITH PURPOSE

CHAPTER TWENTY-THREE   365
    The Forward Mindset—Be Ready
CHAPTER TWENTY-FOUR   375
    The Forward Drive—It Is Well
CHAPTER TWENTY-FIVE   385
    The Forward Proclamation—Move Forward
CHAPTER TWENTY-SIX   399
    The Forward Mission—The Struggle Continues
CHAPTER TWENTY-SEVEN   415
    The Forward Fight—Fighting To Win

PART VII
MOVING FORWARD THROUGH THE IMPOSSIBILITIES OF LIFE

CHAPTER TWENTY-EIGHT   427
    The Forward Flight—
    The Strength To Move Straight Forward
CHAPTER TWENTY-NINE   439
    The Forward Fall—The Suicide of Saul
CHAPTER THIRTY   457
    The Forward Walk—The Valley Walker
CHAPTER THIRTY-ONE   465
    When Forgiveness Makes The Difference—
    Forgiveness Sets the Spirit, Soul, and Body Free

Do You Know Jesus Christ as Your Savior?   473

About the Author   477

Acknowledgements

I would like to express special thanks to God, the Father; God, the Son – Jesus, and God – The Holy Ghost. Without God I could never exist or move at all. I only move forward today after two strokes, because of the grace of God. To my wife, Elder Brenda Jackson Mackey, and our three children, Yolanda, Jordan, and Faith Mackey, thank you for your constant support and encouragement. You are the foundational team that makes the difference and inspires the rest of the team to do the same. Special thanks to my mother, living legend, Dr. Frances W. Mackey of Barto, Florida, and her well known, worldwide More Than Tea Ministries. Special thanks to Elder Vivian Mackey Johnson and Elder Moses Johnson and family of Orlando, Florida. Special thanks to Pastors Frances Mackey Woodside and Tyrone Woodside and family of Winter Haven, Florida. Special thanks to the Mackey and Williams family. To the members of Mount Sinai Baptist Church Cathedral of Roosevelt, New York, God bless you richly. Special thanks to the MSBCC Ministerial Staff - Elder Brenda, Elder Constance Todd, Elder Lester Mackey, Evangelist Terrina Leach, Evangelist Virginia Shim, Rev. Daryl Smith, Minister In Training Sheinedra Leach, Minister In Training Faith Mackey, and Minister In Training Jordan Mackey. Special thanks to Deacon Aaron Scott Jr. and the members of the Deacon Ministry. Special thanks to Trustee James Hodges and the members of the Trustee Ministry. Special thanks to Deaconess Doris Peacock and the members of the Deaconess Ministry. Special thanks to Trustee Margaret Thompson and Sis. Gertha Sawyer and the

Nursing Home Ministry. Special thanks to President Doris Amar and the members of the Missionary Ministry. Special thanks to President Gladys Aycock and the members of Usher's Ministry. Special thanks to Deacon Scott and the Men's Ministry. Special thanks to Deaconess Ernestine Toliver and the Prayer Partner's and the Women's Ministry. Special thanks to Church School Superintendent Deaconess Irene Carter. Special thanks to Youth Director Todd and the members of the Youth Ministry. Special thanks to President Edna Curry and the Voices of Mount Sinai. Special thanks to Brother Dermot Sutherland and the members of the Mentoring Program. Special thanks to every one in the New Members Class. The ministry of Mount Sinai Baptist Church Cathedral of Roosevelt, New York, is moving forward and making a difference every day.

Special thanks to the Mount Sinai Development Corporation Board Members, Executive Director Harold Hamilton Sr., Secretary Edna Curry, Book Keeper Debbie Woodside, Public Relations Rep. Donovan Gordon, and Attorney Michael Williams. Mount Sinai Development Corporation is moving forward and making a difference every day.

Special thanks to the I Support Roosevelt Youth Center of Long Island, Inc. Board Members, Executive Director Harold Hamilton Sr., Secretary Edna Curry, Deacon David Alves, Brother Brick, Public Relations Rep. Donovan Gordon, and Attorney Michael Williams. I Support Roosevelt Youth Center of Long Island, Inc. is moving forward and making a difference every day.

Special thanks to Brother Jacob Dixon and Tutoring Program at I Support Roosevelt Youth Center. Brother Jacob Dixon and Tutoring Program are moving forward and making a difference every day.

Special thanks to Deacon Hamilton, Brother Brick, and Brother Lee

Street for keeping Friday Night Live alive and well every night. Countless young people have graduated and gone on to college and or trade school and got jobs, because you believed in them. Friday Night Live staff you helped to make to vision God gave me a reality. Fright Night Live staff you are moving forward and making a difference every day. Also special thanks to the student volunteers from Hofstra University. Thank you for running the brand new Mentoring Program every Friday.

Special thanks to the Instructors and members of the Self Defense Program at I Support Roosevelt Youth Center. The Instructors and members of the Self Defense Program at I Support Roosevelt Youth Center are moving forward and making a difference every day.

Special thanks to Sis. Mary and the Feeding Program on every Monday morning at 9:00a.m. at MSBCC. Special thanks to Trustee Hodges introducing me to Sis. Mary. Special thanks to Deaconess Toliver and the Feeding Program every Sunday morning at MSBCC after Church School. The Weekly Feeding Programs is moving forward and making a difference every day.

Special thanks to all of the daily and weekly volunteers at Mount Sinai Baptist Church Cathedral, I Support Roosevelt Youth Center of Long Inc., and Mount Sinai Development Corporation. Volunteers you are moving forward and making a difference every day.

Special thank to all of the special events volunteers for the Summer Explosion, Christmas Toy Give-A-Way, Harvest Festival, and the Thanksgiving Day Dinner for the Community. Special event volunteers from all over the local community, state, and nation you are moving forward and making a difference every day.

Special thanks to Mrs. Dixon of Fresh Eyes Proofreading & Editing for your help and assistance since the inception of this book project. Special thanks to Thea of Black Christian Promo for helping to spread the word worldwide. Special thanks to St. Paul Press of Dallas, Texas. It is an honor to work with your company.

Special thanks to Proffesor Serge Martinez and the Staff of the Hofstra University Law Clinic. Your wisdom and insight made all the difference. Special thanks to Attorney Lance Clarke. You have been with us for more than thirty years. You are and mover and a shaker.

Special thanks to Bishop J. Raymond Mackey, Pastor Thomas Bryant, Pastor Donnie McClurkin, Bishop Ronald Carter, Bishop Frank White, Rev. Eric Mallette, Rev. Philip McDowell, Pastor Tyrone Kay, Pastor Darren Brandon, Bishop Orlando Wlson, Pastor Thomas Nins, Pastor Ricardo Hendricks, Bishop Fabian Williams and Executive Pastor Regina Williams, Rev. Willie Reid, Pastor Sylestro Gerald, Pastor Daryl Bass and First Lady Annette Williams Bass, Bishop and Prophetess Pippens, Rev. Ronald Simpkins, Rev. William Watson, Pastor Donnie Baker, and all the distinguished members of the clergy.

Special thanks to Town of Hempstead Supervisor Kate Murray, Councilmembers Anthony J. Santino, Angie M. Cullin, Dorothy L. Goosby, Gary Hudes, James Darcy, Edward A. Ambrosino, Town Clerk Nasin Ahmad, and Receiver of Taxes Donald X. Clavin Jr. Special thanks to Director of Communications and Public Affairs Mike Deery and Staff Members in the Department of Communications and Public Affairs.

Special thanks to Brother Don Roberts, Walking Trustee Jeff Chitty, the Scott family, the Leach & Horsey family, the Todd family, Uncle

Alfred, Aunt Josephine, and Sister Virginia Jones. Thanks for being there. Special thanks to my long time friends, Elder Dorian Joyner and Pastor Michael Burns. Your friendship has made a major difference in my life.

Special thanks to Pam Perry for her awesome words of wisdom over the years. You are America's foremost success coach.

Introduction

Moving Forward After Hurricane Sandy

Let's be honest, most of us underestimate forecasts for storms, but after October 29, 2012, I will never do that again. That was the day Hurricane Sandy, better known as Super Storm Sandy, hit the eastern seaboard, especially in the tri-state area. Little did I know, the thirteenth anniversary of the earthly loss of my father due to complications from colon cancer would foreshadow the astronomical loss of people's lives from Hurricane Sandy. A hurricane is a large tropical storm with extremely intense winds. Still, I did not expect the storm to span 1,100 miles for it to be considered the second costliest hurricane in U.S. history.

When I got up that particular morning, got washed up and dressed for work, I looked out the window and noticed that as early as 8:00 a.m., the high tide waters from the ocean right behind our house were already flooding my block. The forecast was for the super storm to begin later that evening. By the time I went to our car to go to work, the ice cold salt water was already past my knees.

I went to work soaking wet. It was not until after work, when I had returned home that I remembered that my mother-in-law who was in town visiting, would have to walk through the high tide waters to get out of our house. My wife, Brenda, and I decided that it would be better for her to remain where she was. New York State Governor Cuomo and New York City Mayor Bloomberg were also on television stating that if anyone had not evacuated at that point, it would be safer to stay where they were than to risk one's life.

By 6:00 p.m. the winds were strong. At 8:00 p.m. the now 89 miles an hour winds knocked out all electricity in the area. The water from the ocean flooded our streets. My block and the surrounding area looked like the ocean itself. Brenda, my mother-in-law, Elder Bessie Jackson, and I saw large boats floating down the street as we looked out the window. Transformers began to explode. Some of our neighbor's houses burned to the ground.

The alarm on our car went off and would not stop. Then all of a sudden, the car alarm ended. Our car was covered under eight feet of salt water. The basement began to fill up with salt water from the sea and the water began to rise up the stairs on the inside; it went right up to the top step of the high rise house outside. I declared, "Water, you will come no further in Jesus' name."

The raging winds almost blew out the large first floor window. With water already rushing in the basement and up the stairs, the large first floor window being blown out would have meant total destruction for the house. We leaned against the window with all the pressure we could apply and put more duct tape on it. Thankfully, our children slept through the storm.

The next morning, the winds calmed down, the waters receded, and destruction was all around. Ships were on some of the lawns. All our lights were out. We had no heat. Power lines were down and many were on fire. Gas lines were literally miles long. We had to go on odd and even days to get gas in New York. Garages were in other neighbors' front yards. The famous Jones Beach Board Walk was destroyed. The Statue of Liberty had just reopened and now its beloved Ellis Island and Liberty Island were completely demolished. The Freeport Nautical Mile was destroyed. The original Famous Nathan's Restaurant in Brooklyn was totally ruined. Many lost all that they owned in one night throughout the tri-state area. That changed it all. Yet there was an inner yearning to revive, repair, and even rebuild. Once more, God spared our lives in the worst storm experienced in modern history in the tri-state area.

Brenda and I and so many others were determined to honor the memory of those who lost their lives, and by the grace of God, somehow, move forward.

On Valentine's Day of 2013, Brenda and I moved forward and renewed our wedding vows after twenty years of marriage and three children. We were one of eleven Long Island couples whose lives were affected by Hurricane Sandy who renewed their marriage vows at the newly refurbished Bridgeview Yacht Club in Island Park that was also destroyed by the hurricane. Supervisor, Kate Murray, leader of the Town of Hempstead, America's largest township, and the hardest hit by Hurricane Sandy, performed the renewal of all twelve Hurricane Sandy survivors one by one.

Moving Forward Through the Storm

When Deacon Aaron Scott Jr., the current Chairman of the Deacon Board at Mount Sinai Baptist Church Cathedral in Roosevelt, New York, was a youth, he got off of work late one night. That night there was a tremendous snow storm. It was dark. Everything was shut down. He had no one to ride him home to Roosevelt. So he walked from West Hempstead where he worked all the way to

Roosevelt which was miles away. The snow storm was so bad that he could have froze to death. He stayed alive in the severe snow storm by moving forward, walking and not stopping. Moving forward in the severe snow storm, keeping it moving in the severe snow storm kept him warm and kept him alive. Moving forward literally made the difference.

From Genesis to Revelation, the moving forward and making a difference message is clearly declared and decreed. In **Genesis 1:1**, we learn that God is the originator of the moving forward and making a difference message. God is positively progressive and certainly creative for the text states that, **"In the beginning God created the heaven and the earth."**

In **Genesis 1:2**, we are told that the Spirit of our God moved upon the face of the waters, the creation canvas of unfinished masterpieces. The text declares, **"And the earth was without form, and void; and darkness was upon the face of the deep. And the Spirit of God moved upon the face of the waters."**

In **Genesis 1:3**, the one and only Light of the World, Jesus Christ, gave light on the first day of creation long before the sun or moon were made on the fourth day. The text tells us, **"And God said, Let there be light: and there was light."**

This same Jesus, the Lamb slain before the foundation of the world was laid, moved to earth, and came down through forty-two generations. Jesus moved the plan forward down here on earth, being born of the Virgin Mary; He moved forward and had favor with both God and man; He moved forward and was baptized by His cousin, John the Baptist; He moved forward and taught, preached, and healed in a ministry that lasted three and a half years (forty-two months); He moved forward and died on the cross for all of our sins past, present, and future; He moved forward and rose from the dead; and He moved forward and ascended to the right hand of the Father where He is making intercession for the saints. The Apostle John summed up the epitome of the moving forward message by quoting Jesus when he expressed his longing to see Jesus again in Revelation 22:20, which states, **"He which testifieth these things saith, Surely I come quickly. Amen. Even so, come, Lord Jesus."**

Part 1

MOVING FORWARD WITH THE PLAN

CHAPTER ONE

MOVING FORWARD – TAPPING INTO THE YEAR OF INFLUENCE

Genesis 26:12-14:
"Then Isaac sowed in that land, and received in the same year an hundredfold: and the Lord blessed him. And the man waxed great, and <u>went forward</u>, and grew until he became very great: For he had possession of flocks, and possession of herds, and great store of servants: and the Philistines envied him."

I spent seven long years of prayer, planning, being patient, and being persistent in preparation through many meetings and countless detailed documents so that I could sign as Chairman of the Mount Sinai Development Corporation (MSDC). I signed only after an intense and complete lawyer review for a major project known as the Mother Barbara Lee Scott Senior Housing and Workforce Housing funded by the federal government and administered through Nassau County government in New York. After seven long years working closely with Mount Sinai Development Corporation Executive Director Harold Hamilton, Sr. (a leading green technology expert), Hofstra University Law Clinic, the federal government, Nassau County, and the Town of Hempstead, on April 29, 2013, which would have been my father's 75th birthday, I received a contract for the Mount Sinai Development Corporation for $85,000.00 to cover the soft cost for the project. The soft cost consists of the fees for the attorney, architect, appraiser, and project consultant. MSDC Board Member and our Public Relations Representative Donovan Gordon (a former BET Executive and a leading green technology expert) brought me the updated contract which I signed and had notarized by Joni Blenn.

MSDC Board Member Donovan Gordon and Executive Director Harold Hamilton, Sr., immediately took the signed and notarized document to Nassau County and the county immediately gave them a contract for $1.7 million not to exceed $2 million to purchase the land, sub divide the land, and build the Mother Barbara Lee Scott Senior Housing and Workforce Housing with construction work done for free by Habitat for Humanity. I did not sign that document until Attorneys Lance Clarke, Mike Williams, and Lester Wayne Mackey, Sr., reviewed the 65-page document. After the lawyers reviewed it and gave the green light, I signed the document and Joni Blenn notarized it on April 29, 2013. The project was now moving forward from vision to reality. The process was well on its way after seven years of prayer, planning, patience, and persistence (the 4P's). The following week, the Mount Sinai Development Corporation Board, the Mount Sinai Baptist Church, Inc. Board, the Habitat for Humanity Board, and world renowned Architect Angelo Corva were meeting with Town of Hempstead Chairman of Staff Ray Mineo, Planning & Economic Development Commissioner, Building Commissioner John Rottkamp, Building Department Senior Advisors Lou Carnevale and Fred Jawitz (who I worked with on several other building projects for the church and the community). Mount Sinai Baptist Church Cathedral Chairman of the Trustee Board James A. Hodges advised the separate Mount Sinai Development Corporation on getting the required insurance for the newly funded Mother Barbara Lee Scott Senior Housing and Workforce Housing Project. Hodges worked with MSDC Executive Director Hamilton and got the insurance set up so the corporation could move forward to build, rebuild, restore, and revive in Roosevelt, the vicinity, and beyond.

We had sowed in that land over the years. My father and my

grandfather, Rev. Walter Mackey, Sr., who built the Mount Sinai Baptist Church literally with his bare hands had sowed in that land long before me. His sons and colleagues who helped him construct Mount Sinai Baptist Church sowed in that land as well. When I first became Senior Pastor of Mount Sinai Baptist Church Cathedral in Roosevelt, New York, the day after my mentor, spiritual father, and natural father, Rev. Dr. Arthur L. Mackey, Sr., Nassau County's premier Civil and Human Rights leader with national and international impact passed away, I chose to honor them because they deserve to be honored. Not long after becoming pastor, it was announced by New York State Education Commissioner Richard Mills that he was going to close all the schools in Roosevelt, New York.

The Sunday morning after hearing this alarming news, the spirit of prophecy moved within my spirit, soul, and body. I pointed toward the school and prophetically declared and decreed that the schools would not be closed, but that new schools would be built at a time when hardly any new schools were being built in the nation. Then the Spirit of God moved further in my spirit, soul, and body, and led me to take the whole congregation outside and prophetically decree and declare that the Mother Barbara Lee Scott Senior Housing and Workforce Housing Project would be built. At this time, the Mount Sinai Baptist Church Cathedral Church Mother, Barbara Lee Scott, a legend in her own right, the Mother Teresa of Roosevelt, was still alive. Many people thought that I was absolutely insane, but the faithful stayed the course with their new pastor, with their Joshua.

It was not easy, because now I had to commit myself to corresponding action every single day, because faith without works is dead. So after praying all night I went to work at my job at the Town of Hempstead Town Hall in the Department of

Communications, and on my lunch break, I called the then New York State Department of Education Commissioner Richard Mills. He returned my call. I was shocked. Then the Spirit of the Lord moved in my spirit, soul, and body, and began to prophetically declare and decree that New York State Department of Education would not close the schools in Roosevelt. Rather the New York State Department of Education would build new schools in Roosevelt.

Every single day for several years, I asked people by petition, email, in church services, and in meeting announcements to call the New York State Department of Education Commissioner Richard Mills' office and demand that the community's debt be forgiven and new schools be built in Roosevelt which had been socially and economically raped and robbed for way too long. I sent out these emails everyday locally and nationwide to also simultaneously encourage others in the nation who might face the same types of challenges in their community to move forward and engage the system speaking truth to power. New York State Assemblywoman Earlene Hooper and New York State Senator Charles Fuschillo moved forward on this critical issue and came together and hammered out some extremely difficult bipartisan legislation in the New York State Assembly and Senate that rescued the Roosevelt School District and made provision for brand new schools to be built which exist today in Roosevelt, by the grace of God. Like Isaac, we were sowing in that land. During this time, we were also sowing seeds of faith daily behind the scenes for seven years for the Mother Barbara Lee Scott Senior Housing and Workforce Housing Project. Moving forward with the plan of God.

DID YOU KNOW? Isaac was Abraham's promised son. God, Himself, named Isaac. To be named by God—what a thought. Isaac's name means "Laughter." Abraham laughed when he was told he would have a son. Sarah laughed when she overheard this news. Yet, one must flip the script of disbelief and doubt and possess a soul-stirring atmosphere of belly wrenching laughter that believes God to literally demolish the lethal death grip of the age old lies of the enemy within. Abraham was one hundred and Sarah ninety when Isaac was born. Isaac was the half-brother of Ishmael. It was at the age of forty that Isaac married the love of his life, Rebekah. Isaac prayed to God to open Rebekah's womb and she had twins, Esau and Jacob, at the age of sixty. If one will ever move forward from the year of the liar onward and upward to the year of influence, the crucial choice must be made now to bust a major move that will positively impact and influence the remainder of your life and the very destiny of your seed.

3 S'S: THE SEED, THE STARS, AND THE SAVIOR

From Isaac we learn about the 3 S's: the seed, the stars, and the Savior.

1.) The Seed – **Genesis 26:3: "unto thy seed, I will give all these countries"**
2.) The Stars – **Genesis 26:4: "And I will make thy seed to multiply as the stars of heaven"**
3.) The Savior – **Genesis 26:4: "and in thy seed shall all the nations of the earth be blessed."**

Isaac is mentioned 128 times in 21 different books of the Bible. Isaac is first mentioned in Genesis 17:19 and last mentioned in James 2:21.

Dr. Benjamin E. Mays once stated that, "It isn't a disgrace not to reach the stars, but it is a disgrace to have no stars to reach for."

THE POWER OF THEN

"Then Isaac sowed in that land."

Then Isaac sowed in Gerar, the land that God told him to go into. When is your 'then'? You only truly grow if you sow. You only begin to truly live when you give. The very best place to start is right where you are. Don't let the lies, shortcomings, and issues of life stop you from turning over a new leaf by sowing seeds of greatness in the land that you once lived a lie in. Isaac sowed in that land. Sowing in that community, sowing in that church and/or ministry is in all reality a contract with God to move forward from insulting and embarrassing lying behavior to integrity and influence for the advancement of the Kingdom of God. Isaac was caught in a lie concerning Rebekah, his wife, through an extremely embarrassing situation and he was boldly rebuked by the Philistine King Abimelech for his lie. Like his father, Abraham, before him, Isaac lied and called his wife his sister. Genesis 26:7-11 lets us know that Isaac feared that the Philistines would kill him to marry his wife, Rebekah, therefore, Isaac lied so he would not die.

This had to be truly corrected. Yet, Isaac decided to bust a move of major change on the journey of divine destiny, and sowing in that land delivered him from the practice of lying in that land. Sowing in that land gave Isaac's life the much needed structure and discipline to overcome his own personal demons of devastating oppression. Sowing and growing was Isaac's new ground breaking gig. Sowing and growing was Isaac's new cutting edge holy habit. Isaac sowed in that land. Where are we sowing today? Where are you sowing today? Where you sow is where you grow. When Isaac sowed in lies, Isaac grew in lies. Thank God Isaac decided to move forward and sow daily seeds of faith, hope, and love "in that land" which totally transformed his hardcore, negative lying behavior into solid, positive, and daily, godly giving practices.

REAPING THE 100-FOLD SAME YEAR BONUS

"and received in the same year an hundredfold"

Uncanny 100-fold same year breakthrough bonus blessings come to those who move forward in spite of life's most uncomfortable lying issues. These blessings only come to those who completely refuse to live in a lie any more. Now is the time to move forward. Total embarrassment did not run Isaac from that land, because Isaac was busy with a new sowing and growing attitude, with his new positive planting behavior habit, which shattered his old, lying negative behavior habit. Lying is no light matter. Staying a liar can keep one out of Heaven and put one right in the lake of fire.

Revelation 21:8:
"But the fearful, and unbelieving, and the abominable, and murderers, and whoremongers, and sorcerers, and idolaters, and all liars, shall have their part in the lake which burneth with fire and brimstone: which is the second death."

Folks who face the uncomfortable and embarrassing issues of real life and stop lying and start sowing and growing in a godly manner qualify for the 100-fold same year bonus that only God can grant. When we defeat the demons that have been destroying our families for hundreds of years, we qualify for the same year 100-fold blessing: Sowing in that land; Planting in that land; Giving, caring, sharing, and heavy load bearing in that land. It is the new holy habit, the new godly gig that totally destroys the deadly daily routine stronghold of Satan. The 100-fold blessing could be living a life free from drugs. The 100-fold blessing is living a life free of debt. The 100-fold blessing is living a life that is not controlled and manipulated by lies.

THE BLESSING OF THE LORD

"and the Lord blessed him."

Proverbs 10:22 boldly declares, **"The blessing of the LORD, it maketh rich, and he addeth no sorrow with it."**

Isaac was too blessed to be messed over. Isaac was too blessed to be stressed. Isaac moved forward beyond his generational lie and the LORD blessed him. If anyone truly yearns and deeply desires to experience the blessing of the LORD, then overcome the spirit of lying. The actual truth is that in Christ Jesus we are already blessed.

Ephesians 1:3:
"Blessed be the God and Father of our Lord Jesus Christ, who hath blessed us with all spiritual blessings in heavenly places in Christ."

Isaac did not run away when he was caught in a lie. He stopped his lying no matter how well-intentioned it was, and learned how to live a life of sowing and growing that God would bless 100-fold. "And the LORD blessed him."

THE BLESSING OF THE LORD MAKES THE SEEDS OF GREATNESS GROW

"And the man waxed great."

Isaac came into and grew in his own greatness. Isaac had to know the LORD for himself in the dealings of daily life in order to move forward and experience true greatness. For God is greater than any situation and His Holy Spirit resides within blood washed believers.

1 John 4:4:
"Ye are of God, little children, and have overcome them: because greater is he that is in you, than he that is in the world."

We serve a great God and He created us to be a great people.

NOW IS THE TIME TO MOVE FORWARD

"and went forward"
- Bust a move forward for empowerment and progress.
- Make a move forward for growth.
- Take a move forward for success.
- Move forward with the plan of God.

Oprah Winfrey said that, "Every choice in life either moves you forward or keeps you stuck."

The song writer, Israel Houghton, wrote:

I'm not going back, I'm moving ahead
Here to declare to You my past is over in You
All things are made new, surrendered my life to Christ
I'm moving, moving forward.

KEEP ON GROWING. NEVER STOP AT GREATNESS ALONE. ASPIRE TO BE VERY GREAT

"...and grew until he became very great."

- Move forward and grow until we are very great at laughing, learning, living, and loving.
- Move forward and grow until we are very great at sowing and growing.
- Move forward and grow until we are very great at caring, sharing, and heavy load bearing.
- Move forward and grow until we are very great at never ever living a lie.

Rev. Dr. Martin Luther King, Jr. declared and decreed that, "Everybody can be great... because anybody can serve. You don't have to have a college degree to serve. You don't have to make your subject and verb agree to serve. You only need a heart full of grace. A soul generated by love."

TAP INTO THE YEAR OF INFLUENCE

"For he had possession of flocks, and possession of herds, and great store of servants."

Possession of the flock through rock solid godly leadership for influence is leadership. Possession of the herds through rock solid godly leadership for influence is leadership. Leading the great store of workers for leadership is influence.

Move forward to impact and influence the industries of the day for the advancement of the Kingdom of God.

BE PREPARED FOR THE HATERS

God Will Use Your Haters As Your Elevators.

"and the Philistines envied him."

When people envy you, it is a sure sign that you have experienced some form of greatness. When people envy you, it is a sure sign that you have begun to move forward in some manner. The Philistines stopped the wells that Isaac's father, Abraham, dug, and filled them up with dirt. King Abimelech asked Isaac to leave because "you're much mightier than we." People went to war over water rights and wells. People would even kill in that day over water and wells. Isaac led the movement to dig again the well of revival. Isaac moved forward with the plan of God.

We must move forward, onward, and upward, and dig again the modern day wells of revival. Isaac moved forward and pitched his tent in the Valley of Gerar and dwelled there. After Isaac re-dug many wells of revival that his father, Abraham, built he continued to move forward. Genesis 26:23 tells us that Isaac went up to Beersheba, which means "The well of the sevenfold oath." Beersheba was a city located at the southern edge of Israel. Influence on the edge! Moving forward even on the edge! Redigging wells of revival even on the edge! In Genesis 26:24-25, the Lord appeared to Isaac the same night and reconfirmed the blessing He promised to Abraham.

I absolutely love the classic Christian hymn "Onward, Christian Soldiers." Because it so vividly expresses the sense of urgency concerning the moving forward, onward, and upward message.

Sabine Baring-Gould wrote:

> *Onward, Christian soldiers, marching as to war,*
> *with the cross of Jesus going on before.*
> *Christ, the royal Master, leads against the foe;*
> *forward into battle see his banners go!*

Refrain:

> *Onward, Christian soldiers, marching as to war,*
> *with the cross of Jesus going on before.*

CHAPTER TWO

MOVED WITH THE FEAR OF GOD—NOAH MADE A MAJOR DIFFERENCE

Hebrews 11:7:
"By faith Noah, being warned of God of things not seen as yet, moved with fear, prepared an ark to the saving of his house; by the which he condemned the world, and became heir of the righteousness which is by faith."

DID YOU KNOW? Noah, whose name means "comfort" or "relief", moved forward with the fear of God as a ship's captain. Noah moved forward with the fear of God as a vineyard owner. Noah moved forward with the fear of God as the son of Lamech. Noah moved forward with the fear of God as a husband of one wife. Noah moved forward with the fear of God as the father of Shem, Ham, and Japheth. Noah moved forward with the fear of God as father-in-law to his daughters-in-law. Noah moved forward with the fear of God as the grandson of Methuselah, the oldest man to ever live on earth at 969 years young. Noah moved forward with the fear of God as the great grandson of Enoch who walked with God and was not, because God took him, translated him, raptured him.

WHICH IS IT?

Some people would ask, which is it? "God has not given us the spirit of fear" or "be moved with fear"? There is no contradiction at all. God has not given us the spirit of fearing mere man or of fearing the deceptive devil who cannot put us in Heaven or Hell. Yet, we must fear the Lord who *can* put us in Heaven or Hell.

The Apostle Paul states in **Acts 20:24** that **"none of these things move me, neither count I my life dear unto myself, so that I might finish my course with joy, and the ministry, which I have received of the Lord Jesus, to testify the gospel of the grace of God."** It is extremely important to realize that this does not contradict in any way shape or form **Acts 17:28** which declares and decrees that **"For in him we live, and move, and have our being;…"**

Positive and progressive people who move forward with the fear of God and make a positive and progressive difference are not moved by mundane things, foolish stuff that really doesn't matter for they are totally committed to finishing their course with joy.

Scriptures and songs speaking of an oppressed people who shall not be moved in their determination for spiritual, social, political, and economic progress actually points to a people who are actually moving forward with the fear of God and by the grace of God. Key songs of the Civil Rights Movement, such as "I Shall Not Be Moved" and "Ain't Gonna Let Nobody Turn Me Around," clearly pointed to their determination to boldly stand, move forward with the fear of God against the gross sin of segregation, and literally march and move forward, onward, and upward to social and economic justice. That is why it was called the Civil Rights Movement. **Psalm 16:8** declares and decrees that **"I have set the Lord always before me: because he is at my right hand, I shall not be moved."** David would not let the forces of hell move him from his personal and intimate relationship with God on the right hand. It is extremely important to realize that this does not contradict in any way shape or form **Acts 17:28** which declares and decrees that **"For in him** we live, and <u>move</u>, and have our being;…"

If a former alcoholic and or heavy drinker like Noah or a heavy smoker truly sticks to their choice not to be moved to drink alcohol or smoke again, they are actually moving forward in their resistance to drinking and smoking that once destroyed their life. They are actually now a part of a positive and progressive movement of resistance by not being moved by negative and oppressive forces such as constant peer pressure to do the wrong thing. Please also remember that **Hebrews 11:7** declares and decrees that **"By faith Noah, being warned of God of things not seen as yet, <u>moved</u> with fear, prepared an ark to the saving of his house; by the which he condemned the world, and became heir of the righteousness which is by faith."**

When you know who are in Christ and have self awareness and self confidence you won't be so easily influenced to allow someone to pressure you into negative activities through negative peer pressure. It takes inner strength to stand up to people who try to push and pressure you into things you don't want to do.

Alison Corso, a Kent School Services Network community school coordinator who works with Kentwood, Michigan, students selected for a Nickelodeon Nick News interview regarding peer pressure said of negative peer pressure at school. "And I think one of the biggest ways that we can make a difference and move forward to make strides in overcoming peer pressure is being honest, being real and being open about it." Thank God that Noah did not let negative adult peer pressure stop him from moving forward and building the ark as God had told him to do so.

MAJOR LEGISLATIVE ACCOMPLISHMENTS MOVED FORWARD DURING THE CIVIL RIGHTS MOVEMENT WHICH WE STILL NEED TODAY

Major legislative accomplishments moved forward during the Civil Rights Movement first with the positive progressive passage of the **Civil Rights Act of 1964**, that successfully banned discrimination based on "race, color, religion, or national origin" in practices of employment and public accommodations.

Second, the **Voting Rights Act of 1965** moved forward and brought about the revival, restoration, and overall protection of the voting rights of all American citizens including the oppressed. I was deeply disturbed when I learned that on June 25, 2013, the United States Supreme Court struck down key provisions of the Voting Rights Act of 1965. Yes, it is major progress that America has moved forward and elected, an African-American, Barack Obama, twice in a row as United States President. But racial profiling (as practiced by night watchman, George Zimmerman, who shot to death an unarmed young African-American, Trayvon Martin), racial hatred, and blatant out right systematized discrimination still exists in America today. We must continue to move forward and make a difference. The lives of Medgar Evers, Martin Luther King, Jr., and Malcolm X must not be in vain. The lives of Rosa Parks, Fannie Lou Hammer, and Congresswoman Shirley Chisholm must not be in vain. The struggle continues today. Frederick Douglass was right when he said, "If there is no struggle, there is no progress." Wake up! This is an unjust and absolutely horrible changing of the Voting Rights Act of 1965.

Third, the **Immigration and Nationality Services Act of 1965** boldly moved forward the effort to allow immigrants, other than the traditional European immigrants, to enter the United States of America.

Last was the **Fair Housing Act of 1968** that banned discrimination in the sale or rental of housing. African Americans moved forward in politics in the segregated South, and across the entire country, young people in the movement were revitalized to take action and move forward making a lasting difference.

MOVING FORWARD BY FAITH

Hebrews 11:1: "Now faith is the substance of things hoped for, the evidence of things not seen."

DID YOU KNOW? Noah, whose name means "comfort" and "relief", certainly had both the fear of God and deep faith in God for Noah's name is mentioned in the Hall of Faith in Hebrews Chapter 11. Noah's name is moved forward in biblical presentation fifty different times in nine different books of the Bible. That is major. Those nine different books of the Bible are: Genesis, I Chronicles, Isaiah, Ezekiel, Matthew, Luke, Hebrews, I Peter, and II Peter.

MOVING FORWARD WITH THE WARNING OF GOD

God told Noah in detail how men began to move forward in negativity and multiply on the face of the earth, and daughters were born unto them. Now the sons of God moved forward in great error and saw the attractive and lovely daughters of men that they were fair; and they took them wives of all which they chose for themselves. The Lord was greatly angered and said, **"My spirit shall not always strive with man, for that he also is flesh: yet his days** shall be an hundred and twenty years."

Because the sons of God became sexually involved with the daughters of men there were giants birthed in the earth in those days; and also after that, when the sons of God came in unto the daughters of men, and they bear children to them, the same became mighty men which were of old, men of renown.

God was greatly angered when He saw that the wickedness of man was great in the earth, and that every imagination of the thoughts of his heart was only evil continually.

The Lord repented that he had made man on the earth, and God was grieved in His own heart. The Lord told Noah, I will destroy man whom I have created from the face of the earth; both man, and beast, and the creeping thing, and the fowls of the air; for God repented that He had made mankind.

NOAH MOVED FORWARD WITH THE FEAR OF GOD

- God told Noah to build an ark of gopher wood; with rooms in the ark, pitched within and without. Noah moved forward with the fear of God.

- God told Noah to make the ark 450 feet long, 75 feet wide, and 45 feet high. Noah moved forward with the fear of God.

- God told Noah to put only one window in the ark above the door of the ark set in the side thereof; with a lower, second, and third stories on the ark. Noah moved forward with the fear of God.

- God also told Noah that He would bring a flood of waters

upon the earth, to destroy all flesh, wherein is the breath of life, from under heaven; and everything that is in the earth shall die. Noah moved forward with the fear of God.

- God told Noah that I will establish my covenant; and you shall come into the ark, you, and your sons, and your wife, and your sons' wives with you. Noah moved forward with the fear of God.

- God told Noah that every living thing of all flesh, two of every sort shall you bring into the ark, to keep them alive with you; they shall be male and female. Noah moved forward with the fear of God.

- God gave Noah further details of fowls after their kind, and of cattle after their kind, of every creeping thing of the earth after his kind, two of every sort shall come unto you, Noah, to keep them alive. Noah moved forward with the fear of God.

- God clearly told Noah take unto yourself all food that is eaten, and you shall gather it; and it shall be for food for you, and for your family. Noah moved forward with the fear of God.

- Noah quickly moved forward with the fear of God and immediately did according to all that God commanded him, so Noah moved forward and did just as God said. Noah moved forward with the fear of God. Noah moved forward with the plan of God.

MOVING FORWARD IN PREPARATION AND PROCLAMATION

Noah was 480 years young when he started to move forward with the fear of God and built the ark. Back then, 480 years was like 48 years today. The 400's were back then the time of mid-life crisis. People lived much longer. One note of interest is, large dinosaurs existed before the worldwide flood – before the environmental canopy, the firmament of protection, was destroyed from over the earth due to the flood.

The preacher of righteousness and the builder, Noah, moved forward with the 4P's of prayer, planning, patience, and persistence, in preparation over a period of 120 years in the painful process of building the ark.

The powerful preacher of righteousness and the builder, Noah, moved forward with the fear of God in preparation by literally preaching righteousness to all the people he could reach while he built the ark.

The people of the earth had 120 years to move forward to repent and get right with God. No one did so except Noah's family. Noah and his family and all the animals stayed in the ark for seven whole days before the very first drop of rain fell from the sky. God, Himself, moved forward and shut the door of the ark and then God destroyed the entire earth with the great flood. Noah moved forward with the plan of God.

Jesus Christ said of the days of Noah moving forward with preparation and proclamation in **Matthew 24:37-39: "But as the days of Noah were, so also will the coming of the Son of Man** be. For as in the days before the flood, they were eating and drinking, marrying and giving in marriage, until the day that Noah entered the ark, and did not know until the flood came and took them all away, so also will the coming of the Son of Man be."

The Apostle Peter stated in **1 Peter 3:20: "Who formerly were disobedient, when once the Divine longsuffering waited in the days of Noah, while the ark was being prepared, in which a few, that is, eight souls, were saved through water."** The Apostle Peter went on to say in **2 Peter 2:5: "and did not spare the ancient world, but saved Noah, one of eight people, a preacher of righteousness, bringing in the flood on the world of the ungodly."**

MOVING FORWARD WITH THE RAINBOW SIGN

God told Noah, "I will establish my covenant with you, neither shall all flesh be cut off any more by the waters of a flood; neither shall there anymore be a flood to destroy the earth."

God told Noah, whose names means "relief" and "comfort", that this is the token, a sign of the covenant which I make between Me and you and every living creature that is with you, for perpetual generations. Every one of the seven billion people who now live on planet earth ought to move forward and thank God for Noah because if Noah did not obey God's call to build an ark and put his family and the animals on it, we would not be here today. There would be no Black, White, Asian, Italian, Greek, Spanish, Irish, or any other type of people on the face of the earth, because if Noah did not obey God's voice to build the ark no humans would have survived the historic great flood. Thank God that Noah moved forward and fulfilled his destiny and purpose. Your precious pets such as birds, cats, and dogs, or even the animals in the zoo and in the wild would not be here today if Noah did not bring seven clean and two unclean of each and every animal on the entire earth on the ark. **Praise God that Noah moved forward and made a major difference. Without Noah's obedience to the voice of God there would be no human race today on the entire face of the earth today.**

God told Noah, 'I do set my rainbow in the cloud, and it shall be for a token of a covenant between Me and the earth. And it shall come to pass, when I bring a cloud over the earth, that the rainbow shall be seen in the cloud.' Rainbows did not exist on the earth. God himself moved forward the concept as a covenant between God and the earth. God, the Creator, is the original founder of Earth Day. **Psalm 24:1** declares, **"The earth is the Lord's, and the fulness thereof; the world, and they that dwell therein."**

After being in the storm for 40 days and 40 nights; after being on the ark with his family and animals of all kinds for way too long; after sending out a raven to find dry land which never came back; after sending out a dove twice that comes back the second time with an olive branch, proof of dry land; after getting clearance from God to get off the ark stuck on Mount Ararat; after getting drunk on the day of reconstruction; after failing; after falling; after being found drunk and naked, Noah moves forward with the fear of God and gets it right with God. Noah moves forward with the fear of God and his life continues to make a positive and progressive influence and impact. Noah died at 950 years, which is like 95 years today.

CHAPTER THREE

GO FORWARD – GOD'S EXIT STRATEGY

Exodus 14:13-16 (The word "exodus" means "to go out"; "departure"; it's where we get our word "exit" from.)

"And Moses said unto the people, Fear ye not, stand still, and see the salvation of the Lord, which he will shew to you to day: for the Egyptians whom ye have seen to day, ye shall see them again no more for ever. The Lord shall fight for you, and ye shall hold your peace. And the Lord said unto Moses, Wherefore criest thou unto me? speak unto the children of Israel that they go forward: But lift thou up thy rod, and stretch out thine hand over the sea, and divide it: and the children of Israel shall go on dry ground through the midst of the sea."

Condition of Existence – There are some situations in life that absolutely require that you have a highly effective exit strategy, an exodus plan that actually works, to get out of the abusive and oppressive chains of Satan, sin, and modern day slavery which will destroy you with a negative sinful slave mentality if you stay in bondage any longer. Some folk don't want to see you move forward at all, exit and exodus from Satan, sin, slavery, bondage, misuse, and/or abuse, because that means that they would lose their devilish, manipulative control over you. Remember that Moses, the murderer, moved forward and became:

- Moses – The Lawgiver
- Moses – The Prophet of God

- Moses – Author of the Pentateuch
- Moses – Leader of Israel and Leader of the Exodus from Egypt
- Moses' name means – "The one drawn out"

Exodus 2:10 states: **"And the child grew, and she brought him unto Pharaoh and he became her son. And she called his name Moses: and she said, Because I drew him out of the water."**

The three month old baby boy who was drawn out of the Nile River which his mother, Jochebed, placed him in to escape the fury of Pharaoh (who officially ordered the murder of all Hebrew baby boys), would go forward, move forward, and draw out the Israelites from 400 years of slavery in Egypt.

DID YOU KNOW? Moses' name is mentioned in the Bible 804 times in 31 different books of both the Old and New Testaments. Moses is first mentioned in Exodus 2:10 and last mentioned in Revelation 15:3. God would not allow it to be mentioned if it did not matter. Learning from the good, bad, and indifferent experiences in Moses' journey will help us to finally move forward and make a difference.

THE PROPHETIC MESSAGE OF MOSES – "LET MY PEOPLE GO"

Exodus 9:13:
"And the LORD said unto Moses, Rise up early in the morning, and stand before Pharaoh, and say unto him, Thus saith the LORD God of the Hebrews, Let my people go, that they may serve me."

If Pharaoh, if the drug dealer, if the gang leader, if the misuser, if the abuser refuses to let you go, God has His own exit strategy—His very own exodus plan—that truly works.

1.) The Plague of the Nile River Turned To Blood - Let my people go
2.) The Plague of Frogs - Let my people go
3.) The Plague of Lice - Let my people go
4.) The Plague of Flies - Let my people go
5.) The Plague of Cattle - Let my people go
6.) The Plague of Boils - Let my people go
7.) The Plague of Hail and Lightning - Let my people go
8.) The Plague of Locusts - Let my people go
9.) The Plague of Three Days of Darkness - Let my people go
10.) The Plague of the Death of the Firstborn - Let my people go

THE LAST PLAGUE, THE LAST STRAW, ALWAYS LEADS TO DECISIONS THAT CHANGE IT ALL

- Pharaoh's Deadly Decision – Exodus 14:5-9
- The People's Deep Despair – Exodus 14:10-12
- The Prophet Moses' Declaration of Destiny – Exodus 14:13-14

WHEN GOD PUSHES HIS PLAN

THE WISDOM, THE WORD, AND THE WILL OF GOD

The LORD spoke to stuttering Moses in order to push His plan His wisdom, word, and will, and   said "Speak to the children of Israel, that they turn and camp before Pi Hahiroth, between Migdol and the sea, opposite Baal Zephon; you shall camp before it by the sea. For Pharaoh will say of the children of Israel, 'They *are* bewildered by the land; the wilderness has closed them in. Then I will harden Pharaoh's heart, so that he will pursue them; and I will gain honor over Pharaoh and over all his army, that the Egyptians may know that I *am* the Lord. And that is exactly how it happened, because God pushed His plan - wisdom, word, and will, in spite Pharaoh.

When Pharaoh, the King of Egypt, learned that the Israelites had fled for their freedom. The heart of Pharaoh and his workers were turned against the Israelites who did not leave out empty but rather with the gross national profit of Egypt. The Egyptians said, "Why have we done this, that we have let Israel go from serving us? So Pharaoh made ready his chariot and took his people with him. Pharaoh took six hundred choice chariots, and all the chariots of Egypt with captains over every single one of them. TheLord allowed the heart of Pharaoh, the king of Egypt, to be hardened, and Pharaoh viciously pursued the children of Israel; and the children of Israel went out with boldness. So the Egyptians viciously pursued them with all the horses *and* chariots of Pharaoh. Pharaoh's horsemen and his mighty army literally overtook the Israelites camping by the sea beside Pi Hahiroth, which is before Baal Zephon. But God still pushed His plan His wisdom, word, and will in spite Pharaoh.

When Pharaoh, the King of Egypt, drew in extremely close, the children of Israel lifted their eyes filled with utter horror, and behold, the Egyptians marched and moved forward after them. So the Israelites were extremely afraid, and the children of Israel cried out loud to the Lord like never ever before. They complained to Moses, "Because *there were* no graves in Egypt, have you taken us away to die in the wilderness? Why have you so dealt with us, to bring us up out of Egypt? *Is* this not the word that we told you in Egypt, saying, 'Let us alone that we may serve the Egyptians? For *it would have been* better for us to serve the Egyptians than that we should die in the wilderness. But God still pushed His plan His wisdom, word, and will in spite fearful Israelites.

THE WISDOM OF THE LORD - Moses clearly spoke the wisdom of God to the children of Israel, "Do not be afraid. Stand still, and see the salvation of the LORD, which He will accomplish for you today. For the Egyptians whom you see today, you shall see again no more forever. The LORD will fight for you, and you shall hold your peace. The wisdom of the Lord that Moses spoke to the children said in essence don't do nothing at all, just stand still, until God Himself gives some direct and crystal clear marching orders that will make the difference in the situation. The wisdom of the Lord says fear not. The wisdom of the Lord says stand still. The wisdom the Lord says see the salvation of the Lord. The wisdom of the Lord says that the Lord will fight for you to move the plan of God forward. The wisdom of the Lord says hold your peace.

THE WORD OF THE LORD - The LORD, the Prime Mover, spoke His mighty word to Moses, "Why do you cry to Me? Tell the children of Israel to go forward. But lift up your rod, and stretch out your hand over the sea and divide it. And the children of Israel shall go on dry *ground* through the midst of the sea. And I indeed will harden the hearts of the Egyptians, and they shall follow them. So I will gain honor over Pharaoh and over all his army, his chariots, and his horsemen. Then the Egyptians shall know that I *am* the LORD, when I have gained honor for Myself over Pharaoh, his chariots, and his horsemen. The word of the Lord that God gave to stuttering Moses the methodology overcome His speech impediment and speak a crystal clear from the Creator to the children of Israel. The word of God was pure, plain, and simple, "go forward, which means in a nut shell move forward. Before the whole wide world wanted to talk about moving forward from the times of Frederick Douglas to the times of Rev. Dr. Martin Luther King, Jr. As well as before the whole wide world wanted to talk about moving forward from the times of from the times MLK to the current times of President Barack Obama. God said "go forward, move forward, in terms of His wisdom, His word, and His will to free the broken, battered, and bruised members of hurting humanity from slavery in Egypt. God himself started the conservation concerning moving forward and making a difference, and therefore we should never ever unfriend God. Jesus is a friend that sticks closer than a brother. The word of the Lord was go forward. The word the Lord says move forward. The word of the Lord says make a difference.

THE WILL OF THE LORD - The Angel of God, a pre-Bethehemic appearance of the Lord Jesus Christ, who normally moved before the camp of Israel, moved and went behind them to prevent those with a slave mentality from going back into slavery in Egypt. The Lord Jesus Christ got behind the children of Israel to carry out the Father's will, to push the Father's plan, that the children of Israel go forward out of hundreds of years of slavery in Egypt.

Jesus had their back. The pillar of cloud, the Holy Spirit, the Spirit of Christ, the Glory of God, moved from before them where He normally operated and instead the The pillar of cloud, the Holy Spirit, the Spirit of Christ, the Glory of God, stood directly behind the Israelites along with The Angel of God, a pre-Bethehemic appearance of the Lord Jesus Christ. The Holy Spirit had the Israelites back to prevent those with a slave mentality from going back into slavery in Egypt. Jesus and the Holy Spirit showed up on the scene to back up and support the will of the Father that the children of Israel go forward out of slavery. When God the Father pushes His plan the Lord Jesus Christ shows up on the scene. When God the Father pushes His plan the Holy Spirit shows up on the scene. Jesus appears in this case as the Angel of God, and the Holy Spirit appearing this time as the pillar of cloud, the Shekinah, the visible expression of God's presence, who came between the camp of the Egyptians and the camp of Israel. Therefore there was a cloud and darkness *to the Egyptians only,* and Jesus and the Holy Spirit gave light by night *to the Israelites,* so that the Egyptians who wanted to re-enslave the Israelites did not come anywhere near the them at all that night. For Jesus and the Holy Spirit were pushing the perfect plan of the Father. Failure was not an option. Freedom from slavery was the plan that God, the will of the Father, that He was pushing through Jesus and the Holy Spirit on the right on scene facing the Red Sea, the Sea of Reeds. Jesus and the Holy Spirit were right on the scene at the Red Sea to seal the deal on the Father's "Let My People Go message to move the plan of God forward.

STRETCH OUT AND UTILIZE YOUR STAFF: Moses stretched out his hand with his staff over the Red Sea. Moses, the murderer of the Egyptian guard that slew an Israelite slave, is now Moses the deliverer. Moses who used his staff forty years ago to kill an Egyptian guard, is a now a transformed man, and now uses his staff to deliver a people of slavery. Moses used what he had a shepherd's rod, a shepherd's staff. Use what you got for God. Use what you got to free the broken, the battered, and bruised brothers and sisters of hurting humanity. The LORD literally caused the Red Sea to go *back* by a strong east wind all that night, and made the sea into dry *land,* and the waters were literally divided. This was a major miracle of tremendous proportions. The children of Israel moved forward into the midst of the Red Sea on the dry *ground,* and the waters *were* a wall to them on their right hand and on their left. The Egyptians pursued and went after the Israelites into the midst of the Red Sea, with all of Pharaoh's horses, chariots, and horsemen.

THE LORD LOOKS THROUGH THE FIRE: In the morning

watch, after the night season the LORD looked down upon the army of the Egyptians through the pillar of fire and cloud, and the Lord troubled the army of the Egyptians. The Lord took off the Egyptian's chariot wheels, so that they drove them with overwhelming difficulty. They were stuck. The Egyptians said, "Let us flee from the face of Israel, for the LORD fights for them against the Egyptians. The Lord looks through the fire and troubles your enemy. The Lord looks through the fire and troubles your trouble. The Lord looks through the fire and knocks off the wheels of the enemy. God will slow down or even shuts down yours haters, your enemy, in order for Good's children to move forward. The Lord looks through the fire and fights against your enemy to move the plan of God forward.

STRETCH OUT AGAIN: The LORD said to Moses, "Stretch out your hand over the sea, that the waters may come back upon the Egyptians, on their chariots, and on their horsemen. Moses stretched out his hand over the Red Sea again; and when the morning appeared, the sea returned to its full depth, while the Egyptians were fleeing into it. So the jLORD overthrew the Egyptians in the midst of the sea. Then the waters returned and covered the chariots, horsemen, *and* all the army of Pharaoh, the King of Egypt, that came into the sea after them. Not so much as one of them survived. Pharaoh's army was all drowned in the Red Sea. But the children of Israel had walked, moved forward, on dry *land* in the midst of the Red Sea, and the waters *were* a wall to them on their right hand and on their left. At the Red Sea the oppressed were delivered. At the Red Sea the oppressor's army was drowned. Stretch out again and let God finish the plan that He is pushing. Stretch out again and trust God. Stretch out again and let God protect you from the enemy of your soul to move the plan of God forward.

When God pushes His plan, the LORD, the Prime Mover, saves

Israel that day out of the hand of the Egyptians. Israel saw the Egyptians dead on the seashore. When God pushes His plan, Israel saw the great work which the LORD, the Prime Mover, had done in Egypt When God pushes His plan, the children of Israel feared the LORD, and believed the LORD and His servant Moses.

PROPHETIC DECLARATION BIRTHS EFFECTIVE STRATEGY

9 STRATEGIES TO MOVE FORWARD AND MAKE A DIFFERENCE

1.) The Speak to People Strategy - **"And Moses said unto the people."**

Speak to people and not at people. If you want people to show up, speak to them and invite them. If you want people to do something, ask them. Even Jesus spoke to His prospective disciples and said, **"Follow me."**

GO FORWARD & STRATEGICALLY SPEAK SO WE FEAR NOT

2.) The Fear Not Strategy – **"Fear ye not."**

Luke 12:32:
"Fear not, little flock; for it is your Father's good pleasure to give you the kingdom."

2 Timothy 1:7:
"For God hath not given us the spirit of fear; but of power, and of love, and of a sound mind."

Songwriter Carman D. Licciardello wrote:

In myself I've failed the Lord
Then was afraid to try once more
That fire in my soul had fled
That's when Jesus came and said

My spirit gives the strength you need
To raise you up and to succeed
And for vision in the night
To you, I'll give these words of light

Fear not my child
I'm with you always
I feel every pain
And every tear I see.

GO FORWARD & STRATEGICALLY FACE FEAR SO WE CAN STAND

3.) The Stand Still Strategy – **"stand still."**

2 Chronicles 20:17:
"Ye shall not need to fight in this battle: set yourselves, stand ye still, and see the salvation of the LORD with you, O Judah and Jerusalem: fear not, nor be dismayed; to morrow go out against them: for the LORD will be with you."

Joshua 3:8:
"And thou shalt command the priests that bear the Ark of the Covenant, saying, when ye are come to the brink of the water of Jordan, ye shall stand still in Jordan."

Ephesians 6:11-14:

"Put on the whole armour of God, that ye may be able to stand against the wiles of the devil. For we wrestle not against flesh and blood, but against principalities, against powers, against the rulers of the darkness of this world, against spiritual wickedness in high places. Wherefore take unto you the whole armour of God, that ye may be able to withstand in the evil day, and having done all, to stand. Stand therefore, having your loins girt about with truth, and having on the breastplate of righteousness."

Perfecting Faith Church founding pastor, Donnie McClurkin, wrote in his song, Stand:

> *What do you do?*
> *When you've done all you can*
> *And it seems like it's never enough?*
> *And what do you say when your friends turn away*
> *And you're all alone?*
>
> *Tell me, what do you give*
> *When you've given your all and*
> *Seems like you can't make it through?*
>
> *Well, you just STAND*
> *When there's nothing left to do*
> *You just STAND*
> *Watch the LORD see you through*
> *Yes, after you've done all you can*
> *You just STAND.*

GO FORWARD & STRATEGICALLY STAND STILL UNTIL WE SEE

4.) The Salvation of the Lord Strategy - "and see the salvation of the Lord"

A.) The Command to See – (The Command by God to Have Vision) – "and see the salvation of the Lord"

Proverbs 29:18:
"Where there is no vision, the people perish: but he that keepeth the law, happy is he."

2 Chronicles 20:17:
"Ye shall not need to fight in this battle: set yourselves, stand ye still, and see the salvation of the LORD with you, O Judah and Jerusalem: fear not, nor be dismayed; to morrow go out against them: for the LORD will be with you."

Isaiah 52:10:
"The LORD hath made bare his holy arm in the eyes of all the nations; and all the ends of the earth shall see the salvation of our God."

Luke 3:5-6:
"Every valley shall be filled, and every mountain and hill shall be brought low; and the crooked shall be made straight, and the rough ways shall be made smooth; And all flesh shall see the salvation of God."

B.) Overcoming The Control of the Abuser – **"which he will shew to you to day: for the Egyptians whom ye have seen to day, ye shall see them again no more for ever."**

GO FORWARD & STRATEGICALLY SEE HOW TO FIGHT

5.) The Lord Fight For You Strategy – verse 14: **"The Lord shall fight for you, and ye shall hold your peace."**

Fight - Hebrew word - *lacham* // law-kham' // AV -fight, to war, make war, eat, overcome, devoured, ever, prevail.

Deuteronomy 1:30:
"The LORD your God which goeth before you, he shall fight for you, according to all that he did for you in Egypt before your eyes."

Deuteronomy 3:22:
"Ye shall not fear them: for the LORD your God he shall fight for you."

Victory Shall Be Mine, written by John Hason states:

> Verse 1:
> *If I hold my peace,*
> *let the Lord fight my battles;*
> *I know that the victory shall be mine,*
> *victory shall be mine.*
>
> Verse 2:
> *If I walk upright,*
> *all my battles He will fight;*
> *I know that the victory shall be mine,*
> *victory shall be mine.*

Bridge:
Victory shall be mine,
Victory shall be mine.

GO FORWARD & STRATEGICALLY FIGHT SO WE GO FORWARD

6.)   The Go Forward Strategy – verse 15: **"And the Lord said unto Moses, Wherefore criest thou unto me? speak unto the children of Israel, that they <u>go forward</u>."**

7.)

A.) Nothing Moves Forward Until You Speak
B.) Stop Crying and Start Speaking
C.) Listen When The Lord Speaks – verse 15: **"And the Lord said unto Moses, Wherefore criest thou unto me? speak unto the children of Israel, that they <u>go forward</u>."**
D.) Cry When People Die – **"Wherefore criest thou unto me?"**
E.) Be Proactive - Speak Up & Prevent A Slaughter - **"speak unto the children of Israel, that they <u>go forward</u>:"**
F.) Folk Can't Move Forward If You're Silent –Silence means consent. Speak up. Move forward, because your past does not equal your future.

GO FORWARD & STRATEGICALLY LIFT UP

7.) The Lift Up Strategy – verse 16: **"But lift thou up thy rod."**

A.) What You Once Lifted Up and Misused, Now Lift Up And Use To Help The Helpless. Moses, what's in your hand? Verse 16: "But lift thou up thy rod."

John 3:14:
"And as Moses lifted up the serpent in the wilderness, even so must the Son of man be lifted up."

- Lift Up The Name of Jesus! Go Forward! Expand Your Capacity To Lift Up Jesus!
- Praise The Name of Jesus! Go Forward! Expand Your Capacity To Praise Jesus!
- Worship The Name of Jesus! Go Forward! Expand Your Capacity To Worship Jesus!
- Magnify The Name of Jesus! Go Forward! Expand Your Capacity To Magnify Jesus!
- Glorify The Name of Jesus! Go Forward! Expand Your Capacity To Glorify Jesus!

GO FORWARD & STRATEGICALLY LIFT UP SO WE CAN STRETCH OUT

8.) The Stretch Out Strategy – **"and stretch out thine hand over the sea,"** Stretch out your hand over the sea of contradictions of life.

> *Father, I stretch my hands to Thee,*
> *No other help I know;*
> *If Thou withdraw Thyself from me,*
> *Ah! whither shall I go?*

GO FORWARD & STRATEGICALLY STRETCH OUT SO WE CAN GO THROUGH

9.) The Go Through Strategy - **"and the children of Israel shall go on dry ground through the midst of the sea."**

A.) If You're Going To Go Forward You Have To Go Through

I'M GONNA GO THROUGH (Philippians 3:13)
Danniebelle Hall

> *I'm going through, I'm going through*
> *I don't care what the rest of the world decides to do*
> *Made up my mind and I ain't gonna turn around,*
> *Walkin' with my Jesus and I gotta go through*
>> *I'm going through, I'm going through*
>> *I don't care what the rest of the world decides to do*
>> *Made up my mind and I ain't gonna turn around,*
> *No Walkin' with my Jesus and I gotta go through*
> *I started running this Christian race*
> *Counted up the cost to see if I could stand the pace*
> *Turned my back on the world with Heaven in my view*
> *Made up my mind one day and I gotta go through*

GO FORWARD & STRATEGICALLY GO THROUGH SO WE CAN MAKE A DIFFERENCE

2/3rds of God's name is GO!

- Go Forward. Move Forward. Exit out of drug addiction.
- Go Forward. Move Forward. Exit out of insecurity.
- Go Forward. Move Forward. Exit out of abusive relationships.
- Go Forward. Move Forward. Exit out of that violent gang.
- Go Forward. Move Forward. Exit out and lose that weight.

On that note First Lady Michelle Obama has an awesome program entitled *Let's Move! – America's Move to Raise a Healthier Generation of Kids.* Adults could also move forward and make a difference in their health by learning this type of life changing positive and progressive information.

- Go Forward. Move Forward. Exit out of negative thinking.
- Go Forward. Move Forward. Exit out of negative talk.

Helen Keller said that "It is for us to pray not for tasks equal to our powers, but for powers equal to our tasks, to go forward with a great desire forever beating at the door of our hearts as we travel toward our distant goal."

GO FORWARD – GOD'S EXIT STRATEGY

1.) Fear not.
2.) Still Stand.
3.) See The Salvation of The Lord.

Hebrews 11:23-29:
**"By faith Moses, when he was born, was hid three months of his parents, because they saw he was a proper child; and they were not afraid of the king's commandment. By faith Moses, when he was come to years, refused to be called the son of Pharaoh's daughter; Choosing rather to suffer affliction with the people of God, than to enjoy the pleasures of sin for a season; Esteeming the reproach of Christ (Jesus) greater riches than the treasures in Egypt: for he had respect unto the recompence of the reward. By faith he forsook Egypt, not fearing the wrath of the king: for he endured, as seeing him who is invisible. Through faith he kept the passover, and the sprinkling of blood, lest he that destroyed the firstborn should touch them.
By faith they <u>passed through</u> the Red sea as by dry land: which the Egyptians assaying to do were drowned."**

The old Negro Spiritual declared,

> *O Mary don't you weep*
> *Tell Martha not to moan*
> *Pharaoh's army drowned in the Red Sea*
>
> *O Mary don't you weep*
> *Tell Martha not to moan*
> *If I could I surely would*
> *Stand on the rock where Moses stood*
> *Pharaoh's army drowned in the Red Sea*
>
> *O Mary don't you weep*
> *Tell Martha not to moan.*

- Keep Going Forward. Tap Into God's Exit Strategy.
- Keep Going Forward. Declare and Degree That, "I'm coming out with my hands up. I'm coming out with my hands up. Trials come to weigh me down, It's okay. I'm not gonna lose no ground. Got the praise on my lips, word in my heart; I don't have to worry 'cause I'm coming out of this."
- Keep on Moving Forward. Tap Into The Year of Influence.
- Keep it Moving. Move Forward and be a Peace Maker Instead of a Trouble Maker.
- Go Forward From What? Move Forward From What?
- Go Forward, Move Forward From Slavery To Freedom in Jesus!
- Go Forward, Move Forward From Sin To Sanctification in Jesus!
- Go Forward, Move Forward From Serving Satan to Serving The Savior Jesus!
- Go Forward, Move Forward From Ugly, Old, Bad Attitudes To Awesome, Fresh, and New Blessed and Bold Attitudes!

So One Day In Heaven We Will Sing The Song of Moses and The Song of The Lamb (Jesus)!

Revelation 15:3: "And they sing the song of Moses the servant of God, and the song of the Lamb, saying, Great and marvellous are thy works, Lord God Almighty; just and true are thy ways, thou King of saints."

Remember that Moses, the murderer, moved forward, and God strategically worked on him for 40 long years in the Midianite desert, and raised him up as Moses, the servant of God, who will be sung about in Heaven. Moses moved forward with the plan of God. Nelson Mandela was right when he said that, "It is in the character of growth that we should learn from both pleasant and unpleasant experiences." Thank You Jesus! Just imagine what will happen when we go forward, move forward, and embrace God's exit strategy for our deepest shame and finally go through God's entrance strategy for our new name.

> *I've got a new name over in Glory*
> *And It's Mine, Mine, Mine.*

CHAPTER FOUR

MOVING FORWARD IN INTER-GENERATIONAL MINISTRY - "WE WILL GO"

Exodus 10:9:
"And Moses said, <u>We will go</u> with our young and with our old, with our sons and with our daughters, with our flocks and with our herds will we go; for we must hold a feast unto the Lord."

- The Prophetic Message of Moses From God – **"Let My People Go"**
- Moses' Prophetic Response To Pharaoh - **"We Will Go"**

Exodus 9:13:
"And the LORD said unto Moses, Rise up early in the morning, and stand before Pharaoh, and say unto him, Thus saith the LORD God of the Hebrews, <u>Let my people go</u>, that they may serve me."

If Pharaoh, if the drug dealer, if the gang leader, if the misuser, and or abuser refuses to let you go, God has His own exit strategy, His very own exodus plan that truly works. When modern day Pharaoh's heart is hardened to keep us enslaved, we must declare and degree like Moses "<u>We will go</u>."

- The Plague of the Nile River Turned To Blood - Let my people go
- The Plague of Frogs - Let my people go
- The Plague of Lice - Let my people go

- The Plague of Flies - Let my people go
- The Plague of Cattle - Let my people go
- The Plague of Boils - Let my people go
- The Plague of Hail and Lightning - Let my people go
- The Plague of Locust - Let my people go
- The Plague of Three Days of Darkness - Let my people go
- The Plague of The Death of the First Born Son - Let my people go

MOVING FORWARD WITH POSITIVE & PROGRESSIVE CONFESSION

"Moses Said"

What You Say Is A Matter of Life & Death - **Proverbs 18:21: "Death and life are in the power of the tongue: and they that love it shall eat the fruit thereof."** The words we speak either will clear us or convict us. The words we speak literally shape our destiny. A powerful and persuasive word of testimony that is established on the truth of God's love is a major source of strength and victory.

What You Say Truly Matters - Nelson Mandela stated that, "It is never my custom to use words lightly. If twenty-seven years in prison have done anything to us, it was to use the silence of solitude to make us understand how precious words are and how real speech is in its impact on the way people live and die."

Nelson Rolihlahla Mandela was born on July 18, 1918. Nelson Rolihlahla Mandela moved forward and made a major difference as a South African anti-apartheid revolutionary and as a powerful and astute politician who served as President of South Africa for five years from 1994 to 1999. Nelson Rolihlahla Mandela moved forward and made world history as the first black South African to hold the office of the Presidency of South Africa. Nelson Rolihlahla Mandela was the very first person elected in completely multiracial election in the history of South Africa. Nelson Rolihlahla Mandela's presidency and governmental leadership focused on demolishing the lethal legacy of apartheid through taking on institutionalized racism, poverty and inequality, and fostering racial reconciliation amongst all the ages, and stages of the entire South African people. Politically Nelson Rolihlahla was an African nationalist and democratic socialist, he served as the President of the African National Congress (ANC) from 1991 to 1997. Internationally, Nelson Rolihlahla Mandela was the Secretary General of the Non-Aligned Movement from 1998 to 1999. Mandela said, "Do not judge me by my successes, judge me by how many times I fell down and got back up again."

Nelson Rolihlahla Mandela, was a Xhosa born to the well respected royal family named Thembu. Nelson Rolihlahla Mandela proudly went to Fort Hare University and the University of Witwatersrand. Nelson Rolihlahla studied law. Nelson Rolihlahla lived in Johannesburg, South Africa. Nelson Rolihlahla Mandela became involved in the ANC and became a founding member of its Youth League. After the white Afrikaner nationalists of the National Party came to power in 1948 and began implementing the brutally racist policy of apartheid, Nelson Rolihlahla Mandela rose to great prominence in the African National Congress' 1952 Defiance Campaign. Nelson Rolihlahla was elected President of the Transvaal ANC Branch and oversaw the 1955 Congress of the People.

The late Rev. Dr. Martin Luther King, Jr. moved forward and clearly spoke out boldly against the racist policy of apartied in South Africa where Nelson Mandela was unjustly imprisoned when he stated that, "In South Africa today, all opposition to white supremacy is condemned as communism, and in its name, due process is destroyed," Dr. King further stated "A medieval segregation is organized with 20th century efficiency and drive. A sophisticated form of slavery is imposed by a minority upon a majority which is kept in grinding poverty. The dignity of human personality is defiled; and world opinion is arrogantly defied." Working as a lawyer, Nelson Rolihlahla Mandela was arrested time and time again for so called seditious activities and, with the African National Congress core leadership, was prosecuted in the Treason Trial from 1956 to 1961 but he was found not guilty. In 1962 Nelson Rolihlahla Mandela was unjustly arrested, convicted of sabotage and conspiracy to overthrow the racist South African government, and Mandela was unjustly sentenced to life imprisonment in the infamous Rivonia Trial. Nelson Rolihlahla Mandela stated in his book *Long Walk to Freedom* that, "No one is born hating another person because of the color of his skin, or his background, or his religion. People must learn to hate, and if they can learn to hate, they can be taught to love, for love comes more naturally to the human heart than its opposite."

Nelson Rolihlahla Mandela served a long 27 years in prison, first on the infamous Robben Island, and then later in Pollsmoor Prison and also Victor Verster Prison. Mandela said that, "I learned that courage was not the absence of fear, but the triumph over it. The brave man is not he who does not feel afraid, but he who conquers that fear." An intense international campaign lobbied for Mandela's release, which was granted in 1990 amid ever rising civil strife. Nelson Rolihlaha Mandela, a modern day Moses, repeated his legendary defense statement first made during the Rivonia Trial in1964 at the closing of his famous speech delivered in Cape Town, South Africa, on the day he was released from prison 27 years later, on February

11, 1990. "I have fought against white domination, and I have fought against black domination. I have cherished the ideal of a democratic and free society in which all persons will live together in harmony with equal opportunities. It is an ideal which I hope to live for, and to see realized. But my Lord, if needs be, it is an ideal for which I am prepared to die." Nelson Rolihlahla Mandela move forward and made a difference by fighting for people of all ages, all stages, all races, and all classes in South Africa. Mandela also stated that, ""Difficulties break some men but make others. No axe is sharp enough to cut the soul of a sinner who keeps on trying, one armed with the hope that he will rise even in the end." Nelson Rolihlahla Mandela moved forward with the plan of God.

Becoming African National Congress (ANC) President, Nelson Rolihlahla Mandela published his bestseller autobiography and effectively led negotiations with President F.W. de Klerk to abolish apartheid and establish historic multiracial elections in 1994, in which he led the African National Congress to victory. Nelson Rolihlahla Mandela, a modern day Moses, was elected President and formed a Government of National Unity in an attempt to defuse extremely deep ethnic tensions. As President of South Africa, Nelson Rolihlahla Mandela, instituted a new constitution and initiated the Truth and Reconciliation Commission to investigate past human rights abuses. Then South African President Nelson Mandela, was a modern day Moses, in his historic Inaugural Address in Pretoria on May 9, 1994 boldly declared and decreed that, "We enter into a covenant that we shall build a society in which all South Africans, both black and white, will be able to walk tall, without and fear in their hearts, assured of their inalienable right to human dignity – a rainbow nation at peace with itself and the world."

After being sworn in as President of South Africa. Mandela stated that, "Out of the experience of an extraordinary human disaster that lasted too long, must be born a society of which all humanity will be proud." Nelson Rolihlahla Mandela did not run for a second term, and was succeeded by his deputy, Thabo Mbeki. Nelson Rolihlahla Mandela subsequently became a world renowned elder statesman, focusing on charitable work in combating poverty and HIV/AIDS through the Nelson Mandela Foundation.

Nelson Rolihlahla Mandela, a modern day Moses, nevertheless gained great international acclaim for his crystal clear clarion call which was a strong anti-colonial and anti-apartheid position. Mandela believed deeply that, "For to be free is not merely to cast off one's chains, but to live in a way that respects and enhances the freedom of others." Nelson Rolihlahla Mandela, a modern day Moses, received more than 250 awards and various honours, including the world renown 1993 Nobel Peace Prize, the prestigious US Presidential Medal of Freedom, and the Soviet Order of Lenin. The late Nelson Rolihlahla Mandela is held in deep respect and high regard within South Africa, where he is often referred to by his beloved Xhosa clan name, Madiba, or as Tata ("Father"); he is often described as "the father of the nation" for the South African people of all ages and stages of life. Nelson Rolihlahla Mandela, a modern day Moses, stated that "Our human compassion binds us the one to the other - not in pity or patronizingly, but as human beings who have learnt how to turn our common suffering into hope for the future." On the cover of the December 13, 2013 Commemorative Issue of TIME Magazine the late, Nelson Rolihlahla Mandela, was heralded as a mission minded man who moved forward and made a difference in three distinct dimensions of his life as "PROTESTER. PRISONER. PEACEMAKER."

MOVING FORWARD WITH POSITIVE AND PROGRESSIVE DECLARATION

"We Will Go"

The Words You Declare Determine Whether Your Journey Leads To Destiny - **Psalm 118:17: "I shall not die, but live, and declare the works of the Lord."**

> *We Will Go: Just like the ones who came before us*
> *Just like the ones who gave their lives*
> *Lord, we will leave this place with You*
> *And we will go, we will go*
> *Just as You came to earth from Heaven*
> *Humbled Yourself to give Your life*
> *We want to follow and obey You*
> *So we will go, we will go*

MOVING FORWARD WITH INTER-GENERATIONAL MINISTRY

"With Our Young and With Our Old"

Young and Old Moving Forward Together Is A Major Hallmark of The Last Days Ministry

Acts 2:17: "And it shall come to pass in the last days, saith God, I will pour out of my Spirit upon all flesh: and your sons and your daughters shall prophesy, and your young men shall see visions, and your old men shall dream dreams."

- Moving forward with our young and with our old as we go and pray together.
- Moving forward with our young and with our old as we go and study together.

- Moving forward with our young and with our old as we go and walk together.
- Moving forward with our young and with our old as we go and talk together.
- Moving forward with our young and with our old as we go and break bread together.
- Moving forward with our young and with our old as we go and caring, sharing, and bearing one another's burdens.
- Moving forward with our young and with our old as we go and march together onward and upward.

MOVING FORWARD WITH FAMILY RELATIONSHIPS

"With Our Sons and With Our Daughters"

Sons and Daughters Moving Forward With The Family Is A Major Hallmark of The Last Days Ministry - **Acts 2:17: "And it shall come to pass in the last days, saith God, I will pour out of my Spirit upon all flesh: and your sons and your daughters shall prophesy, and your young men shall see visions, and your old men shall dream dreams."**

> *You're my brother, you're my sister*
> *so take me by the hand*
> *Together we will work until He comes*
> *There's no foe that can defeat us*
> *if we're walkin' side by side*
> *As long as there is Love*
> *We will stand*

FATHER AND SON MOVE FORWARD TOGETHER AND GRADUATE MOREHOUSE

One of the most powerful modern day examples of moving forward and making a difference that recently touched the heart of the nation is the true story of my long time friend, a modern day Moses - Elder Dorian Joyner, Sr. and his first born son, a modern day Joshua - Dorian Joyner, Jr., two generations, graduating together from Morehouse College in Atlanta, Georgia. Dorian Sr. and I were next door neighbors, friends growing up in Roosevelt, New York. Thirty years ago, we both preached our initial sermons at the young age of sixteen-years-old at our home church in 1983 (a year before we went to college), Mount Sinai Baptist Church Cathedral in Roosevelt, New York. I am extremely proud of Elder Dorian Joyner, Sr. and Dorian Jr.

My friend Elder Dorian Joyner, Sr. and his son, Dorian Joyner, Jr. graduated together as President Obama gave the commencement address at the recent graduation ceremony. Elder Dorian Joyner Sr. went to Morehouse College between the years of 1984 and 1988, but he left Morehouse to pursue his highly successful business career. In fact I visited him during that time on the campus and we also visited nearby Spellman College during that time. Elder Joyner Sr. went on work as a cutting edge business man and a top senior analyst in the area of data and finance for several top major corporations, including a major law firm in Georgia. Elder Dorian Joyner Sr. is planning to go to law school in the near future and move forward to eventually become a Judge. Elder Joyner Sr. stated concerning graduating with his son that "It's just going to be an exciting time all around," Elder Joyner Sr. further stated "It makes me proud. I watched him struggle through school and he's my firstborn, so it really makes me proud." The dynamic duo of Dorian Sr. and Dorian Jr. literally touched the very heart and soul of the nation far and wide.

Dorian Joyner Jr. was a talented English major at the college. Dorian Jr. has plans to move forward to join the Peace Corps and then attend film school. Dorian Jr. was extremely proud of his father, Dorian Sr. Dorian Jr. stated that, "I'm proud of him as a man for him to come back all these years to pursue something he had when he was my age. So that's awesome. I am proud of him as a man and as my father to grab that diploma and to see his mother, and his brother, and me grab our diplomas together. That's the one thing I'm going to be so happy about."

About three years ago, Elder Dorian Joyner Sr. made up his mind that it was time to move forward on the idea of going back to Morehouse. When Dorian Sr. moved forward and made this choice Dorian Joyner, Jr. was a freshman at the college. I remember him sharing it with me. When Dorian Jr. heard the news this is how the young Joyner responded "I said, 'oh, you're coming back to visit some of your friends?'" he remembered. "Elder Dorian Joyner Sr. said 'no, I'm coming back to be a student. And Dorian Jr. said, 'could you repeat that?'"

Nelson Mandela once stated that, "Education is the most powerful weapon which you can use to change the world." A modern day Moses, Dorian Sr., and a modern day Joshua, Dorian Jr., moved forward together in inter-generational encouragement to support each other in pursuit of excellence in education. This father and son team are world changers who moved forward together and made a major difference in the hearts and minds of the masses. Elder Dorian Joyner Sr. and Dorian Joyner, Jr. moved forward with the plan of God.

MOVING FORWARD WITH OUR FLOCKS

"With Our Flocks"

Psalm 77:20:
"Thou leddest thy people like a flock by the hand of Moses and Aaron."

Psalm 107:41:
"Yet setteth he the poor on high from affliction, and maketh him families like a flock."

Isaiah 40:11:
"He shall feed his flock like a shepherd: he shall gather the lambs with his arm, and carry them in his bosom, and shall gently lead those that are with young."

Luke 12:32:
"Fear not, little flock; for it is your Father's good pleasure to give you the kingdom."

Flocks of sheep in the Holy Scripture are symbolic of the local church.

MOVING FORWARD WITH OUR HERDS

"And With Our Herds"

Don't Compromise With Pharaoh -

Exodus 10:24-26:
"And Pharaoh called unto Moses, and said, Go ye, serve the

Lord; only let your flocks and your herds be stayed: let your little ones also go with you. And Moses said, Thou must give us also sacrifices and burnt offerings, that we may sacrifice unto the Lord our God. Our cattle also shall go with us; there shall not an hoof be left behind; for thereof must we take to serve the Lord our God; and we know not with what we must serve the Lord, until we come thither."

Herds of Cattle – Symbolic of The Mega Church. Herd them in and herd them out.

MOVING FORWARD TOGETHER

Together **"Will We Go"**

We Go Up Together - **Luke 18:31: "Then he took unto him the twelve, and said unto them, Behold, we go up to Jerusalem, and all things that are written by the prophets concerning the Son of man shall be accomplished."**

- Moving forward together in the aftermath of Hurricane Sandy
- Moving forward together In the aftermath of Sandy Hook
- Moving forward together In the aftermath of monthly mass murders
- Moving forward together to be proactive and prevent gun violence

MOVING FORWARD WITH THE LORD

"We Must Hold A Feast Unto The Lord"

- We hold a feast unto the Lord.

- We must feed the hungry.
- We must rescue the perishing.
- We must care for the dying.
- We must clothe the naked.
- We must bear, care, and share.
- We must make a difference
- We must love one another
- We must be saved - **Acts 4:12: "Neither is there salvation in any other: for there is none other name under heaven given among men, whereby we must be saved."**
- We must enter the kingdom through much tribulation - **Acts 14:22: "Confirming the souls of the disciples, and exhorting them to continue in the faith, and that we must through much tribulation enter into the kingdom of God."**
- We must all appear before the judgment seat of Christ – **2 Corinthians 5:10 "For we must all appear before the judgment seat of Christ; that every one may receive the things done in his body, according to that he hath done, whether it be good or bad."**

"We must hold a feast unto the Lord"
- We must move forward together in inter-generational ministry.
- Like Abraham, Isaac, and Jacob from generation to generation.
- We must move forward together in inter-generational ministry.
- Like Jacob laying his hands on his sons and telling them who they are.
- We must move forward together in inter-generational ministry.
- Like the leader of Israel, Moses, and his successor, Joshua.

- We must move forward together in inter-generational ministry.
- Like mother-in-law, Naomi, and daughter-in-law, Ruth.
- We must move forward together in inter-generational ministry.
- Like young David who refused to kill King Saul because he was the Lord's anointed.
- We must move forward together in inter-generational ministry.
- Like old man Simeon and the prophetess Anna and the baby, Jesus.
- We must move forward together in inter-generational ministry.
- Like the Lord Jesus Christ and the little lad with 5 loaves of bread and 2 fish from which the 5000 was fed.
- We must move forward together in inter-generational ministry.
- Like spiritual father, Apostle Paul, and spiritual son, Pastor Timothy.
- We must move forward together in inter-generational ministry.
- Like the younger, John the disciple of Jesus, and the older, Mary the mother of Jesus, taking care of one another.
- We must move forward together in inter-generational ministry.
- Like Jesus receiving support from and giving support to the three Marys: Mary the mother of Jesus, Mary the wife of Cleophas, and Mary Magdalene, and John.

John 19: 25-27:
"Now there stood by the cross of Jesus his mother, and his mother's sister, Mary the wife of Cleophas, and Mary Magdalene.

When Jesus therefore saw his mother, and the disciple standing by, whom he loved, he saith unto his mother, Woman, behold thy son! Then saith he to the disciple, Behold thy mother! And from that hour that disciple took her unto his own home."

We Must Move Forward Together In Inter-Generational Ministry

Like the wise men from afar funding the earthly ministry of Jesus Christ.

Matthew 2:1-2:
"Now when Jesus was born in Bethlehem of Judaea in the days of Herod the king, behold, there came wise men from the east to Jerusalem, And when they were come into the house, they saw the young child with Mary his mother, and fell down, and worshipped him: and when they had opened their treasures, they presented unto him gifts; gold, and frankincense and myrrh."

We Must Move Forward Together In Inter-Generational Ministry

Psalm 100:5:
"For the Lord is good; his mercy is everlasting; and his truth endureth to all generations."

CHAPTER FIVE

MOVED AT THE PRESENCE OF GOD: WHEN GOD MARCHES THROUGH THE WILDERNESS

Psalm 68 (General Hymn of Praise, To the chief Musician, A Psalm or Song of David):

"Let God arise, let his enemies be scattered: let them also that hate him flee before him. As smoke is driven away, so drive them away: as wax melteth before the fire, so let the wicked perish at the presence of God. But let the righteous be glad; let them rejoice before God: yea, let them exceedingly rejoice. Sing unto God, sing praises to his name: extol him that rideth upon the heavens by his name Jah, and rejoice before him. A father of the fatherless, and a judge of the widows, is God in his holy habitation. God setteth the solitary in families: he bringeth out those which are bound with chains: but the rebellious dwell in a dry land. O God, when thou wentest forth before thy people, when thou didst march through the wilderness; Selah: The earth shook, the heavens also dropped at the presence of God: even Sinai itself was moved at the presence of God, the God of Israel."

Condition of Existence – We all have wilderness experiences in our lives that we so desperately need God to go boldly before us and march and move forward through our roughest and toughest wilderness experiences. We all need to be moved at the presence of God in order to go through, march and move forward, and truly come out of our most painful/shameful private and public wilderness episodes. David moved forward with the plan of God and wrote what we know today as Psalm 68 as well as many other classic psalms.

Psalm 68, this spiritual hymn of highly potent prophetic prayer and prophetic praise, reveals how the life, death, resurrection through a clear prophetic reference in Psalm 68:18 to the actual ascension of Jesus Christ would literally defeat the enemies of God.

In Psalm 68 King David describes Prophet and Leader of Israel - Moses' leading, marching and moving the Israelites in prophetic prayer & prophetic praise.

- Prophetic prayer for God's enemies in Psalm 68:1 -2.
- Prophetic prayer for the people of God in Psalm 68:3 -11.

In the remaining verses of Psalm 68, King David describes Moses' marching and moving prophetic praise.

- Prophetic Praise Marching and Moving Through The Wilderness in Psalm 68:7 – 8.
- Prophetic Praise Leads The Wilderness Babies To Canaan Land in 68:9 – 10.
- Prophetic Praise Points To Victory Over The Enemies of God in Psalm 68:1 - 2.
- Prophetic Praise Points To Deliverance Over The Oppressors in Psalm 68:13 -14.
- Prophetic Praise Points To The Presence of God in Psalm 68:15 -17.
- Prophetic Praise Points To The Ascension of Jesus Christ and Salvation Through Jesus Christ in Psalm 68:18 – 20
- Prophetic praise points to Christ victories over His enemies

and Christ favor for the church in Psalm 68:21 -28.
- Prophetic praise points to the growth of the church including the Gentiles in Psalm 68:29 - 31.
- Prophetic prayer is the birthing place of prophetic praise.
- Prophetic praise is God's GPS system to come out of the wilderness.
- Prophetic praise points to the awesome glory and grace of God in Psalm: 32 -35.
- Prophetic prayer and prophetic praise produces a worshiping church.
- Prophetic prayer and prophetic praise produces a word church.
- Prophetic prayer and prophetic praise produces a warrior church.
- Prophetic prayer and prophetic praise produces a witnessing church.
- Prophetic prayer and prophetic praise produces a working church.
- Prophetic prayer and prophetic praise produces a wisdom church.
- Prophetic prayer and prophetic praise produces a whole church.

The Apostle Peter also totally embraced the true prophetic call to move forward by the inspiration of the Holy Ghost and make a difference like the classic examples of the prophets of old when he wrote in **2 Peter 1:21: "For the prophecy came not in old time by the will of man: but holy men of God spake as they were <u>moved by the Holy Ghost</u>."**

Knowledge is power when applied.

THREE LIFE CHANGING "LETS": TO MARCH FORWARD, MOVE FORWARD, AND GO FORWARD IN OUR COMMUNION WITH CHRIST

1.) LET GOD ARISE

According to **Numbers 10:35:**
"And it came to pass, when the ark set forward, that Moses said, Rise up, LORD, and let thine enemies be scattered; and let them that hate thee flee before thee."

These were the very first words that the Prophet Moses and Leader spoke, declared, and decreed every single day before the Nation of Israel as they marched and moved forward during the wilderness experience. As the Prophet and Leader of Israel, Moses spoke. The Ark of the Covenant would be raised to lead the procession. It is extremely important to note that the Ark of the Covenant represented the very presence of God. The Glory of God showed up as a cloud by day and a pillar of fire by night.
Rise up with Jesus Christ or go down with the devil. Moses moved forward with the plan of God.

March forward, move forward with Jesus Christ or go backward with the devil. Make progress with Jesus Christ or make excuses with the devil. Let God arise and let ugly and ungodly attitudes be scattered.

2.) LET HIS ENEMIES BE SCATTERED

Like roaches when the lights come on, let his enemies be scattered. When the true glory of God shows up, his enemies scatter.

3.) LET HIS HATERS FLEE BEFORE HIM –
Let His haters flee, for His haters will be our elevators.
Let His haters flee, for **Proverbs 13:22** states that,

"A good man leaveth an inheritance to his children's children: and the wealth of the sinner is laid up for the just."

Let His haters flee, because you can run from Him, but you can't hide from Him.

Three Life Changing "Lets": Let The Wicked Perish At The Presence of God

THE WICKED PERISH AT THE PRESENCE OF GOD

Psalm 68:2: "As smoke is driven away, so drive them away: as wax melteth before the fire, so let the wicked perish at the presence of God."

Smoke and wax are the two natural examples that show how God is able to handle haters and the wicked. During and after Hurricane Sandy from October 29th until November 12th of 2013, Brenda and I burned candles in the evening darkness and at night for light. In the morning light we blew out the candles and the smoke was driven away, and the wax candles were much shorter, because the fire melted them. When we burn candles during Holy Communion the wax candles always melt before the fire. "I wish somebody's soul would catch on fire burning with the Holy Ghost."

The presence of God totally wears down and destroys the wicked. We need to totally appreciate the blood of Jesus Christ and the grace of God!

When the wicked perish at the presence of God the righteous learn three more life changing "lets".

THREE LIFE CHANGING "LETS": FOR THE RIGHTEOUS

1.) Let the righteous be glad – March forward, move forward, & go forward from sadness to gladness.
2.) Let the righteous rejoice before God.
   A.) Move forward and rejoice before His presence.
   B.) Enjoy, embrace, and get all excited about our communion with Christ.
3.) Let the righteous exceedingly rejoice.

Three life changing "lets" for the righteous lead to four dimensions of singing.

FOUR DIMENSIONS OF SINGING

1.) **The Passion of Singing** – "Sing unto God" – Sing to an audience of one, the only one, the Holy One.
2.) **The Purpose of Singing** – "Sing praises to His name" – Never lose focus to whom we are singing and whose name we are singing.
3.) **The Power of Singing** – "extol him that rideth upon the heavens by his name JAH," "Extol" means to command "raising a song."
   - Singing Must Extol God's Name — JAH – Raise a praise In song about JAH, the Righteous Rider upon the heavens.

- JAH is a contraction for the name of God, Jehovah, that is used only in prophetic poetry (Ps. 68:4).
- Always remember that God Is JAH, Jehovah, the Righteous Rider who can take us higher than we've ever been before!

Ride on King Jesus
No man can-a-hinder me
Ride on King Jesus
Ride on
No man can-a-hinder me
No man can-a-hinder me
In that great getting up morning
Fair thee well, fair thee well
In that great getting up morning
Fair thee well, fair thee well

4.) The Pleasure of Singing - "and rejoice before him." Singing must move us so deeply marching forward, moving forward, onward, and upward to rejoice before Jesus, JAH, Jehovah, the Blessed Redeemer.

The ultimate goal of singing is to move the believer forward to rejoice right before the weighty presence of God.

Charles Wesley got it right when he wrote:

O for a thousand tongues to sing
My great Redeemer's praise,
The glories of my God and King,
The triumphs of his grace!

The four dimensions of singing heightens our awareness of His holy habitation.

HOLY HABITATION MAKES THE MAJOR DIFFERENCE IN MARCHING & MOVING FORWARD

Psalm 68:5 speaks clearly concerning the fatherless and widows. Widows and the orphans were particularly vulnerable in the ancient world and even so today. God's word literally commanded the Children of Israel to care, share, and bear the burden for the fatherless and widows (Ex. 22:22; Deut. 10:18; Ruth 4:14, 15).

GOD IS A FATHER OF THE FATHERLESS ONLY IN HIS HOLY HABITATION.

Psalm 22:3: "But thou art holy, O thou that inhabitest the praises of Israel."

God is a Judge of the widows only in His holy habitation. I truly love the word of the classic Gospel song entitled, "God Is."

> Verse 1:
> *God is my protection.*
> *God is my all in all.*
> *God is my guide and direction.*
> *God is my all in all.*
>
> Verse 2:
> *God is my joy in time of sorrow.*
> *God is my all in all.*
> *God is my today and tomorrow.*
> *God is my all in all.*

Chorus:
God is the joy and the strength of my life,
He moves all pain, misery, and strife.
He promised to keep me, never to leave me.
He's never ever come short of His word.

I've got to fast and pray, stay in His narrow way,
I've got to keep my life clean everyday;
I want to go with Him when He comes back,
I've come too far and I'll never turn back.
God is, God is, God is, God is, God is, God is, God is, God is
God is my all in all.

Holy Habitation Is The Birthing Place of God's Set Up Plan.

GOD'S SET UP PLAN

God sets the solitary in families.

Psalm 68:6—the solitary. Since the family culture was the very heart and center of Israelite community, those outside of its structure were left all alone and found themselves in dire need.

Solitary – One, lone, lonely as in solitary confinement.
One can be lonely, but not alone.
"God gives the lonely a permanent home." - (Jerus)
God brings out those bound with chains.
"He leads out the prisoners to prosperity." - (RSV)
Rebellious dwell in a dry land.

God's set up plan prepares us for when God marches through our public and private wilderness experiences.

WHEN GOD MARCHES THROUGH THE WILDERNESS

"O God, when thou <u>wentest forth</u> before thy people."

Battle Hymn of The Republic clearly describes how God's truth marches on.

> *Mine eyes have seen the glory of the coming of the Lord;*
> *He is trampling out the vintage where the grapes of wrath are stored;*
> *He hath loosed the fateful lightning of His terrible swift sword;*
> *His truth is marching on.*
> *Glory! Glory! Hallelujah! Glory! Glory! Hallelujah!*
> *Glory! Glory! Hallelujah! His truth is marching on.*

"when thou didst march through the wilderness"

Psalm 68:7—"march through the wilderness." The specific spiritual reference is to the forty years of the nation of Israel's wanderings in the wilderness.

- When God marches through the wilderness, things must move forward.
- When God marches through the wilderness things will move forward come hell or high water.
- When God marches through the wilderness only the obedient will enter the Promise Land.
- When God marches through the wilderness Mount Sinai is moved by the presence of God.
- When God marches through the wilderness Mount Sinai shakes, quakes, smokes, and burns with the Shekinah Glory of God.

- When God marches through the wilderness Moses is moved by the presence of God and is allowed to see the Promise Land, yet not enter, but shows up in the New Testament on the Mount of Transfiguration with Elijah, and the Blessed Redeemer, Jesus Christ, the express image of the glory of God.
- When God marches through the wilderness Joshua is moved by the presence of God and leads the Wilderness babies and crosses the Jordan River to actually enter the Promise Land.
- When God marches through the wilderness the rebellious, the haters, and the enemies of God in the ranks of the children of Israel are scattered and die in the wilderness never seeing the Promise Land. The spirit of rebellion is like witchcraft. It's a killer.

Isaiah 1:19: "If ye be willing and obedient, ye shall eat the good of the land."

- When God marches through the wilderness the disobedient will die in the wilderness.
- When God marches through the wilderness the disobedient will wander for 40 years in a desert that they could have marched forward through in 40 days.

Psalm 68:6: "but the rebellious dwell in a dry land."

DON'T DIE IN THE WILDERNESS THAT GOD WANTS YOU TO COME OUT OF!

2 Corinthians 1:20: "For all the promises of God in him are yea, and in him Amen, unto the glory of God by us."

March forward, move forward, go forward! Follow God's presence, and come out of the wilderness! Bishop Gary Oliver who has ministered in word and song at Mount Sinai wrote in his awesome song "Marchin and Movin".

> *We're marchin' and movin' onward and upward*
> *The kingdom of God is on a forceful advance*
> *We are takin' dominion over the darkness*
> *Tearin' down the works of the enemy's hands*
>
> *(Chorus)*
> *We've got the victory*
> *We've got the victory*
> *We've got the victory*
> *By the blood of the Lamb*

Don't let the wilderness mentality destroy you! The following old Negro spiritual told us how to move forward and come out of the wilderness.

> *Tell me, how did you feel when you*
> *Come out (come out of the wilderness)*
> *Come out (come out of the wilderness)*
> *Come out (come out of the wilderness)*
> *Tell me, how did you feel when you*
> *Come out (come out of the wilderness)*
> *Leaning on the Lord?*
>
> *(Chorus)*
> *I'm leaning (leaning on the Lord; leaning on the Lord)*
> *I'm leaning (leaning on the Lord; leaning on the Lord)*
> *Oh, yes, I'm leaning (leaning on the Lord; leaning on the Lord)*
> *Who died on Calvary*

God Marches Through The Wilderness to Make Sure That All The Wilderness Babies Will Make It Into The Promise Land

- Wilderness babies were birthed in the trial.
- Wilderness babies were birthed in the deepest trouble.
- Wilderness babies were birthed in the toughest times.
- Wilderness babies were birthed in tragedies.
- Wilderness babies were birthed in the worst of times.
- Wilderness babies respected their present leader, Moses.
- Wilderness babies respected their future leader, Joshua.
- Wilderness babies absolutely refuse to die in the wilderness.
- Wilderness babies were raised daily on prophetic prayer and prophetic praise.
- Wilderness babies don't have a slave mentality.
- Wilderness babies don't mind marching and moving onward and upward until they get to the Promise Land.
- Wilderness babies catch the vision of victory & never give up!

SELAH STATE OF MIND

Selah: *celah* // seh'-law // 1) to lift up, exalt, a technical musical term showing accentuation, pause, interruption.

Selah [pause, and calmly think of that]!— Amplified Bible

I am in a selah state of mind. Selah praise is the type of praise that makes me pause, and commune with Christ, as I think of His goodness. A selah state of mind propels me into the next dimensions of intimate praise and worship.

When I think of the goodness of Jesus
And all He's done for me
My soul, my soul cries out
Hallelu, hallelujah
I thank God for saving me

Selah moments teach us to be sensitive to and to move at the presence of God. Yes I am a native New Yorker and in a New York state of mind, but I am also a praiser and worshiper. I am in a selah state of mind and I am moved at the presence of God.

MOVED AT THE PRESENCE OF GOD

Psalm 68:8: "The earth shook, the heavens also dropped at the presence of God: even Sinai itself was moved at the presence of God, the God of Israel."

Exodus 19:18: "And Mount Sinai was altogether on a smoke, because the Lord descended upon it in fire: and the smoke thereof ascended as the smoke of a furnace, and the whole mount quaked greatly."

- God is on the move.
- God's church must be on the move.
- God's church must be marching and moving forward in consistent communion with Jesus Christ.
- Embrace The Move of God!!!
- Embrace The Presence of God!!!

Psalm 68:18: "Thou hast ascended on high, thou hast led captivity captive: thou hast received gifts for men; yea, for the rebellious also, that the Lord God might dwell among them." Ephesians 4:8: "Wherefore he saith, When he ascended up on

high, he led captivity captive, and gave gifts unto men."

The rebellious children of Israel died in the wilderness and never entered the Promise Land. Their wilderness babies, their off-spring, their children did enter the Promise Land. Now thank God for Jesus Christ who ascended on high and successfully put His very own precious blood on the Mercy Seat. Therefore, today, the rebellious can get right with God. The rebellious can repent today. The rebellious can receive forgiveness through the Blood of Jesus Christ today.

Moses was absolutely rebellious, but he got right with God and communicated with Jesus Christ on the Mount of Transfiguration. Paul was totally rebellious, but he got right with God and had consistent communion with Christ.

We were totally rebellious, dead in trespasses and sins, but got right with God, and now have consistent communion with Christ.
Get right with God and do it now. Get right with God and He will show you how. Down at the cross where He shed His Blood, get right with God. Get right. Get right with God.

God is a God of Another Chance Through the Blood of Jesus Christ. Robert Lowry was absolutely right when he penned the classic hymn

> *What can wash away my sin?*
> *Nothing but the blood of Jesus.*
> *What can make me whole again?*
> *Nothing but the blood of Jesus.*

Not just for Moses or Paul, but for every rebellious sinner like you and me, and every other ever born. That's the good news. That's the gospel of Jesus Christ!

CHAPTER SIX

MAKING A DIFFERENCE BY SETTING FORWARD & RAISING THE STANDARD - WHAT FLAG ARE YOU MARCHING AND MOVING UNDER?

Numbers 2:17: Then the tabernacle of the congregation shall set forward with the camp of the Levites in the midst of the camp: as they encamp, so shall they <u>set forward</u>, every man in his place by their standards.

1.) **The Tabernacle of The Congregation – The Tent of Meeting** also better known as the Tabernacle of Moses.

The Gate – Jesus Is The Gate.

John 14:6: "Jesus saith unto him, I am the way, the truth, and the life: no man cometh unto the Father, but by me."

The fence surrounded the entire Tabernacle of Moses. Outer Court – With it's brazen altar and brazen laver. The outer court was 150 feet long, 75 feet wide, and 7 ½ feet high.

The tent inside the outer court included the inner court and the most holy place was 45 feet long, 15 feet wide, and 15 feet high.

Inner Court, aka, the holy place – with it's table of shewbread, golden candlestick, and altar of incense.

The Vail
The Cloud
The Most Holy Place – With the Ark of the Covenant

Hebrews 8:1-5:
"Now of the things which we have spoken this is the sum: **We have such an high priest, who is set on the right hand of the throne of the Majesty in the heavens; A minister of the sanctuary, and of <u>the true tabernacle, which the Lord pitched, and not man.</u> For every high priest is ordained to offer gifts and sacrifices: wherefore it is of necessity that this man have somewhat also to offer. For if he were on earth, he should not be a priest, seeing that there are priests that offer gifts according to the law: <u>Who serve unto the example and shadow of heavenly things, as Moses was admonished of God</u> when he was about <u>to make the tabernacle: for, See, saith he, that thou make all things according to the pattern shewed to thee in the mount.</u>"**

SHALL SET FORWARD

- We shall go forward.
- We shall march forward.
- We shall move forward.
- We won't be like the foolish and rebellious generation that was barred by God, Himself, from entering the Promise Land, because of their disobedience.
- We will be like the obedient generation who actually entered, Yes, literally entered the Promise Land, Canaan Land, because of their obedience.

Obedience is the catalyst of change that moves a people forward into the Promise Land. We shall set forward, yes, we will move forward and learn what not to do from the teacher named failure, and what to do from the teacher named success, in order to enter in.

In his awesome book entitled Failing Forward, John Maxwell, wrote that, "The more you do, the more you fail. The more you fail, the more you learn. The more you learn, the better you get." Dr. Benjamin E. Mays was right when he declared and decreed that," It must be borne in mind that the tragedy of life does not lie in not reaching your goal. The tragedy of life lies in having no goal to reach." Don't fear failure for failure is a God-ordained opportunity to turn your personal predicament inside out and make your life a captivating forward journey.

LEVITES IN THE MIDST OF THE CAMP – WORSHIPERS IN THE MIDST OF THE CHURCH

When the Levitical priesthood & families of working worshipers had a goal to function in the camp efficiently and effectively, the movement and the masses marched forward. When worshipers function in the camp, the movement, and the masses march forward. Marching with a mindset for change. We shall overcome. We shall get ahead.

The Patriarch Jacob had twelve sons, who ultimately transitioned into being the leaders of the twelve tribes of Israel. Twelve representing the government of God. Christian concept of twelve disciples and the twelve apostles called by Jesus is also based on the government of God.

According to Genesis 35:23 and 26 Levi was Jacob's third son by, Leah, his wife. The Levites were clearly the descendants of Levi.

According to Exodus 6:13, 16-20 Levi was the High Priest Aaron and Deliverer Moses' great-grandfather. Levi was also the father of Gershon, Kohath, and Merari, who became key leaders of three main sections of the Levites.

The word Levite, very often refers to the tribe of Levi in its entirety. The priestly sons of Aaron made up the Levitical priesthood. (1Kings 8:4; 1Chronicles 23:2; Ezra 1:5; John 1:19) Priestly duties were confined to the male members of Aaron's family, with the rest of the Levite tribe as served as their assistants, dismantling, and carrying the tabernacle (Numbers 3:3, 6-10) as the children of Israel traveled as a church in the wilderness.

Each of these Levite families had a specific assigned place according to scripture, a family of working worshipers literally surrounding the entire tabernacle of Moses in the wilderness with an atmosphere of praise and worship. The High Priest Aaron's Kohathite family camped to the east side, in front of the tabernacle of Moses. The rest of working worshipers known as the Kohathites camped on the south side. The worshipers known as the Gershonites camped on the west side, and the working worshipers known as Merarites camped on the north side.

When the time was right to set forward, moved forward, marched forward.

The High Priest Aaron and his priestly sons took down the veil dividing the Inner Court from the Most Holy and covered the table of shew beard, alter of incense, brazen laver, brazen alter, golden candlestick, and the ark of the covenant.

Numbers 4:5-6:
"And when the camp setteth forward, Aaron shall come, and his sons, and they shall take down the covering vail, and cover the ark of testimony with it: And shall put thereon the covering of badgers' skins, and shall spread over it a cloth wholly of

blue, and shall put in the staves thereof."

KOHATHITES SET FORWARD

The working worshipers known as Kohathites then set forward, moved forward, marched forward carried the covered table of shew beard, alter of incense, brazen laver, brazen alter, golden candlestick, and the ark of the covenant.

On the south side of the Tabernacle of Moses there was 151,450 people from the tribes of Gad, Simeon, and Reuben with Kohath, but the levitical priesthood were in the midst, were in the middle of the camp with Moses, Aaron, and Aaron's priestly sons in front. Today take action now. Now is the time set forward, Move forward, march forward, onward and upward for deeply intimate, passionate, potent, and pure worship must be at the core center, inner court of the church. The Kohathites moved forward with the plan of God.

GERSHONITES SET FORWARD

The working worshipers known as Gershonites set forward, moved forward, marched forward bringing all of the tent cloths, screens, courtyard hangings, and tent cords from the tabernacle of Moses. On the west side of the Tabernacle of Moses there was 108,100 people from the tribes of Benjamin, Manassah, and Ephraim with Gershon, but the levitical priesthood, were in the midst, were in the middle of the camp with Moses, Aaron, and priestly sons of Aaron at the front. Today take action now. Now is the time to set forward, move forward, march forward, onward and upward for deeply intimate, passionate, potent, and pure worship must be at the core center, inner court of the church. The Gershonites moved forward with the plan of God.

MERARITES SET FORWARD

The working worshipers known as Merarites set forward, moved forward, marched forward handling all of the panel frames, pillars, socket pedestals, tent pins and cords of the courtyard surrounding the tabernacle of Moses. The Merarites moved forward with the plan of God.

MOVING FORWARD ON THE NORTH SIDE

On the north side of the Tabernacle of Moses there were 151,600 people from the tribes of Dan, Asher, and Naphtali with Merriam, but The Leviticus Priesthood were in the midst, were in the middle of the camp with Moses, Aaron, and the Priestly Sons of Aaron in the Front. Today take action now. Now Is the time to set forward, Move forward, march forward, onward and upward for deeply intimate, passionate, potent, and pure worship must be at the core center, inner court of the church.

MOVING FORWARD ON THE SOUTH SIDE

On the south side of the Tabernacle of Moses there was 151,450 people from the tribes of Gad, Simeon, and Reuben with Kohath, but The Levitical Priesthood were in the midst, were in the middle of the camp with Moses, Aaron, and the Priestly Sons of Aaron in the Front. Today take action now. Now is the time to set forward, move forward, march forward, onward and upward for deeply intimate, passionate, potent, and pure worship must be at the core center, inner court of the church.

MOVING FORWARD ON THE EAST SIDE

On the east side of the Tabernacle of Moses there were 186,400 people from the tribes of Judah, Issachar, and Zebulon, but The Levitical Priesthood were in the midst, were in the middle of the camp with Moses, Aaron, and Aaron's Priestly Sons were. Today take action now. Now is the time to set forward, move forward, march forward, onward and upward for deeply intimate, passionate, potent, and pure worship must be at the core center, inner court of the church.

MOVING FORWARD ON THE WESTSIDE

From the west side camp to the east side camp around the Tabernacle of Moses and from the overlapping north side camp to the south side camp around the Tabernacle of Moses it made the sign of the cross. It all pointed to the Prime Mover, our Lord and Savior, Jesus Christ.

WHEN LEVITES ENCAMP/WHEN WORSHIPERS ENCAMP

When levitical priesthood encamp the masses set forward. When worshipers encamp the masses move forward and start marching.

- Yes, we still do need to set forward, move forward, march for jobs.
- Yes, we still do need to set forward, move forward, march for economic and social justice.
- Yes, we still do need to set forward, move forward, march for the very soul of our local villages, towns, counties, states, and nation which are in jeopardy of being corrupted from within and without.

We are New Testament, new covenant priests who must set forward, march forward, onward and upward.

Revelation 1:6: "And hath made us kings and priests unto God and his Father; to him be glory and dominion for ever and ever. Amen."

Revelation 5:10: "And hast made us unto our God kings and priests: and we shall reign on the earth."

WORSHIP CHANGES THE ATMOSPHERE

John 4:22-24:
"Ye worship ye know not what: we know what we worship: for salvation is of the Jews. But the hour cometh, and now is, when the true worshipers shall worship the Father in spirit and in truth: for the Father seeketh such to worship him. God is a Spirit: and they that worship him must worship him in spirit and in truth."

Marching and Moving In Order

- Know your place. Mind your business. March and move in order.
- Know your lane. Mind your responsibility. March and move In Order.

WHAT PLACE ARE YOU IN?

- We can only set forward when we are in our place.
- We can only set forward when we are in our purpose.
- If you're in somebody else's place, get out.
- Stay in your God-given place. It is from there that you will move forward. Flow and grow in your God-given purpose.
- Stay In your God-given lane. It is from there that you will

move forward. Make great gains of victory in your God-given lane.

- Don't bring hell in someone's lane!!!
- Don't bring demonic rebellion in someone's lane!!!
- Don't bring devilish disobedience in someone's lane!!!
- Don't bring deceptive foolishness in someone's lane!!!
- Don't bring dangerous sin and satan into someone's lane!!!

- Get the hell out of their God-given lane!!!
- Get the demonic rebellion out of their God-given lane!!!
- Get the devilish disobedience out of their God-given lane!!!
- Get the deceptive foolishness out of their God-given lane!!!
- Get dangerous sin and satan out of their God-given lane!!!

Move forward, set forward and know that pleading the blood of Jesus prevails!!!

We are trying to serve the Lord. Were setting forward. Were marching forward. Were moving forward, onward and upward. We don't want to run you over. Get the hell out of our Lane. Get the demonic rebellion out of our Lane. Get devilish disobedience out of our lane. Get the deceptive foolishness out of our lane. Get dangerous sin and satan out of our lane. Move forward, set forward and know that pleading the blood of Jesus prevails.

Don't sell crack and all types of damnable and lethally dangerous dope on our corners or in our communities. Get the hell out, demonic rebellion out, devilish disobedience out, and deceptive foolishness out of our God-given lane. Get dangerous sin and satan out of our God-given lane. Pleading the blood of Jesus prevails. Don't church gossip on our corners or in our communities. Get the destructive hell, rebellion, disobedience, and foolishness out of our

God-given lane. Get deadly sin and satan out of our God-given lane. Pleading the blood of Jesus prevails. Don't let gangster style, gang style, kill, shoot, and loot on our corners or in our communities. Get the damaging hell, rebellion, disobedience, and foolishness out of our God-given lane. We mean business we are setting forward, marching forward, moving forward, onward, and upward. The blood of Jesus prevails!!!

WHAT FLAG ARE YOU MARCHING AND MOVING UNDER?

- Are you marching and moving under the church gossip gang's flag?
- Are you marching and moving under the bloods gang's flag?
- Are you marching and moving under the crips gang's flag?
- Are you marching and moving under the religious assassins gang's flag?
- Are you marching and moving under the political assassin gang's flag?
- Are you marching and moving under the negative peer-pressure gang's flag?
- Or are you marching and moving under the blood of Jesus crew, the army of the Lord, the blood washed believers Flag?

The Christian song "We Are Soldiers" truly drives home the moving forward and making a difference message.

We are soldiers in the army
We got to fight, although we have to cry
We got to hold up the blood stain banner
We got to hold it up until we die

Verse
My father was a soldier
he had her hand on the gospel plow,
But one day he got old
he couldn't fight anymore
he said 'I've got to stand here and fight anyhow!'

THE TRAGIC SHOOTING OF TRAYVON MARTIN

The tragic shooting of Trayvon Martin by night watchman George Zimmerman on the night of February 26, 2012, in Sanford, Florida, is a horrible situation that showed the drastic need to mend the vast racial divide in America. February  is African-American history month. Trayvon Martin had no weapon on that night in February. Yet he was profiled and followed by George Zimmerman. Trayvon Martin was returning from the store where he picked up a bag of Skittles candy and an Iced Tea drink. Trayvon Martin was a 17-year-old African American high school student who profiled and judged by Zimmerman as a threat. My heart and soul goes out to Trayvon Martin's mother and father and the entire family. George Zimmerman, is a 28-year-old man of mixed-race. Zimmerman has a Hispanic mother and a White father. Zimmerman was an overzealous neighborhood watch coordinator for the gated community in Sanford, Florida, where Trayvon Martin was visiting his father and where the fatal shooting that shocked the nation occurred.

Zimmerman profiled Martin as a trouble maker and called the police. Zimmerman was clearly told by the Police dispatcher not to pursue the matter and to stay in his car. Foolishly Zimmerman did not listen and took matters in to his own hands that took Trayvon Martin's life with the fatal gunshot that never should have happened. Had Zimmerman listened Trayvon Martin would still be alive today. The police arrived within two minutes of the fatal gunshot. George Zimmerman was taken to jail, he was treated for his non-fatal head injuries. Zimmerman was questioned for five hours, but he was eventually released under the supposition the shooting was in self-defense. Six weeks later after intense national and international outcry from the concerned public George Zimmerman was charged with murder by a new prosecutor for the State of Florida.

George Zimmerman's trial began on June 10, 2013, in Sanford. On July 13, 2013, a jury of six women, all of the jurors with exception of one was white, found Zimmerman not guilty of the charges of second-degree murder and of manslaughter. Cartoons, charts, and dummies covered up the only facts known beyond a shadow of a doubt in the case that being that George Zimmerman was clearly told not pursue Trayvon Martin who was unarmed and Zimmerman shot Martin in the heart. Only Trayvon Martin who is dead, George Zimmerman, and God know the entire truth. We must move forward and make a difference by pushing to get unjust laws that allow the unjust murder of young black males to be changed. Across the nation the concerned masses began to march in protest against this unjust verdict.

Unbelievable!!! This unjust verdict condones the killing of an unarmed black young male. Let us all pray for the Martin family. The struggle continues!!! With this unjust verdict Trayvon Martin was killed twice and true justice was also shot in her very heart and soul. Rev. Dr. Martin Luther King Jr. was right when he moved forward and stated in the letter from the Birmingham Jail that "Injustice anywhere is a threat to justice everywhere." Justice lost in this case and the racist good ole boys system of "just us" won. It's not over. The struggle continues. Key provisions in the voters rights act were recently struck down by the Supreme Court and the life of a young black male is not valued in America. The struggle continues today.

Stevie Wonder moved forward and vowed to not perform in any state that has a "stand your ground" law. Wonder stated that "For the gift that God has given me and for whatever I mean, I've decided today that until the 'stand your ground' law is abolished in Florida, I will never perform there again." Stevie Wonder further stated that, "Wherever  I find that law exists, I will not perform in that state or in that part of the world." We must move forward and make a difference in the backwards world full of racial profiling. "These laws try to fix something that was never broken," Attorney General, Eric Holder recently moved forward and stated at the NAACP Convention held at the Orange County Convention Center in Orlando, Florida. Attorney General Holder further stated that, "There has always been a legal defense for using deadly force if - and the 'if' is important - no safe retreat is available. But we must examine laws that take this further by eliminating the common sense and age-old requirement that people who feel threatened have a duty to retreat, outside their home, if they can do so safely." In spite of this deep pain let us all keep the peace. So Trayvon Martin will rest in peace.

I was deeply moved in my heart and soul when almost one week after the unjust George Zimmerman Trial not guilty verdict United States of America President Barack Obama moved forward spoke from his heart and soul concerning the tragic killing of Trayvon Martin, the not guilty verdict, and race relations in America.

President Obama stated that, "When Trayvon Martin was first shot, I said that this could have been my son. Another way of saying that is, Trayvon Martin could have been me 35 years ago," I can relate to that as a black man. Push for truth and justice as we are empowered by the grace and mercy of God to move forward, set forward, and make a difference.

SET FORWARD & RAISE THE STANDARD

- Set forward and raise the standard. Move forward and love your neighbor as you love yourself.

- Set forward and raise the standard. Pay your bills. Keep your word. Build good credit. Move forward and build your reputation. Rebuild, repair, restore, and revive your name.

Proverbs 22:1 States That "A good name is rather to be chosen than great riches, and loving favour rather than silver and gold." Even God, Himself keeps His word, or else His name would be no good.

Psalm 138:2: "I will worship toward thy holy temple, and praise thy name for thy lovingkindness and for thy truth: for thou hast <u>magnified thy word above all thy name</u>."

- Set forward and raise the standard. Learn to forgive. Move forward and raise the standard don't let bitterness and unforgiveness eat you up alive.

- Set forward and raise the standard. Rebuild, repair, restore, and revive broken, battered, and bruised relationships that only time can heal through the grace of God.

When the time was right to set forward, move forward, and march forward, The High Priest, Aaron, and his priestly sons took down the veil dividing the Inner Court from the Most Holy and covered the table of shewbread, altar of incense, brazen laver, brazen altar, golden candlestick, and the Ark of the Covenant. This discipline layed the groundwork for the leaders, learners, and Levites who actually moved forward and made a difference by entering the promise land after the death of Moses and all the Israelites who were not supportive of Moses. Moses' successor, Joshua, who strategically moved forward with the plan of God led these leaders, learners, and Levites in the promise land.

CHAPTER SEVEN

LEADERS, LEARNERS, & LEVITES – GO AFTER IT

Joshua 1:10-11:
"Then Joshua commanded the officers of the people, saying, <u>Pass through</u> the host, and command the people, saying, Prepare you victuals; for within three days ye shall <u>pass over</u> this Jordan, to <u>go</u> in to <u>possess the land</u>, which the Lord your God giveth you to <u>possess it</u>."

Joshua 3:1-3:
"And Joshua rose early in the morning; and they removed from Shittim, and came to Jordan, he and all the children of Israel, and lodged there before they <u>passed over</u>. And it came to pass after three days, that the officers went through the host; And they commanded the people, saying, When ye see the ark of the covenant of the Lord your God, and the priests the Levites bearing it, then ye shall remove from your place, and <u>go after it</u>."

- Every leader must be a learner – Must have a teachable spirit.
- Every leader must learn from the Lord.
- Every leader must learn from their spiritual leader.
- Every leader must learn from the Levitical priesthood.

Nelson Mandela was right when he stated that "Real leaders must be ready to sacrifice all for the freedom of their people." Joshua literally sacrificed his whole life to be Moses' minister and he was Moses' successor. Joshua would move on to lead the Israelites into the Promise Land. Joshua moved forward with the plan of God.

DID YOU KNOW? - Joshua means "Jehovah saves." Joshua is mentioned 201 times in the Bible in eight books: Exodus, Numbers, Deuteronomy, Joshua, Judges, I Kings, I Chronicles, and Hebrews. Joshua was a well-trained soldier. Joshua was the National Leader of Israel. "Yeshua," "Joshua" and "Jesus" are all essentially the same name. In fact, Joshua had followed Moses since he was a youth freed from the vicious chains of slavery. We first see Joshua at the battle with the Amalekites, where Aaron and Hur held up Moses' hands, and Joshua led the battle. (Exodus 17:8-13) Then Joshua shows up all through the trek to the Promised Land. Learning from the good, bad, and indifferent experiences in Joshua's journey will help us to finally move forward and make a difference. John Maxwell in his book entitled *You Win Some, You Learn Some* wrote that, "The lessons you have the opportunity to learn will be presented to you in various forms. Fail to learn the lesson and you get stuck, unable to move forward. Learn the lesson and you get to move forward and go to the next one."

LEADERS, LEARNERS, & LEVITES RISE EARLY

Joshua rose early - **"And Joshua rose early in the morning"**

Joshua 6:12: "And Joshua rose early in the morning, and the priests took up the ark of the Lord."

Joshua 7:16: "So Joshua rose up early in the morning, and brought Israel by their tribes; and the tribe of Judah was taken."

Joshua 8:10: "And Joshua rose up early in the morning, and

numbered the people, and went up, he and the elders of Israel, before the people to Ai."

Moses rose early - **Exodus 8:20:** "And the Lord said unto Moses, Rise up early in the morning, and stand before Pharaoh; lo, he cometh forth to the water; and say unto him, Thus saith the Lord, Let my people go, that they may serve me."

Jesus rose early - **Mark 16:9:** "Now when Jesus was risen early the first day of the week, he appeared first to Mary Magdalene, out of whom he had cast seven devils."

It is not positive or progressive to rise early and worry - **Psalm 127:2:** "It is vain for you to rise up early, to sit up late, to eat the bread of sorrows: for so he giveth his beloved sleep."

It is not positive or progressive to rise early and drink wine – **Isaiah 5:11:** "Woe unto them that rise up early in the morning, that they may follow strong drink; that continue until night, till wine inflame them!"

- Rise early and pray!
- Rise early and read your Bible!
- Rise early and meditate!
- Rise early and exercise!
- Rise early and prepare for your day!
- Rise early and get yourself together!
- Rise early and prepare to move forward spiritually, socially, politically, and economically!

LEADERS, LEARNERS, AND LEVITES REMOVE FROM SHITTIM AND MOVE FORWARD

"and they removed from Shittim"
Shittim // Myjv // Shittiym // shit-teem' // Shittim = "the acacias"
a) Place of Israel's encampment between the conquest of the Transjordanic region and crossing the Jordan into Canaan
b) A place west of Jerusalem.

- Remove from mess.
- Remove from stress.
- Remove from less.
- Remove from pest.
- Remove from not being blessed.
- Remove from not getting God's best.
- Remove from all the rest.
- Remove from Shittim.

Move Forward & Get Out of Shittim – The conquest of Transjordan region must move forward to the actual crossing of the Jordan River and entrance into Canaan land.

"If you can't fly then run, if you can't run then walk, if you can't walk then crawl, but whatever you do you have to keep moving forward."
--Martin Luther King Jr.

LEADERS, LEARNERS, & LEVITES COME TO JORDAN

"and came to Jordan," river Jordan = "descender"

a) The river of Palestine running from the roots of Anti-Lebanon to
the Dead Sea a distance of approx 200 miles (320 km)

- Come to Jordan and prepare to follow.
- Come to Jordan and prepare to walk by faith.
- Come to Jordan and prepare to go a way that you have never been before.
- Come to Jordan and prepare to leave mediocrity.
- Come to Jordan and prepare to leave compromise.
- Come to Jordan and prepare to make a difference.
- Come to Jordan and prepare to move forward!

LEADERS, LEARNERS, & LEVITES LODGE BEFORE THEY PASS OVER

"...he and all the children of Israel, and lodged there before they passed over."

- Remember where we came from before moving forward and passing over.
- Remember how the Lord brought us through before moving forward and passing over.
- Remember to get rest before moving forward and passing over.
- Remember to be at your best before moving forward and passing over.

Rev. Dr. Martin Luther King, Jr. said, "If we are to go forward, we must go back and rediscover those precious values - that all reality hinges on moral foundations and that all reality has spiritual control."

LEADERS CHECK ON LEARNERS

"And it came to pass after three days, that the officers went through the host"

- Leaders check on learners so be your brother's keeper.
- Leaders check on learners so help restore those who have fallen from grace.
- Leaders check on learners so stay in touch and pray for those you are responsible for.
- Leaders check on learners so don't let anyone fall through the cracks.
- Leaders check on learners so be a big brother and a big sister in Christ.
- Leaders check on learners so be a good neighbor.
- Leaders check on learners so love one another.
- Leaders must move forward with the plan of God.

LEADERS COMMAND LEARNERS TO SEE THE ARK

"And they commanded the people, saying, When ye see the ark of the covenant of the Lord your God."

Nelson Mandela stated, "Lead from the back — and let others believe they are in front."

- Leaders command learners to see the best even in the worst of times.
- Leaders command learners to see what the Lord Is strategically moving forward through.
- Leaders command learners to see when to strategically move forward themselves.

- Leaders command learners to see what represents the presence of the Lord.

Ark of the Covenant. The first piece of the tabernacle's furniture for which precise directions were delivered. Exodus 25:1 gives us a description of the tabernacle: It appears to have been an oblong chest of shittim (acacia) wood, 2 1/2 cubits long by 1 1/2 broad and deep. Within and without gold was overlaid on the wood, and on the upper side or lid, which was edged roundabout with gold, the mercy-seat was placed. The ark was fitted with rings, one at each of the four corners, and through these was passed staves of the same wood similarly overlaid.

LEVITES BEAR IT

"and the priests the Levites bearing it"

- Levites bear it!
- Priests bear it!
- Those who respect the presence of God bear It!
- Blood washed believers who care and share will bear It!

Deuteronomy 10:8: "At that time the Lord separated the tribe of Levi, to bear the ark of the covenant of the Lord, to stand before the Lord to minister unto him, and to bless in his name, unto this day."

1 Peter 2:9: "But ye are a chosen generation, a royal priesthood, an holy nation, a peculiar people; that ye should shew forth the praises of him who hath called you out of darkness into his marvellous light."

Revelation 1:6: "And hath made us kings and priests unto God and his Father; to him be glory and dominion for ever and ever. Amen."

Revelation 5:10: "And hast made us unto our God kings and priests: and we shall reign on the earth."

LEADERS, LEARNERS, & LEVITES REMOVE FROM THEIR PLACE

"then ye shall remove from your place"

- Remove from your place.
- Remove from the past disgrace.
- Remove from doubt.
- Remove from sin.
- Remove from bad tradition.
- Remove from controlling folk.
- Remove from the land of not enough and move forward into the land of more than enough.

Mary, Mary got it right in their hit single, "Go Get It"

Go get it, Go Get it, Go get it, Go get it, Go get it
Go get yo blessing
Go get it, Go get it, Go get it, Go get it, Go get it, Go get it
It's yo time, it's yo time, it's yo time, it's yo time

LEADERS AND LEARNERS GO AFTER IT

"and go after it."

- Go after it. Move forward and be a worshiping church!

- Go after It. Move forward and be a word church!
- Go after It. Move forward and be a warrior church!
- Go After It. Move forward and be a witnessing church!
- Go After It. Move forward and be a working church!
- Go After It. Move forward and be a wisdom church!
- Go After It. Move forward and be a whole church!

Dr. Benjamin E. Mays was right when he said that, "Every man and woman is born into the world to do something unique and something distinctive and if he or she does not do it, it will never be done."

MOVING FORWARD & GOING AFTER IT WITH THE PROSPER PROGRAM

Over the last 25 years I have worked as a Community Research Assistant in the Town of Hempstead Office of Communications and Public Affairs. During the time I have been deeply honored not only to write for many distinguished elected officials, but also on occasion to give tours to youth groups at town hall. One of the youth groups that have toured town hall over the last few years is the PROSPER Program. I shared with them that the town of Hempstead which was established in 1644 and is older than the United States of America itself. I shared with them that town Hempstead is the largest township in America. Larger than our nation's capitol, Washington, D.C. and the state of Alaska. I bring the students to the Marriage License Division of the Town Clerk's Office, the Law Library of the Town Attorney's Office, and the System and Data Computer Lab. Students in the PROSPER (People Reaching for Opportunities to Succeed Personally, Educationally and Realistically) program are enrolled in a positive and progressive school-to-career program with an emphasis on attendance retention that provides service to students in grades 10 through 12 from

Freeport and Westbury High Schools.

This year, 40 students received PROSPER certificates of completion, and of the eight participating seniors, six will be graduating from their respective high schools and move forward on to either college, employment or military service—something they would not have ever achieved without the help of PROSPER Program.

Jim Molle, the PROSPER Coordinator and his staff work closely with the students at Abilities, Inc., located at the Viscardi Center (formerly Abilities!) in Albertson, New York. For 60 years, Abilities, Inc. has been able to maintain a critical balance between job seekers with disabilities and the interests of companies.

The PROSPER program was created in 1997 to address New York State educational and vocational mandates within a unique pre-vocational environment that moves forward and bridges the gap between high school and the professional world. Over 800 students have enrolled in the program over the years and the school has partnered with the likes of the Town of Hempstead, Adelphi University, Hofstra University, SUNY Old Westbury, and Nassau Community College, as well as the collaboration of members of the business community including but not limited to Covanta Energy, Cedar Creek Water Pollution Plant, Mercy Medical Center, Adecco Group NA, Holocaust Museum, Long Island Crisis Center, Quest Diagnostics, the United States Army and United States Navy.

Mississippi's Fred McDowell put it this way:

> *You got to move*
> *You got to move*
> *You got to move, child*

You got to move
But when the Lord
Gets ready
You got to move

Go After It. Move Forward. Now we must backup and get a clear understanding of exactly what happened before Joshua and the obedient next generation of Israelites moved forward and entered the promise land. This information is extremely important because it lays the legal groundwork for Jesus to move forward from heaven into the earth realm fully God and fully man born of a woman, Mary. God the Father will make sure that the body of Jesus will be prepared in the most colorful way possible. So everyone can relate.

Part 2

MOVING FORWARD THROUGH THE PAIN

CHAPTER EIGHT

MOVING FORWARD FROM PROSTITUTION TO PROCLAMATION – THE SCARLET THREAD OF REDEMPTION

Joshua 2:1: "And Joshua the son of Nun sent out of Shittim two men to spy secretly, saying, Go view the land, even Jericho. And they went, and came into an harlot's house, named Rahab, and lodged there."

Joshua 2:18: "Behold, when we come into the land, thou shalt bind this line of scarlet thread in the window which thou didst let us down by: and thou shalt bring thy father, and thy mother, and thy brethren, and all thy father's household, home unto thee."

Our condition of existence is found in the truth that we all need to move forward from the dangerous abuses and misuses of our very own potential from one degree to another in order to walk in our very own divine purpose and destiny. In one form or another we all need to move forward from the prostitution of hidden potential in order move into the moment and place of our deliverance, and the proclamation of divine purpose and destiny.

Did You Know?: Rahab's name means breadth. Rahab, the prostitute, protected the two Israelite secret spies sent out of Shittim across the Jordan River by Moses' successor, Joshua, to view, to spy out the promise land, from being brutally killed by Jericho's King. Rahab was born and raised in Jericho. Rahab was a prostitute who found redemption in the Lord. Rahab was a prostitute who found safety through the scarlet thread of redemption given to her by two Israelite spies whose life she protected by hiding them in her house from the King of Jericho. When the walls of Jericho would finally fall down after Joshua's army marched around it seven times and then shouted. Rahab's family would be the only family to survive Joshua's battle of Jericho, because the scarlet thread of redemption was in her window. Rahab the redeemed sister from Jericho is mentioned directly by name precisely eight different times in four different books of throughout the breadth of the Bible. Eight represents a new day and four represents the earth and the four winds of the earth. One book in the Old Testament mentions Rahab and three books in the New Testament mention Rahab, the redeemed sister, whose name means breadth. Learning from the good, bad, and indifferent experiences in Rahab's journey will help us to finally move forward and make a difference. Rehab moved forward through the pain of the destruction of Jericho, her home.

Rahab's testimony teaches us the true meaning of **Ephesians 3:17-19:**

"That Christ may dwell in your hearts by faith; that ye, being rooted and grounded in love,
May be able to comprehend with all saints what is the breadth, and length, and depth, and height;
And to know the love of Christ, which passeth knowledge, that ye might be filled with all the fulness of God."

DID YOU KNOW? - That the four books that mention Rahab's name which means "breadth" cross the very breadth of the Holy Bible are Joshua, Matthew, Hebrews, and James. Rahab, the redeemed sister, is first mentioned in Joshua 2:1 and is last mentioned in James

2:25. Rahab is a redeemed sister from Jericho who moved forward and made a most meaningful difference in spite of the overwhelming pain of her past. Rahab's past most certainly did not equal her future. We must also be motivated by Rahab and move forward realizing that our broken, battered, and bruised past does not equal our blessed, bountiful, and beneficial future. Learning from the good, bad, and indifferent experiences in Rahab's journey will help us to finally move forward and make a difference.

MOVING FORWARD FROM LYING TO LEARNING

Joshua 2:4: "And the woman took the two men, and hid them, and said thus, There came men unto me, but I wist not whence they were."

Rahab, moved forward and made a major difference through the process of moving from lying to learning the fear the Lord. Rahab was learning to lean on the Lord.
Rahab was moving forward from prostitution to proclamation as she leaned on the Lord to spare her and her family's life.

Learning to lean, learning to lean
I'm learning to lean on Jesus
Finding more power than I'd ever dreamed
I'm learning to lean on Jesus

MOVING FORWARD & LEARNING TO FEAR THE LORD
– RAHAB'S REHAB

Joshua 2:11:
And as soon as we had heard these things, our hearts did melt,

neither did there remain any more courage in any man, because of you: for the LORD your God, he is God in heaven above, and in earth beneath.

Rahab's confession of faith moved forward her new found spiritual connection as she mentions the Lord four times and God twice in terms that are clear statements of faith. Joshua 2:9 -13. The fear of the Lord was moving Rahab forward from the constant practice of prostitution to the constant proclamation of the Lord. Rahab's rehab, Rahab's rehabilitation from the practice of prostitution was found in her deeply abiding reference and more importantly reverence of the Lord God both in word and in deed. God was not finished with Rahab and God is not finished with us today. Thank God for Rahab's crystal clear proclamation that, **"for the LORD your God, he is God in heaven above, and in earth beneath."**

MOVING FORWARD & LEARNING TO FIGHT FOR THE FAMILY

Joshua 2:12-13:
Now therefore, I pray you, swear unto me by the LORD, since I have shewed you kindness, that ye will also shew kindness unto my father's house, and give me a true token:
And that ye will save alive my father, and my mother, and my brethren, and my sisters, and all that they have, and deliver our lives from death.

Rahab moved forward and was deeply concerned about delivering lives from death. We must move forward and be deeply concerned about delivering lives from death. Rahab moved forward and fought for the life of her father. Rahab moved forward and fought for the life of her mother. Rahab moved forward and fought for the life of her brothers. Rahab moved forward and fought for the life of her sisters. Rahab moved forward and fought for her family. We must move forward and fight for the family today.

MOVING FORWARD & LEARNING TO LISTEN

Joshua 2:21:
And she said, According unto your words, so be it. And she sent them away, and they departed: and she bound the scarlet line in the window.

Rahab moved forward and listened to the words of the two Israelite secret spies sent out of Shittim and across the Jordan by Joshua. After they safely departed from Jericho she put the scarlet thread in her window just as the two Israelite spies said. Many people are destroyed both within and without simply because they never learn to move forward and listen to instructions that will help them in life.

FAITH IN PECULIAR PLACES

A.) Moving Forward and Finding Faith in the God While in Jericho.
The two Israelite spies moved forward and surprisingly found faith in God being practiced in Jericho by Rahab. The two Israelite secret spies sent out of Shittim and across the Jordan by Joshua moved forward and found faith in peculiar places.

B.) Moving Forward and Finding Faith in God at a Harlot's House.
The two Israelite spies moved forward and surprisingly found faith in God being practiced at Rahab, the harlot's house. The harlot was now called to holiness. Rahab was forever changed. The prostitute was now called to higher place of praise. The two Israelite secret

spies sent out of Shittim and across the Jordan by Joshua moved forward and found faith in peculiar places.

C.) Moving Forward and Finding Faith and Not Finding Fault.
The two Israelite spies moved forward and surprisingly found faith in God being practiced by Rahab, both in word and in the deed of protecting their lives from the King of Jericho who wanted them dead. The two Israelite secret spies sent out of Shittim and across the Jordan by Joshua moved forward and found faith, and not fault in peculiar places.

DELIVERANCE FROM DESTRUCTION – THERE IS A REDEEMER

The Scarlet Thread of Redemption – Saved the Spies, Rahab & Her Family – There is a Redeemer
The Blood on the Doorpost – Saved the Israelites – There is a Redeemer

The song writer, Keith Green got it right when he penned the legendary words:

There is a redeemer,
Jesus, God's own Son,
Precious Lamb of God, Messiah,
Holy One,

Jesus my redeemer,
Name above all names,
Precious Lamb of God, Messiah
Oh, for sinners slain.

Thank you oh my father,

For giving us Your Son,
And leaving Your Spirit,
'Til the work on Earth is done.

THE BENEFITS OF MOVING FORWARD IN OBEDIENCE – WHAT'S IN YOUR WINDOW?

Rahab the harlot, Rahab the prostitute, moved forward and became Rahab the Jewess, because the scarlet thread of redemption was in her window. Rahab had a spiritual rehab, a spiritually extreme makeover, and Rahab was totally transformed by the renewing of her mind and was never the same again. What's in your window?

Rahab the harlot, Rahab the prostitute, moved forward and became Rahab the wife of Salmon of the tribe of Judah (Matthew 1:5), because the scarlet thread of redemption was in her window. Rahab had a godly rehab, a godly extreme makeover, and Rahab was totally transformed by the renewing of her mind and was never the same again. What's in your window?

Rahab the harlot, Rahab the prostitute, moved forward and became Rahab the mother of Boaz – the Kinsman Redeemer (Matthew 1:5), because the scarlet thread was in her window. Rahab had a prayerful rehab, a prayerfully extreme makeover, and Rahab was totally transformed by the renewing of her mind and was never the same again. What's in your window?

Rahab the harlot, Rahab the prostitute, moved forward and became Rahab the other mother in law of Ruth, the wife of her own son, Boaz, because the scarlet thread of redemption was in her window. Rahab had a motivational rehab, a motivationaly extreme makeover, and Rahab was totally transformed by the renewing of her mind and was never the same again. What's in your window?

Rahab the harlot, Rahab the prostitute, moved forward and became Rahab the Great Great Grandmother of King David (Matthew 1:5-6), because the scarlet thread of redemption was in her window. Rahab had an inspirational rehab, an inspirationally extreme makeover, and Rahab was totally transformed by the renewing of her mind and was never the same again. What's in your window?

Rahab the harlot, Rahab the prostitute, moved forward and became Rahab an Ancestor of Jesus Christ (Matthew 1:1-16), because the scarlet thread of redemption was in her window. Rahab moved forward and had a vision of a new purposeful life, a new gig, a new walk, a new talk, that was far better than prostitution. Rahab had a transformational rehab, a transformationally extreme makeover, and Rahab was totally transformed by the renewing of her mind and was never the same again. What's in your window?

What's in your window? Is a godly vision in your window? Is a godly mission in your window? Is a godly life, purpose and future in your window? Is the scarlet thread of redemption in your window? Is the blood of the lamb in your window? Yes, is the blood of Jesus Christ, in your window, is the redeeming blood of Jesus Christ in your world view, that you move forward and see your whole life, purpose and future through? Or do you just say God bless America ceremonially, and only quote scripture in times of disaster. Now is the time to move forward and be proactive and not only reactive. Be like Rahab and move forward before the walls come down. Be like Rahab and move forward before massive destruction comes to where you live.

- Rahab moved forward and heard.
- Rahab moved forward and believed.
- Rahab moved forward and took action.

- Rehab moved forward through the pain of destruction.

Have you moved forward and heard? Have you moved forward and believed? Have you moved forward and taken action?

Rahab had a profession, but the scarlet thread of redemption moved her forward and gave her a place of prominence for all time to come. The scarlet thread saved the spies, saved Rahab, and saved her family. Have you been saved? Have you been rescued? Have you been redeemed?

Rahab's name which means "breadth" literally makes it into the great Hall of Faith found in Hebrews Chapter 11. There was more to Rahab than what meets the eye. This is a big deal. This is major. This cannot be minimized, but rather maximized for the glory of God. The former prostitute, Rahab, is now shown as a major proclaimer of the faith both in word and deed in Hebrews Chapter 11, the legendary Hall of Faith.

Hebrews 11:31: "By faith the harlot Rahab perished not with them that believed not, when she had received the spies with peace."
James 2:25: "Likewise also was not Rahab the harlot justified by works, when she had received the messengers, and had sent them out another way?"

Now the word "justified" means just as if one never sinned. That is the awesome type of redemption that Rahab received from the Lord.

Even When The Walls Come Down All Around You - Rahab had a house, but the scarlet thread of redemption moved her forward and gave her a home and a future even when the walls of Jericho came down. Even when the walls of life and strife come down on you, you can thrive and survive if you put your total trust in God.

The old Negro spiritual titled, "Joshua Fought The Battle of Jericho" breaks the story down.

Joshua fought the battle of Jericho
Jericho Jericho
Joshua fought the battle of Jericho
And the walls come tumbling down

Up to the walls of Jericho
He marched with spear in hand
Go blow them ram horns, Joshua cried
'Cause the battle is in my hands

Then the lamb ram sheep horns began to blow
The trumpets began to sound
Old Joshua shouted glory
And the walls came tumblin' down

God knows that
Joshua fought the battle of Jericho
Jericho Jericho
Joshua fought the battle of Jericho
And the walls come tumbling down

Down, down, down, down, down
Tumblin' down

PREVIEW OF THE COMING ATTRACTION - Rahab the harlot, Rahab the prostitute, had selling power, but the scarlet thread of redemption moved Rahab forward and gave Rahab a preview of better coming attractions. It foreshadowed Rahab's True Savior, the Lord and God of Israel that she spoke of, Jesus Christ, the lamb who was slain before the foundation of earth, who washes away all the sins of the world as far as the east is from the west.

Even today, people need to move forward and stop prostituting their time, tithe, and talent. Not giving God the time of day in prayer, meditation, and Bible Study is prostituting our time. Move forward so God can redeem the time. Not giving God the time of day in our financial giving is prostituting our tithe. Move forward and bring your tithe to the storehouse. Not giving God the time of day with our gifts is prostituting our talent. Move forward and utilize your talent for God's glory. Moved forward, boldly march around the walls and finally shout so the walls of prostituting time, tithe, and talent will come down. President Franklin D. Roosevelt was right on target when he stated that, "The only limit to our realization of tomorrow will be our doubts of today. Let us move forward with strong and active faith."

When the walls of life come falling down all around you, you can find safety and shelter in the scarlet thread of redemption, the precious blood of the Savior, Jesus Christ. Move forward and put your time, tithe, and talent under the blood of the Lamb, the soul saving blood of Jesus Christ, our Wounded Healer.

"Nothing but the Blood" by Robert Lowry (1876), is still relevant today, for that classic Christian hymn says:

What can wash away my sin? nothing but the blood of Jesus;
What can make me whole again? nothing but the blood of Jesus.
O precious is the flow that makes me white as snow;
No other fount I know, nothing but the blood of Jesus.

God had to teach Moses to overcome his stuttering and speak to the children of Israel that they may "go forward". Those lessons from Moses taught Joshua and the next generation of Israelites how to move forward, how to cross the Jordan and enter the Promised Land. Joshua's passion to enter the Promised Land led him to send out spies to spy on the promise that he and Caleb had spied out for their leader, Moses many years before. Those whom Joshua sent out to spy the land had their lives saved by Rahab, and they spared Rahab's life. By saving Rahab's seed, they would move the message forward one more important step closer to the earthly birth of Jesus, the Prime Mover.

DID YOU KNOW? Rahab whose name means "breadth" discovered the power of friendship through the scarlet thread of redemption in her window given by Joshua's spies. Rahab did not remain a prostitute. She married Salmon and they had a son named Boaz. Thank God for Jesus that Rahab taught her son, Boaz, about the power of friendship, Rahab's seed, Rahab's son, Boaz, would move matters one step closer to the physical earthly birth of Jesus, the Redeemer, who was moved with compassion to die for sins of all humanity past, present, and future.

CHAPTER NINE

MOVING FORWARD IN THE POWER OF FRIENDSHIP – THE TRUE TEST OF FRIENDSHIP

Ruth1:13-17:
Then she said, Let me find favour in thy sight, my lord; for that thou hast comforted me, and for that thou hast spoken friendly unto thine handmaid, though I be not like unto one of thine handmaidens.

And Boaz said unto her, At mealtime come thou hither, and eat of the bread, and dip thy morsel in the vinegar. And she sat beside the reapers: and he reached her parched corn, and she did eat, and was sufficed, and left.

And when she was risen up to glean, Boaz commanded his young men, saying, Let her glean even among the sheaves, and reproach her not:

And let fall also some of the handfuls of purpose for her, and leave them, that she may glean them, and rebuke her not.

So she gleaned in the field until even, and beat out that she had gleaned: and it was about an ephah of barley.

The key question is can we be a resourceful friend in the time of the after effects of famine? Famine is defined as extreme scarcity of food, starvation, a tremendous shortage. Can we be a friend to the bitter person who is broken, battered, and bruised, even angry at

God in the after effects of famine. Can you be a friend to a bitter person who is in deep need of inner healing and essential wholeness during the after effects of the famine? Wholeness is absolutely essential to being an overcomer; to being a survivor and not a statistic.

The book of Ruth begins during a time of famine. **Ruth 1:1** states, **"Now it came to pass in the days when the judges ruled, that there was a famine in the land. And a certain man of Bethlehemjudah went to sojourn in the country of Moab, he, and his wife, and his two sons."**

Naomi and her husband, Elimelech, and two sons, Mahlon and Chillion, survived the famine, but Naomi lost them all to death in Moab after the famine in Bethlehem. The after effects of famine whether direct or indirect can be deadly. Naomi's family survived the food famine in Bethlehem. Only to experience the brutally harsh and utterly bitter famine of the soul from the deepest pains of death in Moab. In other words, the natural famine in Bethlehem only foreshadowed the three close family deaths of Elimelech, Mahlon and Chillion, and famine of the soul experienced by the sole survivor, Naomi. Will our version of friendship pass God's timeless test of friendship during the after effects of famine? Folks don't need anybody to pull them down any further during the after effects of famine and failure. Folks need true friends who will help lift them up and out during the time of the after effects of famine.

Henry David Thoreau moved the true philosophy of friendship forward when he wrote, "The most I can do for my friend is simply be his friend."

THE TEST OF TRUE FRIENDSHIP AFTER THE FAMINE

After the famine, Naomi, her husband, and two sons went to Moab. Moab means "of his father." Moab was the name of Lot's son from an incestuous relationship with his own oldest daughter. Moab is the nation that descended from Lot's son.

Now Elimelech was Naomi's husband who died first after the famine. He did not die in the famine in Bethlehem. Elimelech died in Moab after the famine in Bethlehem.

DID YOU KNOW? Elimelech's name means "My God is King." Naomi's husband, Elimelech, the father of her beloved sons, Mahlon and Chillon, became the first victim to death after the famine, but the very meaning of his name foreshadows that his God, the King, is able to move matters forward and is able to free the family from the lethal famine of the soul. With Naomi and Ruth, the family will move forward. The family will survive and even thrive with some major players coming into the picture over different periods of time. This family will move forward in spite of the horrible pain of losing Elimelech, Mahlon and Chillion, who were the family providers and protectors for Naomi, Orpah, and Ruth. The meaning of Elimelech's name, "My God is King", will guide, move, and transition the surviving members of this family through some mountains filled with bitterness. Nevertheless, "My God Is King" is a word that will even keep the bitter moving forward to finally get better. It's a process. Let's learn more about the process through the details of the journey.

DID YOU KNOW? Naomi's name literally means "my delight, my joy, the sweet one, pleasant". Naomi was the wife of Elimelech, the mother of Mahlon and Chillion, and the mother-in-law of Orpah and Ruth. After Naomi's husband, Elimelech died, her sons Mahlon, which means "sick", and Chillion, which means "pining" married Moabites women named Orpah and Ruth. After about ten years of marriage in Moab both Mahlon and Chillion died. The after effects of famine: the sickness caused by starvation that you survived can still kill you even ten years later without the proper nourishment and medical attention. Yes, Naomi's name means "my delight", yet Ruth 1:20-21 accurately records how Naomi truly felt. Naomi was experiencing emptiness and a bitter, deep and painful famine of the soul. Naomi did not feel pleasant, delightful, sweet, or joyful at all. Naomi said call me Mara. Call me bitter. Mara means bitterness. Yet, inspite of Naomi's deepest hurt and bitterness, Naomi still was there to help her hurting daughters-in-law: Orpah and Ruth. Naomi is a representative of the Holy Spirit, because like the Holy Spirit, Naomi still moves on the face of the waters with darkness on the face of the deep where there is no light yet. So don't let Naomi's bitterness fool you. The hurting mother still acknowledges God as the Almighty. She is bitter, but she is still a believer who will process her overwhelming pain and push to move forward. Even if she is angry, she is not going to fall into sin. She will get it all out and process the pain.

Verses 20-21:
And she said unto them, Call me not Naomi, call me Mara: for the Almighty hath dealt very bitterly with me. I went out full and the Lord hath brought me home again empty: why then call ye me Naomi, seeing the Lord hath testified against me, and the Almighty hath afflicted me?

The emptiness of Naomi makes me recall a faithful sister in the Lord whose first born child died in the hospital just a few days after her precious birth. The mother had bonded with her first child, but now the child is dead. In the hospital bed, the mother held in her arms a dead baby. I was at a conference in Washington, D.C. and left the conference to come home and preach the funeral and comfort the family. There was a small casket at the altar in the church with the baby in it. The mother said "I am going home empty." Many years later, this dear sister in the Lord was pregnant again, but the child died inside her. She had to have a procedure to induce the delivery of the dead baby. The mother said "I am going home empty again."

Many years later, my wife, Brenda, called me to the phone and the prayerful husband of this mother who has two babies located in heaven in the arms of Jesus said she is giving birth right now, and I heard the baby cry. I prayed for the baby over the phone as he was being born. Brenda, the children, and I went to visit them a few days later. That baby boy is whole and healthy and in kindergarten today, because his mom and dad moved forward in faith after experiencing the excruciatingly painful emptiness of life's ups and downs.

DID YOU KNOW?: Orpah's name literally means "gazelle". Orpah was a Moabite woman, a Moabite widow, the wife of the late Chillion, the deceased son of Naomi. Orpah was the sister-in-law of Ruth. Both Orpah and Ruth said in Ruth1:10 that, "surely we will return with thee unto thy people." But bitter and empty, Naomi honestly laid it on the line pure, plain, and simple. In essence, Naomi said, "I don't have any more sons in my womb to be your husbands, Orpah and Ruth. I am too old for another husband, Orpah and Ruth. If I had a husband tonight and got pregnant, Orpah and Ruth, you would not wait until my sons grew up. Orpah and Ruth, the hand of the Lord is gone against me."

Ruth 1:14 states, **"And they lifted up their voice, and wept again: and Orpah kissed her mother in law; but Ruth clave unto her.**

Ruth moved forward in the power of friendship with Naomi. The true test of friendship goes beyond a kiss! The test of friendship goes way beyond a hug! Orpah went back home unto her gods in Moab according to Ruth 1:15. Ruth and Naomi moved forward through the pain.

EIGHT LIFE-CHANGING PRINCIPLES

The Book of Ruth is outlined with eight life changing principles that teach believers to move forward in the power of friendship. So we can also pass the test of true friendship. These eight principles are the principles of: faith, favour, friendship, the field, the feet, finishing, fame, and family.

1.) THE PRINCIPLE OF FAITH - Ruth, a Moabite woman, a beautiful woman of color, a Moabite widow, moved forward with the principle of faith. Ruth moved forward and found both faith and friendship in spite of the failures of life.

Ruth 1:16:
And Ruth said, Intreat me not to leave thee, or to return from following after thee: for whither thou goest, I will go; and where thou lodgest, I will lodge: thy people shall be my people, and thy God my God:

Ruth, the daughter-in-law of Naomi, through the thick and thin of real life, moved forward and boldly declared in **Ruth 1:16, "for whither thou goest, I will go; and where thou lodgest, I will lodge: thy people shall be my people, and thy God my God."** In stating this, Ruth moved forward and renounced the idol gods of Moab for the God of Israel. Ruth and Naomi moved forward through the deepest pain.

DID YOU KNOW?: Ruth whose name means "friendship" is

mentioned 13 times in the Bible. First in the Old Testament Book of Ruth 1:4 and last in the New Testament Book of Matthew 1:5. Ruth moved forward in the power of true faith in God and friendship that positively and progressively impacted both Old Testament believers back in the day and New Testament believers right now. Ruth tapped into the principle of faith.

Deep frustration represented by Naomi and deep faith represented by Ruth, and at other times vice-versa, helps this dynamic duo decide to move forward in spite of the pain of overwhelming personal loss. Ruth and Naomi walked close to a 100 miles up many mountains to return to Bethlehem from Moab. Ruth and Naomi moved forward together through the deepest pain.

2.) THE PRINCIPLE OF FAVOUR - Ruth, a Moabite widow, moved forward with the principle of favour. Ruth moved forward and found both favour and friendship with Boaz.

Ruth 2:13:
Then she said, Let me find favour in thy sight, my lord; for that thou hast comforted me, and for that thou hast spoken friendly unto thine handmaid, though I be not like unto one of thine handmaidens.

Boaz, the kinsman redeemer who fell in love with Ruth gave favour to Ruth, and Boaz told his hard-working staff in essence, fellas, let fall also some of the handfuls of purpose for Ruth, the Moabitess, and leave those handfuls of purpose, that Ruth may glean them, and don't rebuke Ruth for moving forward and going after those handfuls of purpose. Bless Ruth, revive Ruth, and restore Ruth. Ruth rushed forward and gleaned in the field until even, and Ruth rushed forward and beat out what she had gleaned: and it was about an ephah of barley, thirty pounds of barley. Ruth moved forward as a reaper.

Ruth, the reaper, had the favour of God, and God gave Ruth the reaper favour with Boaz, the kinsman redeemer, a distant relative of Elimelech, who would become an extremely significant player in the picture for Ruth and her mother-in-law, mentor and best friend, Naomi. Ruth tapped into the principle of favour.

3.) THE PRINCIPLE OF FRIENDSHIP - Ruth's name actually means "friendship". Ruth most certainly moved forward with the principle of friendship. Ruth moved forward and found true friendship with her mentor and mother-in-law, Naomi. Ruth's friendship helped Naomi process her bitterness, and be the strong guide to point Ruth in the right direction. They were both widows. They both needed resources. They both needed each other's friendship and support, and they both had to remember the meaning of Elimelech's name, "My God is King." Nelson Mandela stated, "I like friends who have independent minds because they tend to make you see problems from all angles." Listen to the words of Ruth speaking to the kinsman redeemer, Boaz, who fell in love with her. Naomi prepared her well. Naomi helped Ruth move forward and see life from all angles. Ruth and Naomi moved forward together through the overwhelming pains of widowhood.

Ruth 2:13:
Then she said, Let me find favour in thy sight, my lord; for that thou hast comforted me, and for that thou hast spoken friendly unto thine handmaid, though I be not like unto one of thine handmaidens.

As stated before, Ruth's name means "friendship". Thomas Aquinas was right when he stated, "There is nothing on this earth more to be prized than true friendship." Let us move forward today and make a major difference simply through the power of true friendship.

Solomon put it this way in **Proverbs 17:17: "A friend loveth at all times and a brother is born for adversity."** Let us move forward today and make a major difference simply through the power of true friendship. Ruth was not a weak fair weathered friend, here today and gone tomorrow. Ruth was a rock solid friend to her mother-in-law, Naomi. Naomi was a rock solid mentor, mover and shaker type of friend to Ruth.

Ruth and Naomi, the daughter-in-law and mother-in-law tag team moved forward and made a difference through their encouragement and support of one another. It makes me think of the song titled, "Thank You For Being a Friend" by Andrew Maurice Gold. This song is best known as the opening theme song of the old television sitcom, *The Golden Girls*. Ruth, the daughter-in-law, and Naomi, the mother-in-law, moved forward as God's golden girls, survivors of the toughest storms of life. Mr. Gold's famous song says:

Thank you for being a friend
Traveled down the road and back again
Your heart is true. Your a pal and a confidant
I'm not ashamed to say
I hope it always will stay this way
My hat is off, won't you stand up and take a bow.
And if you threw a party
Invited everyone you knew
You would see the biggest gift would be from me
And the card attached would say
Thank you for being a friend.

THREE ENSLAVED WOMEN SET FREE

May 6, 2013 was the day that three young women from Cleveland, Ohio, named Amanda Berry, Georgina "Gina" DeJesus, and Michelle

Knight were delivered from their decade of deep bondage after Amanda Berry moved forward in the power of friendship and escaped her brutal slavery and called the police. The three enslaved woman were freed from a house owned by Ariel Castro, the suspect in their kidnappings. A six-year-old daughter of Amanda Berry was born while Amanda was enslaved. The rapist, Ariel Castro, is the father. The precious six-year-old young child was also saved from the brutal bondage.

Concerned neighbor Angel Cordero quickly responded to the alarming sound of a woman screaming, but was apparently unable to communicate with the women inside the house, since he spoke very little English at all. Another concerned neighbor, Charles Ramsey, an African-American, who quickly moved forward and got with Angel Cordero at the door and said that a woman, later identified as Amanda Berry, told him that she was being enslaved in the house with her six-year-old baby. Because the door was locked, the concerned neighbors moved forward and made a difference together by kicking a hole in the bottom of the locked door, and Amanda Berry, praise God, crawled through, moved forward to freedom, carrying her precious six-year-old daughter with her. Amanda Berry moved forward in the power of friendship and got to the nearby home of another deeply concerned Spanish-speaking neighbor and Amanda called 911, saying, "Help me, I'm Amanda Berry ... I've been kidnapped and I've been missing for 10 years. And I'm here, I'm free now."

Michelle Knight disappeared in Cleveland, Ohio in the year 2002 at the young age of 21-years-old, thank God she is free now. Amanda

Berry disappeared in the year 2003 at the young age of 16-years-old. Thank God she is free now. Georgina "Gina" DeJesus disappeared in the year 2004 at the young age of 14-years-old, thank God she is free now. While enslaved in the house by the rapist oppressor, Ariel Castro, the three women all had pregnancies, at least one surviving live birth that we know of today (Amanda Berry's six-year-old daughter), and there were many miscarriages and brutal beatings. The three women were also bound with literal chains and ropes of oppression by their sick rapist oppressor on many occasions.

Ariel Castro, a school bus driver, was arrested on the date of May 6, 2013. The enslaved women were all set free because they moved forward in the power of friendship and made a major difference. This was modern day slavery, sex slavery. On May 8th, Ariel Castro, a known wife abuser, was finally charged with four counts of kidnapping and three counts of rape, charges that carry prison sentences of ten years to life. Ariel Castro received a sentence of life in prison plus 1000 years. However, he committed suicide in his jail cell on September 4, 2013. Like Ruth and Naomi, these three enslaved broken, battered, and bruised women, moved forward in faith inspite of the deepest pains of real life to discover new life on the other side of the jagged edged sword of enslavement and daily oppression. Like Ruth and Naomi, they worked hard and worked smart together and moved forward to be free from the brutal chains of enslavement.

Forsaken, long forgotten, left all alone on an island of anger and bitterness, this is a condition of existence that many women can relate to sadly too often. Whether it is aftershock of a brutal divorce or separation, the death blows of infidelity and unfaithfulness in marriage, or a mate who ignores you, who will not hold you and care for you, God hears your cry for wholeness and this book will show you His answer for your deepest pains, problems and predicaments.

Naomi had gone on to move forward from the famine. Naomi had gone on to move forward after three major family funerals for her husband and two sons. Naomi would go on to move forward after many farewells to family and friends. Naomi had a lot of losses. Ruth staying by the side of Naomi caring, sharing, and heavy load bearing made a major difference in Naomi's life. Also, Naomi staying by the side of Ruth with love, care, and concern in spite of deep bitterness. Naomi, the widow from Bethlehem, needed to overcome deep bitterness, and Ruth, the Moabite widow, needed the boldness to live her life with purpose. Motherly mentoring and rock solid friendship made the difference for this dynamic duo.

Ralph Waldo Emerson stated, "A man's growth is seen in the successive choirs of his friends." Move forward in the power of true friendship.

MOVING FORWARD IN THE POWER OF FRIENDSHIP AT VIRGINIA UNION UNIVERSITY

As a student majoring in religion and philosophy at Virginia Union University in Richmond, Virginia, in the 1980's, a group of preachers, student scholar friends, and I had the distinct privilege of meeting some of the greatest African-American leaders on the scene at that time. The Honorable Douglas Wilder, a distinguished VUU graduate who would move forward to become the first African-American elected as governor of the state of Virginia, would always speak a positive and progressive word into our lives. Bishop Desmond Tutu of South Africa spoke for Virginia Union during this time. The late great Rev. Dr. Samuel Dewitt Proctor, a former VUU College President and former Pastor of New York's world renown Abyssinian Baptist Church spoke an awesome word into our lives. When the Reverend Jesse Louis Jackson Sr. was running for the presidency of the United States of America we had the privilege of meeting him when he spoke on our campus. Elder Bernice King (a student at Spelman College in Atlanta, Georgia, at the time), the daughter of the late Rev. Dr. Martin Luther King, Jr., also spoke at VUU and we had the privilege of meeting her as well. Many years later when I became pastor of my home church, Mount Sinai Baptist Church Cathedral in Roosevelt, N.Y., Elder Bernice King would come and preach at the church as did her beloved grandfather, Rev. Dr. Martin Luther King, Sr., in 1980.

I served as VUU Presidential Fellow, a special assistant to the then President of VUU, Dr. S. Dallas Simmons. When I was presented with the VUU Presidential Fellow Award during a special ceremony, an awesome neuro-surgeon who just wrote a bestselling book and had successfully disconnected the adjoined heads of Siamese twins, Dr. Ben Carson, was the keynote speaker who presented me with the VUU Presidential Fellow Award. He was the newest hero of African-American history and the university chapel was packed beyond capacity to see black history's newest hero face to face. My preacher and student scholar friends and I experienced many special moments moving forward in the power of friendship that would change the course of our lives forever. Like meeting Stokely Carmichael and seeing him cry as a grown man as he spoke of how Rev. Dr. Martin Luther King, Jr., touched his life. We received a black perspective and many behind the scenes moments that challenged us to move forward and make a difference universally.

During this time, there was a song that played loudly as we walked the streets of Richmond, Virginia, together as friends. In the halls, in the malls, and even in the bathroom stalls you would hear the words by a group named Whoudini. I did not own any secular music, but I clearly remember the words that were played everywhere at that time and season in my life.

> *Friends*
> *How many of us have them?*
> *Friends*
> *Ones we can depend on*
> *Friends*
> *How many of us have them?*
> *Friends*
> *Before we go any further, let's be*
> *Friends*

If you are so blessed to have just one or even two rock solid friends in your life then you are a blessed and wealthy person indeed. Also when couples date, court, go out, it always pays to just be friends first and foremost. It is important to find out what people are like when they get mad. You could end up marrying a serial killer when you rush things and there is no moving forward with true friendship or courtship. Long before Elder Brenda and I moved forward and got married we moved forward and dated and developed a solid friendship by getting to know each other.

4.) THE PRINCIPLE OF THE FIELD - Ruth moved forward with the principle of the field. Ruth, a Moabite widow, a beautiful woman of color, was on a mission to move forward and glean in the fields of harvest. Be like Ruth and glean and gather the harvest. The Church must glean and gather the harvest of souls. According to Ruth 2:15-17, when Ruth moved forward to glean, the kinsman redeemer, Boaz, commanded his young male workers, let Ruth glean even among the sheaves, and don't reproach Ruth. This makes me think of the hymn written by Knowles Shaw titled, "Bringing in the Sheaves":

> *Sowing in the morning, sowing seeds of kindness,*
> *Sowing in the noontide and the dewy eve;*
> *Waiting for the harvest, and the time of reaping,*
> *We shall come rejoicing, bringing in the sheaves.*

Remember Boaz told his working men in essence fellas let fall also some of the handfuls of purpose for Ruth, and leave them, that Ruth may glean them, and don't rebuke Ruth, bless Ruth. Ruth gleaned in the field until even, and Ruth beat out what she had gleaned: and it was about an ephah of barley. Ruth moved forward as a reaper. Ruth tapped in to the principle of the field.

5.) THE PRINCIPLE OF FEET - Ruth, a Moabite woman, a beautiful woman of color moved forward with the principle of feet. Ruth 3:4-17 breaks it down. Naomi had a positive and progressive plan to provide a husband and a home for her daughter-in-law and best friend, Ruth. One day Ruth's mother-in-law Naomi said to her, **"My daughter, I must find a home[a] for you, where you will be well provided for."**

DID YOU KNOW? Naomi (who is symbolic of the Holy Spirit) told Ruth (who is symbolic of the church) that when Boaz the son of Rahab the ex-prostitute (who is symbolic of Jesus Christ) lays down, mark the place where he shall lay, and, Ruth, you go in, and uncover Boaz' feet, and you lay down at the kinsman redeemer's feet; and Boaz will tell you what to do. THIS IS BETTER THAN A SOAP OPERA. Ruth moved forward and told Naomi, her mentor, mother in law, and true friend, that all that you said unto me Naomi that I will do.

Ruth went down to the floor, and did according to all that her mentor, mother-in-law, and best friend, Naomi, told her. When the kinsman redeemer, Boaz, had eaten and drank to his hearts content, and his heart was merry, Boaz went to lie down at the end of the heap of corn: and Ruth moved forward, she came ever so softly, and uncovered his feet, and Ruth, the Moabitess, laid down at Boaz' feet.

At midnight Boaz was afraid, and turned over: and wow, a woman lay at his feet. Boaz said, Who are you? Ruth answered, I am Ruth your handmaid: spread therefore your skirt, your covering, your provision over your handmaid; for you are a near kinsman. Ruth moved forward and actually proposed to Boaz, the kinsman redeemer. Ruth moved forward with her request, because Ruth represented and foreshadowed the church. Boaz represented and foreshadowed Jesus Christ, and Naomi represented and foreshadowed the Holy Spirit, who is called alongside to help us. Naomi, Ruth, and Boaz all moved forward in the power of friendship. Naomi, Ruth, and Boaz all passed the test of true friendship.

Because Boaz was in their family line, Ruth wanted him to redeem her and reclaim her inheritance. Boaz was drawn to her, like Christ loves the church and would lay His life down for it. There was a natural, God-given attraction between Ruth and Boaz.

Boaz who had fallen in love with Ruth said, Blessed be you of the Lord, my daughter: for you have shown more kindness in the latter end than at the beginning, inasmuch as you followed not young men, the young bucks, whether poor or rich.

Boaz continued to state, now, my daughter, fear not; I will do to you all that you require, for all the city of my people do know that you,

Ruth, a Moabite widow, are a virtuous woman. Boaz said, now it is true that I am thy near kinsman: however there is a kinsman closer than I am. Wait this night, and, it shall be in the morning, that if the closer kinsman will perform unto you, Ruth, the role of a kinsman, well; let him do the kinsman's responsibility: but if he will not do the responsibility of a kinsman to you, Ruth, then will I do the responsibility of a kinsman to you, Ruth, as the Lord liveth: lie down until the morning. They did not have sexual relations. They were not married. Boaz promised to marry Ruth if the kinsman ahead of him, more closely related to her did not. Boaz wanted to marry Ruth.

Ruth lay down at Boaz' feet until the morning: and Ruth, the Moabite widow, rose up before anyone could know another. Boaz said, Let it not be known that a woman came into the floor. Boaz, the kinsman redeemer, respected Ruth as a virtuous woman. Boaz did not want Ruth's good mission to be evil spoken of by witnesses.

Like Ruth who moved forward and laid down at the feet of Boaz, we need to come before Christ in that same humility.

Boaz also said to Ruth, Bring the veil that you, Ruth, have upon you, and hold it. And when Ruth held it, Boaz measured six measures of barley, and Boaz laid it on her: Boaz blessed Ruth, and Ruth moved forward and went into the city. When Ruth came to her mother-in-law, Naomi, Ruth said, who are you, my daughter? And Ruth told Naomi all that Boaz had done to her. Ruth said, these six measures of barley Boaz gave me; for Boaz said to me, Go not empty unto thy mother in law, Naomi. Naomi was empty from the death of her husband and two sons. Boaz wanted Naomi to experience fullness of joy again. Ruth truly tapped into the principle of feet.

Ruth laying at the feet of the kinsman redeemer, Boaz, foreshadows and moves forward the extremely important teaching of all things being put under the feet of Jesus Christ, the Head of the church. **Ephesians 1:22: "And hath put all things under his feet, and gave him to be the head over all things to the church."**

6.) THE PRINCIPLE OF FINISHING - Ruth moved forward with the principle of finishing. Ruth 3:18 tells about Naomi telling Ruth to "Sit still, my daughter, until you, Ruth, know how this matter will fall: for the kinsman redeemer, Boaz, will not be at rest until he has finished your request. No, Boaz will not sleep until he has moved forward, until Boaz has finished the thing this day, Ruth." This is another classic example found in the Holy Scripture, the holy writ, of how statements such as "sit still", "stand still", "I shall not be moved" are the language of a divine set up to move forward God's perfect agenda and finish the course. The kinsman redeemer in front of Boaz wanted to purchase Elimelech's land, but refused to marry Ruth, because he did not want lose his own estate, his own inheritance. This opened up the door for Boaz to redeem Elimelech's land and marry Ruth.

Ruth 4:5-10:
Then said Boaz, What day thou buyest the field of the hand of Naomi, thou must buy it also of Ruth the Moabitess, the wife of the dead, to raise up the name of the dead upon his inheritance.

And the kinsman said, I cannot redeem it for myself, lest I mar mine own inheritance: redeem thou my right to thyself; for I cannot redeem it.

Now this was the manner in former time in Israel concerning redeeming and concerning changing, for to confirm all things; a man plucked off his shoe, and gave it to his neighbour: and

this was a testimony in Israel.

Therefore the kinsman said unto Boaz, Buy it for thee. So he drew off his shoe.

And Boaz said unto the elders, and unto all the people, Ye are witnesses this day, that I have bought all that was Elimelech's, and all that was Chilion's and Mahlon's, of the hand of Naomi.

Moreover Ruth the Moabitess, the wife of Mahlon, have I purchased to be my wife, to raise up the name of the dead upon his inheritance, that the name of the dead be not cut off from among his brethren, and from the gate of his place: ye are witnesses this day.

DID YOU KNOW?: When Boaz receives the other kinsman redeemer's plucked off shoe that represented ownership, the finishing of that act allows him to redeem and marry Ruth. This act of Boaz moving forward and finishing the thing, finishing the assignment, finishing the job, so Ruth receives redemption clearly foreshadows the finished work of Jesus Christ on the cross of Calvary. Boaz truly tapped into the principle of finishing.

John 19:30: "When Jesus therefore had received the vinegar, he said, It is finished: and he bowed his head, and gave up the ghost."

7.) THE PRINCIPLE OF FAME - The Book of Ruth moved forward with the principle of fame. Moving forward from famine to fame. The kinsman redeemer, Boaz, moved forward and made a major difference by gladly purchasing Ruth as his wife when the other kinsman did not, and Ruth became famous in Bethlehem.

Ruth 4:11: "And all the people that were in the gate, and the elders, said, We are witnesses. The Lord make the woman that is come into thine house like Rachel and like Leah, which two did build the house of Israel: and do thou worthily in Ephratah, and be famous in Bethlehem."

Boaz, the kinsman redeemer, was made famous in Israel, and Naomi moved forward from bitterness to blessedness. With the spirit of rough and tough true friendship Naomi went from deep seated bitterness to overflowing blessings.

Ruth 3:17: "And she said, These six measures of barley gave he me; for he said to me, Go not empty unto thy mother in law."

Have you been empty too long? You don't have to be empty any more. You don't have to be bitter any more. You can be a friend of God and be blessed of the Lord like Naomi.

Ruth 4:14: "And the women said unto Naomi, Blessed be the Lord, which hath not left thee this day without a kinsman, that his name may be famous in Israel."

Boaz in Bethlehem. The wealthy kinsman redeemer in Bethlehem. Bethlehem literally means "house of Bread." Bethlehem a city of Judah. Bethlehem of King David. Bethlehem the birthplace of Jesus, my Lord & Savior. Bethlehem of Zebulun.

8.) THE PRINCIPLE OF FAMILY - The Book of Ruth moved forward with the principle of family. Ruth moves forward into the family line of King David and Jesus Christ. Ruth 4:13-17 and Matthew 1:5 breaks this down very clearly. Boaz, the kinsman redeemer, Boaz, the son of the redeemed ex-prostitute, Rahab, took Ruth, the daughter in law of Naomi, and Ruth became Boaz' wife. Boaz clearly understood the importance of moving forward in the power of redeeming friendship. His mother, the redeemed prostitute, Rahab, was a true friend to the Israelite spies who in turn moved forward and spared her life as discussed in detail in the earlier chapter entitled "The Scarlet Thread of Redemption – Moving Forward From Prostitution to Proclamation." Rahab the former prostitute was now the other mother-in-law of Ruth, the Moabitess. Rahab moved forward and saved the two Israelite spies, and her blessed son, Boaz, moved forward and redeemed Ruth from ruin. When Boaz, the son of a former prostitute made love to his wife, Ruth, the Lord gave Ruth conception, and Ruth bare a son. Ruth was faithful and fruitful. The women said unto Naomi, Blessed be the Lord, which has not left you this day without a kinsman, that Boaz' name may be famous in Israel. Boaz, Ruth's second husband, the kinsman redeemer, was a righteous restorer of Naomi's bitter life, and a needful nourisher of Naomi's old age also foreshadows our blessed Redeemer, Jesus Christ. Naomi's daughter-in-law, Ruth, who loved her, was better to Naomi than seven sons. Naomi took the child, and laid the child in her bosom, and became nurse to Ruth and Boaz' son. The neighbors of Naomi, women of Bethlehem, named the grandchild of Naomi and they called his name Obed: he is the father of Jesse, the father of King David. Now these are the generations of Pharez: Pharez seed was Hezron, And Hezron's seed was Ram, and Ram's seed was Amminadab, And Amminadab's seed was Nahshon, and Nahshon's seed was Salmon, And Salmon's seed was Boaz, and Boaz's seed was Obed, And Obed's seed was Jesse, and Jesse's seed was David. Through the lineage of David, Jesus Christ was born of Mary, the seed of woman who would crush the head of the serpent. Boaz's name means "fleetness". Boaz did not flee from his responsibility. Boaz moved forward and made a difference with the power of true friendship. Boaz, the kinsman redeemer, did not flee, just as Jesus did not flee. Jesus hung right there and died on that old rugged cross for you and I.

DID YOU KNOW? Boaz, the kinsman (moda in Hebrew meaning relative) redeemer foreshadows Jesus Christ, our blessed Redeemer, the friend of sinners. King Solomon got it right in Proverbs 18:24, "A man that hath friends must shew himself friendly: and there is a friend that sticketh closer than a brother." Jesus, Blessed Redeemer, known far and wide as the friend of sinners. Move forward and make a difference in the power of true friendship. **Matthew 11:19: "The Son of man came eating and drinking, and they say, Behold a man gluttonous, and a winebibber, a friend of publicans and sinners. But wisdom is justified of her children."**

Johnson Oatman, Jr., hit the nail right on the head when wrote the classic hymn "No Not One".

There's not a friend like the lowly Jesus,
No, not one! No, not one!
None else could heal all our soul's diseases,
No, not one! No, not one!

Refrain

Jesus knows all about our struggles,
He will guide till the day is done;
There's not a friend like the lowly Jesus,
No, not one! No, not one!

Moving forward with the true test of friendship will teach us the 7 P's of Friendship.

THE 7 P'S OF FRIENDSHIP

1.) THE POWER OF FRIENDSHIP - Move forward and make a difference through the positive and progressive power of friendship. Like Ruth who said to Naomi in essence, "we are moving forward together."

Ruth 1:16:
"And Ruth said, Intreat me not to leave thee, or to return from following after thee: for whither thou goest, I will go; and where thou lodgest, I will lodge: thy people shall be my people, and thy God my God."

2.) THE PURPOSE OF FRIENDSHIP - Move forward and make a difference through the positive and progressive purpose of friendship. Like Ruth who clave and held on for dear life to her mother-in-law, mentor, and friend, Naomi.

Ruth 1:14 states "And they lifted up their voice, and wept again: and Orpah kissed her mother in law; but Ruth clave unto her.

3.) THE PRACTICE OF FRIENDSHIP - Move forward and make a difference through the positive and progressive practice of friendship. Like Naomi looking out for the future safety and security of her daughter in law and dear true friend, Ruth.

Ruth 3:1 NIV One day Ruth's mother-in-law Naomi said to her, "My daughter, I must find a home[a] for you, where you will be well provided for.

4.) THE PRODUCTIVITY OF FRIENDSHIP - Move forward and make a difference through the positive and progressive productivity of friendship. Like Boaz, the kinsman, redeemer looking out for both Ruth and Naomi.

Ruth 3:17 And she said, These six measures of barley gave he me; for he said to me, Go not empty unto thy mother in law.

5.) THE PATIENCE OF FRIENDSHIP - Move forward and make a difference through the positive and progressive patience of friendship. Like Boaz taking every step necessary to finally redeem and marry Ruth. Nelson Mandela once stated that, "I like friends who have independent minds because they tend to make you see problems from all angles."

Ruth, the Moabitess, moved forward and made a difference by waiting patiently for her new husband, Boaz, the kinsman redeemer. Single ladies, move forward and make a difference with divine destiny and powerful purpose. While you are patiently waiting on your own personal Boaz, don't ever settle for any of his dangerous and destructive relatives which Pastor Jentezen Franklin named as: Broke-az, Lyin-az, Cheatin-az, Dumb-az, Dirty-az, Drunk-az, Cheap-az, Crazy-az, Lockedup-az, Goodfornothing-az, Lazy-az, and single ladies of divine destiny and powerful purpose especially don't get involved with his dangerous and destructive cousin Beatinyo-az. Single ladies of divine destiny and powerful purpose patiently wait on your Boaz and make sure he really respects You-az, a true woman of worship, a designer's original created to move forward and make a major difference!

Ruth 4:10 Moreover Ruth the Moabitess, the wife of Mahlon, have I purchased to be my wife, to raise up the name of the dead upon his inheritance, that the name of the dead be not cut off from among his brethren, and from the gate of his place: ye are witnesses this day.

6.) THE PRECISION OF FRIENDSHIP - Move forward and make a difference through the positive and progressive precision of friendship. Like Ruth meeting Boaz and finding the favour and friend that she needed so her life would be forever changed.

Ruth 2:13 Then she said, Let me find favour in thy sight, my lord; for that thou hast comforted me, and for that thou hast spoken friendly unto thine handmaid, though I be not like unto one of thine handmaidens.

7.) THE PAIN OF FRIENDSHIP - Move forward and make a difference through the positive and progressive pain of friendship. Like Naomi working through her own painful bitterness while still simultaneously moving forward and mentoring Ruth to be redeemed. It was painful but Naomi moved forward and made a lasting difference by processing her public and private pain and moving from bitterness to blessedness. Oh yes the pain of friendship is real. Ruth and Naomi moved forward through the pain.

Ruth 1:20 And she said unto them, Call me not Naomi, call me Mara: for the Almighty hath dealt very bitterly with me.

21 I went out full and the Lord hath brought me home again empty: why then call ye me Naomi, seeing the Lord hath testified against me, and the Almighty hath afflicted me?

Ruth 2:20 And Naomi said unto her daughter in law, Blessed be he of the Lord, who hath not left off his kindness to the living and to the dead. And Naomi said unto her, The man is near of kin unto us, one of our next kinsmen.

Yes moving forward and passing the test of true friendship can be painful at times. Moving forward and passing the test of true friendship cost Jesus Christ his life. The friend of sinners moved forward and paid the ultimate price to save any sinners who would call on His name.

I love the classic hymn "What A Friend We Have In Jesus" written by Joseph M. Scriven.

> *What a friend we have in Jesus,*
> *All our sins and griefs to bear!*
> *What a privilege to carry*
> *Everything to God in prayer!*
> *Oh, what peace we often forfeit,*
> *Oh, what needless pain we bear,*
> *All because we do not carry*
> *Everything to God in prayer!*

Believe that God is still working all the circumstances of your life to His glory and your ultimate good. Like Ruth and Naomi, move forward inspite of the pain, step out in faith and allow God to surprise you with joy and fulfillment that only He can bring. Before we begin to look at what the New Testament teaches in more detail concerning moving forward and making a difference. Let us look closely at the book of Job, because we cannot talk about moving forward and making a difference without discussing the very first biblical book ever written. The Book of Job written by Moses. Job's testimony will certainly bring fresh new meaning to the subject matter of moving forward and making a difference. Job provides the reader with one of the most powerful testimonies of moving forward inspite the deepest pain anyone could experience in life. Only the testimony of Jesus Christ, Himself, and the early martyrs of Christianity goes any further. Let's move forward and hear from our Brother Job.

CHAPTER TEN

MOVING FORWARD IN A BACKWARDS WORLD
LIFE ON THE LEFT HAND OF GOD

Job 23:8-12:
Behold, I go forward, but he is not there; and backward, but I cannot perceive him: On the left hand, where he doth work, but I cannot behold him: he hideth himself on the right hand, that I cannot see him: But he knoweth the way that I take: when he hath tried me, I shall come forth as gold. My foot hath held his steps, his way have I kept, and not declined. Neither have I gone back from the commandment of his lips; I have esteemed the words of his mouth more than my necessary food.

James 5:11:
Behold, we count them happy which endure. Ye have heard of the patience of Job, and have seen the end of the Lord; that the Lord is very pitiful, and of tender mercy.

DID YOU KNOW? Job's name literally means, "Where is the Father?" The subject matter of "Moving Forward and Making A Difference" cannot be completely addressed from a biblical world view with addressing the timeless and time tested testimony of Brother Job. Brother Job teaches us how to trust God even when we can't trace His presence in our present problem and predicament. The book of Job was the very first book written that was included in the canonized Scripture of the Old Testament even before Genesis. It is believed that Moses wrote the Book of Job. Job is mentioned in three books of the Bible, both in the Old and New Testament. Job's name which means, "Where is the Father?" is recorded a total of 56 times in the Bible. Learning from the good, bad, and indifferent experiences in Job's journey will help us to finally move forward and make a difference. Job moved forward through the pain.

Who was Job in the first place and why is he important in this biblical world view conversation concerning "Moving Forward and Making A Difference"? Job 1:1 -3 clearly tells the reader exactly who Job was.

Job was a man from the land of Uz. Job was a man who was perfect and upright. Job was a man who feared God, and eschewed evil. Clearly, Job was moving forward spiritually.

Job was the father of seven sons and three daughters. Job continually sent and sanctified with burnt offerings for his children's potential sins of cursing God in their hearts after partying hard. Clearly, Job moved forward in caring for his family.

Job owned seven thousand sheep, three thousand camels, five hundred yoke of oxen, and five hundred she asses. Job possessed a very great household. Job had the lush and plush home of the rich and famous. Job was clearly the greatest, the richest of all the men of the east during his day. Job clearly moved forward in the area of wealth long before multi-millionaires liked Donald Trump, Oprah Winfrey, and Bill Gates.

Now Job 1:6 -22 declares that there was a day when the sons of God came to present themselves before the Lord, and Satan, the devil, the old serpent, Lucifer, came also among them. And the Lord said to Satan, Where have you come from? Then Satan answered the Lord, and said, From going to and fro in the earth, and from walking up and down in it. The Lord said to Satan, Have you considered my servant Job, that there is none like him in the earth, a perfect and an upright man, one that fears God, and escheweth evil?

Satan quickly answered the Lord, and said, Does Job fear God for nothing?

Have you not made a hedge about him, and about his house, and about all that Job has on every side? You have blessed the work of Job's hands, and Job's substance is increased in the land.

Satan said, but put forth your hand now, and touch all that Job has, and Job will curse You to Your face.

The Lord said to Satan, Behold, all that Job has is in your power; only upon Job put not forth thine hand. So Satan went forth from the presence of the Lord.

So there was a day when Job's sons and daughters were eating and drinking wine in their oldest brother's house. There came a messenger unto Job, and said, the oxen were plowing, and the asses feeding beside them: and the Sabeans fell upon them, and took them away. They have slew the servants with the edge of their sword; and I only am escaped alone to tell you.

While Job's surviving servant was yet speaking, there came also another, and said, the fire of God is fallen from heaven, and has burned up the sheep, and the servants, and consumed them; and I only am escaped alone to tell you.

While that surviving servant was yet speaking, there came also another, and said, the Chaldeans made out three bands, and fell upon the camels, and have carried them away, and slew the servants in charge of the camels with the edge of their sword; and I only am escaped alone to tell you.

While that surviving servant was yet speaking, there came also another, and said, your sons and your daughters were eating and drinking wine in their oldest brother's house: and, behold, there came a great wind from the wilderness, and smote the four corners of the house, and it fell upon the young people, and they are dead; and I only am escaped alone to tell thee. Job's children were all dead. The majority of Job's staff was dead, and all of Job's animals that brought in his wealth were dead.

Then Job, whose name means "Where is the Father"? Arose, and rent his mantle, and shaved his head bald, and fell down upon the ground, and moved forward in worship to God, the Heavenly Father, in the midst of the brutally painful losses he had just experienced. Victor Kiam said that, "Even if you fall on your face, you're still moving forward." Job moved forward through the pain.

Job said, Naked came I out of my mother's womb, and naked shall I return thither: the Lord gave, and the Lord hath taken away; blessed be the name of the Lord. Job moved forward and blessed the Lord. In all this Job sinned not, nor charged God foolishly.

Again there was a day when the sons of God came to present themselves before the Lord, and Satan came also among them to present himself before the Lord. The Lord said to Satan, From where have you come? And Satan answered the Lord, and said, From going to and fro in the earth, and from walking up and down in it. The Lord said to Satan, Have you considered my servant Job, that there is none like him in the earth, a perfect and an upright man, one that fears God, and escheweth evil? Still he holds fast his integrity, although you move Me against him, to destroy him without cause.

Satan answered the Lord, and said, Skin for skin, yes, all that a man hath will he give for his life. But put forth Your hand now, and touch his bone and his flesh, and he will curse You to thy face. The Lord said unto Satan, Behold, he is in thine hand; but save his life. So went Satan forth from the presence of the Lord, and smote Job with sore boils from the sole of his foot to the top of his head.

Job took a potsherd to scrape himself with it all over; and Job sat down among the ashes. Job has now gone from riches to rags in the ashes of life.

1.) MOVING FORWARD IN A BACKWARDS WORLD: In **Job 2:9,** the foolish unnamed wife says to Job at the lowest point in his entire life **"Do you still retain your integrity? Curse God, and die."** Job's wife could not comprehend how Job could maintain his integrity to move forward and worship God when his entire life was going backwards in utter destruction and Job could not even feel God's presence. Job was moving forward, maintaining his integrity, maintaining his worship, in a backwards world full of death, desperation, dirt, disease, and deep depression. Job was now living life on the left hand of God. **Job 23:8** states, **"Behold, I go forward, but he is not there; and backward, but I cannot perceive him."**

2.) LIFE ON THE LEFT HAND OF GOD: Job, whose name means "Where is the Father"? Still moved forward and worshiped the Heavenly Father in his backwards world full of death, desperation, dirt, disease, and deep depression. Job was living life on the left hand of God where God was working the night shift.

Psalm 16:11 declares, **"Thou wilt shew me the path of life: in thy presence is fulness of joy; at thy right hand there are pleasures for evermore."** Job was not feeling the presence of God in the fulness of joy. Job was temporarily blocked from the right hand of God where there are pleasures for evermore. Job's pleasure season was put on hold for a season. Yet Job moved forward and trusted God even when he could not trace God's presence within his present plight and condition of existence. Job was living life on the left hand of God where God was working the night shift. Job moved forward and backward through the pain.

Job was moving forward in his integrity and worship long before the Bible was ever written. Job had no Bible. No spiritual television, radio, or internet programs. Job only could move forward and trust God in his backwards world full of the 5 D's -- death, desperation, dirt, disease, and deep depression. Job was living life on the left hand of God. This was a season were Job would not experience the type of victory from God's right hand that the rich man, Job, once enjoyed as the psalmist speaks of in **Psalm 98:1: "O sing unto the Lord a new song; for he hath done marvellous things: his right hand, and his holy arm, hath gotten him the victory."** No, no, no, Job was moving forward in integrity and worship in his newly found backwards world full of death, desperation, dirt, disease, and deep depression. Job was living life on the left hand of God, the hand that allows a world full of death, desperation, dirt, disease, and deep depression for His ultimate unfolding plans, precepts, provisions, and purposes. Unlike His right hand that protects us and crushes the enemy with punishment.

Mark 12:36 declares, **"For David himself said by the Holy Ghost, The Lord said to my Lord, Sit thou on my right hand, till I make thine enemies thy footstool."** Job was moving forward even though he did not feel God's presence in a backwards world full of death, desperation, dirt, disease, and deep depression.

3.) LONGING FOR REST FOR THE WEARY FROM A BACKWARDS WORLD: Yet without a Bible, (because the Old or New Testaments were not yet written) and yet without a preacher, Job spoke of place in **Job 3:17** where, **"the wicked cease from troubling; and there the weary be at rest."** Job was deeply depressed and wished that he was never born or still born. Yet he moves forward speaking of God, trusting God in tragedy even when he can't feel God in his backwards world full of death, desperation, dirt, disease, and deep depression. Job was living life on the right hand of God. God is working it out in the night shift for Job, but Job can't see Him. **Job 23:9** spells it out **"On the left hand, where he doth work, but I cannot behold him: he hideth himself on the right hand, that I cannot see him:"**

Noted best-selling author and world renown speaker, John Maxwell, stated that, "To achieve your dreams, you must embrace adversity and make failure a regular part of your life. If you're not failing, you're probably not really moving forward." Job's health failed him. Job's business failed him. Job's wife failed him. Job's backwards friends failed him, but Job found the way to move forward in a backwards world full of deep pain and torment.

I call our current culture back to the consideration of the scriptural Christ centered world view and the cross of Christ to move forward with eternal meaning and make a difference that matters in this life and the life to come.

Move forward and make a difference that echoes through eternity. Many of our major colleges and universities in the United States were founded men and women of meaning who moved forward with a Christ centered world view.

Passing phony political litmus test is not what is most important. What is most important is whether one loves all people even those thy disagree with. What is most is that one would put their very life on the line for all members of hurting humanity. Jesus loved and died for all hurting humanity even those he most clearly disagrees with.

Therefore secular society needs to pay much closer attention to the Christ centered worldview. For it was the Christ centered world view that gave us concepts such as churches, social work, hospitals, feeding programs, schools, and counseling. Just to name a few.

Before Hurricane Sandy and the many mass shootings when President Obama, who is now essentially the most powerful man in the world, verbalized and emphasized a Christ centered world view of marriage as between a man and women only as then candidate Senator Obama at his highly televised debate at Pastor Rick Warren Saddleback Church during his first presidential campaign against fellow Senator John McCain.

The book of Job cleary teaches all of hurting humanity one main lesson of life that the judgment of God not always necessarily what God does. Rather on many occasions the judgment of God is what God allows.

When President Obama evolved or flip flopped on his public view on marriage to embrace same sex marraige that the Holy Bible clearly calls an abomination.

All hell broke loose in terms of drought, hurricane/super storms, wild weather patterns, and tragic mass murder shootings at malls, movie theatres, and schools. God in His broken hearted judgment was forced to lift His hand of protection because America was to grown to respect what God commands in terms of marraige being between a man or a woman. You can not get more scientific than what happens when God's hand of protection is lifted. To many only want to the Bible to swear on for the oath of office or quote after tradgedies, but never to abide by it in public policy. This is the very downfall that must be quickly corrected with a compassionate nondiscrimatory Christ centered world view that many movers and shakers of old held on to for dear life. Evidently for goods reasons. To get America moving forward and not backwards.

We must pray for our President. When President Richard Nixon was caught in the Watergate scandal I prayed for him. When our nation went through the Iran hostage crisis during President Jimmy Carter's administration I prayed for him and the hostages. When President Ronald Reagan was shot I prayed for him. When the USA went war in Iraq under the leadership of the elder President George Bush I prayed for him. When President Bill Clinton went through hard times I prayed for him. When the younger President Bush went through the aftermath of the tragedy of 9/11 terrorist attacks I prayed for him. Therefore I most move forward and pray for President Barack Obama when he is right and also when he is dead wrong. Since the days of my youth I followed the news and prayed for all of the United States of America Presidents who were white. Well I must also move forward and pray for this current President who is black.

Being the first black in the most influential position of leadership in the whole entire world is tremendously historic. Being the first black in the most influential position of leadership in the whole entire world and to move forward to obey the Creator, the Prime Mover, God, boldly in public policy with a Christ centered world view is absolutely life changing and needed right now. To whom much is given. Much is required. I am not a hater. I am a celebrator. I celebrate the possibility of better days that come through repentance. Judgement begins at the house of God. So I move forward and repent first and call on others to do the same in the house of government.

It is imperative to be not to the left or the right, but rather in the center of God's will. This is critically important spiritually and politically. If we truly love our current President with the love of God. We should have no problem saying that pushing for public policy that contradicts the crystal clear definition of marriage as between a man and women only by Jesus Christ, the Son of God, is only continue to cause God to lift His hand of protection on America. That is no light issue. That is a major issues. Only those who truly care for our President and nation would even bring it up.

4.) JOB'S BACKWARDS FRIENDS: Job is even wounded in the house of his own three friends words. Job's so-called friend, Bildad, radically rebukes Job and tells him, 'your personal sin has brought the judgment of God to your life.' Job's second so-called friend, Zophar, rebukes Job telling him, 'no one can understand what God does, in so many words, whatever will be will be.' Job's third so-called wise friend, Eliphaz, tells Job, 'the men of wisdom have always suffered from sin brings suffering.' Job is upset with his friends and yes, yes, yes, Job is even upset with God. It is all unfair to Job, a righteous man, fears God, and never embraces evil.

5.) MY REDEEMER LIVES EVEN IN MY BACKWARDS WORLD: Yet without the advent of Christian or Jewish radio, television, or internet programs. Yet before the Redeemer, Jesus Christ, died on the cross of Calvary for the sins of all humanity, Job whose name means "Where is the Father"? states clearly in **Job 19:25: "For I know that my redeemer liveth, and that he shall stand at the latter day upon the earth:"** Job is clearly moving forward in his integrity and worship in a backwards world full of the death of his own darling children and dedicated staff, daily desperation, daily dirt, daily disease, and daily deep depression.

6.) THE TURNING POINT IS WHEN YOU ARE HEALED ENOUGH TO PRAY FOR YOUR MEAN BACKWARDS FRIENDS – DOUBLE FOR YOUR TROUBLE

Job 42:10: And the Lord turned the captivity of Job, when he prayed for his friends: also the Lord gave Job twice as much as he had before.

Job 42:12-17 tells us of God moving forward Job with double for his trouble.

The Lord blessed the latter end of Job more than his beginning. The Lord moved Job forward with double for his trouble. Job was blessed with fourteen thousand sheep, six thousand camels, a thousand yoke of oxen, and a thousand she asses.

Job was also blessed with a new family of seven sons and three daughters.

Job called the name of the first daughter, Jemima; and the name of the second daughter, Kezia; and the name of the third daughter, Kerenhappuch. In all the land were no women found so fair as the daughters of Job: and Job gave his three daughters an inheritance among their brothers. Job moved forward and made a major difference. Job lived a hundred and forty years. Job moved forward to see his sons, and his sons' sons, even four generations. Job died as a blessed man and not as a stressed man being old and full of days.

Job moved forward in a backwards world full of the 5 D's -- death, desperation, dirt, disease, and deep depression. Job move forward from riches to rags and back to true riches with double for his trouble. In his book entitled "Failing Forward" John Maxwell wrote that we should, "Fail early, fail often, but always fail forward." Now, let us move forward and learn from our own failures more about the conviction of communion, so we can learn how to truly move forward with biblically based backbone. **Job 19:25** declares and decrees that, **"For I know that my redeemer liveth, and that he shall stand at the latter day upon the earth:"** Job could move forward with meaning even in the middle of a backwards world, because his Redeemer was with him, God with us, through the thick and the thin. Job moved forward through the pain.

CHAPTER ELEVEN

MOVING FORWARD IN PRAISE INSPITE OF PAIN – THE MANDATE OF THE PALM TREE CHRISTIAN

John 12:12 -19

Every single human being ever born or to be born on the face of the entire earth was and is called by God, the Creator, the Prime Mover, to move forward in positive and progressive praise. Let everything that has breathe praise the Lord. Move forward and make a difference in everyday life, in spite of the presence of overwhelming pain. This is our common condition of existence. This is the common link amongst all hurting humanity. Let us move forward with a positive and progressive mindset. No pain, no gain. No cross, no crown. Progress must never be stopped solely because of the presence of overwhelming pain. The progress, purpose, and plan of Jesus, the Prince of Peace, was not stopped, blocked, or hindered by the painfully unholy collaboration of an unruly rebellious disciple, religious cronies, and greedy governmental and political phonies plotting to kill Jesus of Nazareth. Even if you know that you're going to die Lord Jesus, to be killed my Jesus, yes crucified Jesus for speaking truth to power, move forward my Jesus in powerful praise in spite of pulsating pain. Even if the many cronies and phonies mixed in the massive crowd of the faithful cry out next week "crucify Him, crucify Him", move forward in highly potent and passionate praise my Lord Jesus in spite of paralyzing pain. Even if you're unjustly whipped to a bloody pulp and moved from judgment hall to judgment hall Jesus, move forward in positive and progressive praise Jesus in spite of the deeply demoralizing and penetrating pain. Jesus you're my Savior, my ultimate hero, my motivator, my friend that sticks closer than a brother. Let us learn from Jesus, who knows all about our troubles. Never forget inner strength from God will keep us moving forward and making a difference even when physical strength says it is impossible to go any further. God deeply desires blood washed believers in the Lord Jesus Christ to move forward and make a difference as Palm Tree Christians with a positive and progressive mindset, mission, and mandate in a real world full of the jagged edged issues of life. THANK YOU JESUS!!!

1. MOVING FORWARD AT THE PEOPLE'S PARADE

JOHN 12:12: "On the next day much people that were come to the feast, when they heard that Jesus was coming to Jerusalem"

People from all over the known world of that time in history, His-story, are in the great city of Jerusalem waiting on extremely long lines and longing with greatly heightened anticipation just to see Jesus, the miracle worker, Jesus, the wonder worker. Jesus Himself is ready to triumphantly move forward into Jerusalem.

The people moved forward and proudly paraded at Passover because they yearned so deeply to just see Jesus Christ, who moved forward and made a difference. Yes, Jesus, who literally changed water into wine at the wedding in Cana of Galilee, His first public miracle.

The people moved forward by pulling, pushing, and proudly parading at Passover, because they yearned so deeply to just see Jesus Christ, who moved forward and made a difference. Yes, Jesus Christ who opened the eyes of the blind.

The people moved forward pulling, pushing, and proudly parading at Passover because they yearned so very deeply to just see Jesus

Christ, who moved forward and made a difference. Yes, Jesus Christ who fed the 5000 with a little boy's lunch of two fish and five loaves of bread.

The people moved forward pulling, pushing, and proudly parading at Passover because they yearned so deeply to just see Jesus Christ, who moved forward and made a difference. Yes, Jesus Christ who literally calmed the stormy sea by just speaking the legendary words "peace be still."

The people moved forward pulling, pushing, and proudly parading at Passover, because they yearned so very deeply to just see Jesus Christ, who moved forward and made a difference. Yes, Jesus Christ who literally raised His own close friend Lazarus, whose name means "whom God helps", from the dead.

The people who move forward pulling, pushing, and proudly parading at Passover just to see Jesus Christ, the Lamb of God, are about to move forward to the next level, the next dimension of divine destiny with the people's praise.

As I journey through the land, singing as I go,
Pointing souls to Calvary—to the crimson flow,
Many arrows pierce my soul from without, within;
But my Lord leads me on, through Him I must win.

Refrain:
Oh, I want to see Him, look upon His face,
There to sing forever of His saving grace;
On the streets of glory let me lift my voice,
Cares all past, home at last, ever to rejoice.

2. MOVING FORWARD AMIDST THE PEOPLE'S PRAISE

John 12:13: "Took branches of palm trees, and went forth to meet him, and cried, Hosanna: Blessed is the King of Israel that cometh in the name of the Lord."

The people's praise marvelously marches and majestically moves forward with tremendously deep passion and penetration in the worship experience as the people wave palm branches, palms of praise, for the one and only Prince of Peace, Jesus Christ.

The palm branch is a classic symbol of precious peace, true triumph over tragedy, the valiant vision of victory, and most importantly life eternal for the overcomer in Christ Jesus. The positive and progressive palm branch symbolism was best made known and moved forward in the everyday life and business activities in the lands of the Bible, the ancient Eastern Mediterranean world.

Natural high energy foods are produced from the potent date palm. The coconut and date are just two the many popular healthy foods that come from palms. Palm oil and palm wine are all still consumed and drank all over the world. The seeds of the palm are burnt to make charcoal. Palm seed oil is still utililized in many cosmetics and soaps. The fruit of the palm is still utilized as good medicine to fight colds, fevers, sore throats, stomach problems, and sexually transmitted disease such as gonorrhea. Huts, early homes and habitats for the humanity were made with palms to shade and protect people from the harsh elements. The gum of the palm tree's trunk is utilized to medically aid urinary problems and to stop direahea. Palms are also still used to make hand-woven baskets. The Bible refers to Palms in the Eastern Mediterranean world 35 times. The Palm Tree moves and bows before God when major storms move through the land, and stand majestically back up after the storm.

The palm was considered to be extremely special and even extremely sacred in the spiritual beliefs of the Mesopotamian people. The Jews clearly utilized the palm as the centerpiece in their seven day Sukkot Festival, also known as the biblical Feast of Tabernacles. The first mention of this particular popular festival featuring the palm tree is found in Leviticus 23:39 which states "Also in the fifteenth day of the seventh month, when ye have gathered in the fruit of the land, ye shall keep a feast unto the Lord seven days: on the first day shall be a Sabbath, and on the eighth day shall be a Sabbath. 40 And ye shall take you on the first day the boughs of goodly trees, branches of palm trees, and the boughs of thick trees, and willows of the brook; and ye shall rejoice before the Lord your God seven days. 41 And ye shall keep it a feast unto the Lord seven days in the year. It shall be a statute for ever in your generations: ye shall celebrate it in the seventh month."

In the Christian movement, the palm branch, the palm of praise, is clearly associated with what is commonly known in many Christian churches around the whole world as Palm Sunday. When according to reliable I witness accounts accurately recorded in biblical history that palm branches were wondrously waved in an awesome acclamation of worship and praise to Jesus, at the triumphal entry. The precise prophetic fulfillment of the moving forward of the Jewish Messiah, Jesus Christ into Jerusalem. Psalm 92:12 declares that, "The righteous shall flourish like the palm tree: he shall grow like a cedar in Lebanon." This positive and progressive word of scripture is actually engraved on my father's tomb stone. My dad, Rev. Dr. Arthur L. Mackey, Sr. was a Palm Tree Christian who moved forward and made a difference for jobs, justice, and freedom. God deeply desires blood washed believers in the Lord Jesus Christ to move forward and make a difference as Palm Tree Christians with a positive and progressive mindset, mission, and mandate in a real world full of the jagged edged issues of life. THANK YOU JESUS!!!

The legendary palm of praise is also representative of the valiant vision of victory of blood washed Christian martyrs who endured the brutal torturing pain of persecution with the overcoming spirit, which overcame the vicious brutality of the oppressor as referred to in the Book of Revelation. Let us move forward with a positive and progressive mindset. No pain, no gain. No cross, no crown.

Noted best-selling author and retired neuro-surgeon, the living legend, Dr. Benjamin Carson, who had spoke into my life at the ceremony when I was named as the Presidential Fellow at Virginia Union University in Richmond, Virginia, during my college days more recently stated that, "The most important thing for me is having a relationship with God. To know that the owner, the creator of the universe loves you, sent His Son to die for your sins; that's very empowering. Knowing Him and knowing that He loves me gives me encouragement and confidence to move forward." Dr. Carson is a Palm Tree Christian, a true leader of leaders with worldwide influence and impact, who is still standing tall, positive and progressive in the very best sense of the word, moving forward and making a difference.

Yes it was a majestic palm tree's branch that was one of the main iconic images associated with victory in ancient Rome and rewarded to the mighty Roman gladiators and warriors who fought until the bloody death of their opponent. Even the early Greeks proudly presented the glorious green palm branch to the most highly effective athletes who gained the victory in the sweat, pain, and heavy heat of their classic sporting competitions.

The palm has also become a classic symbol appearing on many secular governmental seals such as the United States of America, United Nations; the states of Illinois, Florida, Pennsylvania, New Hampshire, and Hawaii; and many flags from all over the entire world.

When I go to Florida to visit my mother and sisters there are Palm Trees all over majestically lined up decorating the beautiful landscape of Orlando and many other scenic areas in the state. When I fly into the Orlando Airport I can see the awesome and wonderful sight of all of the splendid Palm Trees as we approach the airport for landing. When I was at a recent Pastor's and Leadership Conference in Orlando, Florida, the Palm Trees literally lined the entire Orlando community with an overwhelming atmosphere of elegance and excellence.

The people's praise marvelously marches and moves forward with great momentum and deep passion as the people try to out run each other just to meet and greet Jesus face to face in the flesh.

The people's praise majestically marches and moves forward with deep passion as the people cry, as the people boldly shout, from the depths of their souls "Hosanna: Blessed is the King of Israel that cometh in the name of the Lord."

Let all the people praise Thee.
Let all the people praise Thee,
Let all the people praise Thy Name
Forever and forevermore.

3. MOVING FORWARD FULFILLING THE PEOPLE'S PROPHECY

John 12:14-16: "And Jesus, when he had found a young ass, sat thereon; as it is written, Fear not, daughter of Sion: behold, thy King cometh, sitting on an ass's colt. These things understood not his disciples at the first: but when Jesus was glorified, then remembered they that these things were written of him, and that they had done these things unto him."

The people's prophecy precisely proclaimed in Zechariah 9:9 moves forward in a whole new dimension of fascinating fulfillment found as Jesus, the King of Kings, humbly rides into Jerusalem on sitting a donkey. Not riding in on a strong stallion as a mighty military leader coming to conquer Rome, but on a donkey, a colt, an ass. Zechariah 9:9 proclaimed with precise prophetic accuracy "Rejoice greatly, O daughter of Zion; shout, O daughter of Jerusalem: behold, thy King cometh unto thee: he is just, and having salvation; lowly, and riding upon an ass, and upon a colt the foal of an ass."

The people's prophecy proclaimed in Zechariah 9:9 marvelously moves forward in a new dimension of fascinating fulfillment as Jesus, the King of Kings, rides into Jerusalem embodying the meaningful message "Fear not" for King Jesus has moved forward, the King Jesus has comes in humility riding on donkey.

Earlier when Jesus and His twelve disciples moved forward close to the city of Jerusalem, moved forward to Bethpage and Bethany, moved forward at the Mount of Olives. Jesus sent forward two of His disciples on a meaningful ministry mission. Jesus said to them, "Go your way into the village over against you: and as soon as you enter into it, you shall find a colt tied, whereon never man sat; loose him, and bring him." Jesus continued to say "if any man say unto you, Why do ye this? say ye that the Lord hath need of him; and straightway he will send him hither." The two disciples moved forward, and found the colt, the donkey, the ass tied by the door without in a place where two ways met; and the two disciples loosed the donkey. One of them that stood there said to the two disciples, What are you doing loosing the colt? The two disciples that Jesus sent said to them even as Jesus had commanded: and they let them go. The two disciples brought the colt, the donkey, the ass to Jesus, and cast their garments on the donkey. Then Jesus sat on the donkey. Let me reemphasize that many in the multitude then spread their garments all along the way. Other disciples cut down branches off the trees, palms of praise, and placed them all along the way that Jesus rode. The disciples that moved forward before, and those that followed, marched forward crying, "Hosanna; Blessed is he that cometh in the name of the Lord: Blessed be the kingdom of our father David, that cometh in the name of the Lord: Hosanna in the highest." This is how it happened, this exactly how it went down when Jesus moved forward and entered into Jerusalem.

The people's prophecy proclaimed by the minor prophet in Zechariah 9:9 moves forward into a whole new dimension of fascinating fulfillment as Jesus rides into Jerusalem and His very own daily twelve disciples, don't even fully understand, clueless, they just don't totally get it yet, until Jesus moves forward, ascends in glorification to the Father above after His crucifixion, resurrection, and ascension.

When Jesus, the King of Kings, moved forward and rode in triumphantly into Jerusalem, Jesus' grace rode and rolled right in for you and I.

When Jesus, the Lord of Lords, moved forward and rode in triumphantly into Jerusalem, Jesus' mercy rode and rolled right in for you and I.

When Jesus, the Prince of Peace, moved forward and rode in triumphantly into Jerusalem, Jesus' forgiveness rode and rolled right in for you and I.

Ride on King Jesus!
No man can hinder him
Ride on King Jesus!
No man can hinder him

4. MOVING FORWARD AS THE PEOPLE'S PREACHER

John 12:17-18: "The people therefore that was with him when he called Lazarus out of his grave, and raised him from the dead, bare record. For this cause the people also met him, for that they heard that he had done this miracle."

Jesus, the Lamb of God, was the people's preacher because Jesus truly cared for plain ordinary folk, ordinary people with an extraordinary future like Lazarus, whose name means "whom God helps."

Jesus, the Wonder Worker, was the people's preacher because Jesus made a major difference by raising a dead situation by simply saying "Lazarus come forth." Lazarus, which simply means "whom God helps", move forward.

Jesus, the Son of God, was the people's preacher because Jesus met the people where they were, and they wanted to meet and greet Jesus too for themselves. The people wanted to touch Jesus. The people wanted to see Jesus no matter what. The Greeks who came from far to worship at the feast told the disciple Philip, "Sir, we would see Jesus." Jesus had his hand on the pulse of the people. Jesus had His heart on the pulse of our public and private sin. Jesus had His hand and heart on the pulse of our personal pain. Yes, the Lord Jesus had His hand and heart on the pulse of the perilous plight of all the people. Let us move forward with a positive and progressive mindset. No pain, no gain. No cross, no crown.

5. MOVING FORWARD IN SPITE OF THE PHARISEE'S PROTEST.

"The Pharisees therefore said among themselves, Perceive ye how ye prevail nothing? behold, the world is gone after him."

The Pharisees' protest reveals their bitterly deep seething anger over the rising popularity of Jesus, and clearly uncovers the truth that haters could not ever stop, prevail over, or even prevent Jesus from moving forward and making a difference with His holistic message, ministry, and mission. Some of the Pharisees mixed in the multitude said to Jesus, "Master, rebuke thy disciples." Jesus answered and said to them, "I tell you that, if these should hold their peace, the stones would immediately cry out." Now I don't want any stones shouting out the praise that I must shout out to my God. I don't want any rocks rolling out praise for me. When Jesus moved forward near Jerusalem, Jesus beheld the city, and overwhelmingly wept over it. There was some major, major, major pain there inside of Jesus. Some deep and painful inner hurt that Jesus was processing. Jesus said with His heart overwhelmingly full of plenty of pain, "If thou hadst known, even thou, at least in this thy day, the things which belong unto thy peace! but now they are hid from thine eyes." Plotters and haters don't want peace, therefore they are spiritually blinded. Jesus heart was full of major deep pain, because the city had taken for granted the many prophets sent directly from God the Father, Jesus the Son, and the Holy Spirit, that we read about in the Old Testament sent from God and ignored in that city. They will pay dearly for it, Jesus continues to state, "For the days shall come upon thee, that thine enemies shall cast a trench about thee, and compass thee round, and keep thee in on every side, and shall lay thee even with the ground, and thy children within thee; and they shall not leave in thee one stone upon another; because thou knewest not the time of thy visitation." Now Jesus, the Messiah, was right there and they knew not the time of their visitation. They did not appreciate Jesus. The religious, governmental, and political high place powers that be, plotters and haters had their focus in all the wrong places and missed the time of their visitation. Even when Jesus combination of religious, governmental, and political plotters and haters had Him crucified on the cross of Calvary missing the time of their visitation and thought that they could possibly stop Jesus from moving forward and "the world going after Him." In spite of it all Jesus still took His mighty message, ministry, and mission underground and conquered the unholy trinity of death, hell, and the grave before rising again with all power in His hands.

6. MOVING FORWARD IN SPITE OF THE PALMS OF PAIN

Matthew 26:67: "Then did they spit in his face, and buffeted him; and others smote him with the palms of their hands."

For every palm of praise in life face it there are also so many hateful vicious and violent palms of pain. For every positive and progressive person who is honestly doing the right thing. Face it there are outright misusers and outright abusers who are oppressively doing the worst wrongful and treacherous things, and can end up in prison for it based on today's law.

Mark 14:65: "And some began to spit on him, and to cover his face, and to buffet him, and to say unto him, Prophesy: and the servants did strike him with the palms of their hands."

John 18:22: "And when he had thus spoken, one of the officers which stood by struck Jesus with the palm of his hand, saying, Answerest thou the high priest so?"

Never forget that Jesus is a wounded Healer. Jesus clearly understood paralyzing pain, because He was an abused Savior. Smitten, rejected, and terribly tortured by His haters. Now the palm of pain went way beyond a simple spit and hit for Jesus. Jesus beard was literally and painfully ripped off His face. Jesus had a crown of sharp thrones literally and painfully pushed on His head. Jesus was literally and painfully whipped on His bloody back throughout the night with 39 lethal lashes demonically designed for death. Jesus literally and painfully had both bloody hands nailed to a rugged wooden cross. Jesus had both bloody feet literally and painfully nailed to a rugged wooden cross. Jesus was literally and painfully pierced in His bloody side with a Roman soldiers spear. Jesus was literally and painfully misused and even abused as He took on the sins of all humanity until He died, moved forward and rose again, and moved forward again and ascended to His Father. So we know that we are somebody extremely special, the King's kids, Christ's children, brought with the price of Jesus precious blood, and we don't have to be in or stay in any abusive, oppressive, and or toxic relationships.

7. MOVING FORWARD WITH THE PALM OF TOTAL PRAISE

Revelation 7:9-10: "After this I beheld, and, lo, a great multitude, which no man could number, of all nations, and kindreds, and

people, and tongues, stood before the throne, and before the Lamb, clothed with white robes, and palms in their hands; And cried with a loud voice, saying, Salvation to our God which sitteth upon the throne, and unto the Lamb."

The palm of total praise is not limited to a phony religious crowd where some people praise Jesus for one day only, and some of the same people plot against Jesus one week later saying "crucify Him, crucify Him."

The palm of total praise will only end up in the hands of the totally committed overcomers who truly endured the hard, harsh and heavy pulsating pain of public and private persecution until they pushed out their very last breathe.

The palm of total praise is only for a mighty massive multitude of the redeemed in the Lord Jesus Christ made up of real ordinary people like you and I from all ethnic groups, all nationalities, and all languages. Real ordinary people who in spite of the paralyzing pain of persecution moved forward, onward, and upward and finally made it to heaven. A number that no mere man made calculator could ever count. A number that no mere human being could or would ever be able to add or tally up. God deeply desires blood washed believers in the Lord Jesus Christ to move forward and make a difference as Palm Tree Christians with a positive and progressive mindset, mission, and mandate in a real world full of the jagged edged issues of life. THANK YOU JESUS!!!

Part 3

MOVING FORWARD WITH THE PRINCE OF PEACE

CHAPTER TWELVE

MOVING FORWARD WITH MEANING – THE IMPACT OF THE FORWARD DREAM

Matthew 1:18-25

1.) **THE FORWARD MESS**

18 Now the birth of Jesus Christ was on this wise: When as his mother Mary was espoused to Joseph, before they came together, she was found with child of the Holy Ghost.

Joseph was experiencing a major forward mess, a major life changing transition from his perspective. Joseph was experiencing a major forward mess, a major life changing transition from his vantage point. His Bride-to-Be is pregnant. Joseph is dealing with a major change. Joseph is dealing with a major transition in his relationship with Mary, because Joseph is not the father of this baby. Joseph must be thinking that Mary cheated on me. Joseph feels brutally betrayed. He thinks in enhance that his Dollie is pregnant by another Charlie. We know that Mary was impregnated with child of the Spirit of God. Mary was impregnated with child of the Holy Ghost, but Joseph was hurting real bad. Joseph was going through a forward mess. Any way you cut it Joseph is not Jesus biological father.

2.) **THE FORWARD STRESS**

19 Then Joseph her husband, being a just man, and not willing to make her a public example, was minded to put her away

privily.

Feeling utterly disgraced Joseph wanted put Mary in hiding and not move forward with a meaningless marriage. Joseph was hurting real bad. Joseph had some overwhelming forward stress, but he still had love in his heart for Mary. Religious Jews in that particular time would publically stone to death a woman who was found pregnant outside of marriage. Joseph felt brutally betrayed. Joseph was going through hot and heavy forward stress, but Joseph still had some love in his heart for Mary. Joseph had enough love in his heart for Mary to not want to see Mary viciously stoned to death by a religious mob as a public example. In the midst of Joseph's deepest forward stress he had the mindset to make forward decision to hide Mary and save her life.

3.) THE FORWARD DREAM

20 But while he thought on these things, behold, the angel of the Lord appeared unto him in a dream, saying, Joseph, thou son of David, fear not to take unto thee Mary thy wife: for that which is conceived in her is of the Holy Ghost.

In the midst Joseph's ferocious forward mess. In the midst of Joseph's fiery forward stress. As a tired Carpenter named Joseph thought on these things the angel of the Lord showed up in Joseph's God-given forward dream. A forward dream for Joseph's forward mess. A forward dream for Joseph's forward stress. A forward dream for Joseph's inner and outer forward scream.

In essence the angel of the Lord said in a nutshell or in street language that Joe, descendent of King David. Joe don't fear. Fear not at all Joe. Joe you will make it through this major transition I your life. Joe it is not as bad as it looks. Joe I know that you feel that your relationship with Mary is meaningless. Joe I know that you feel that it now impossible for you to move forward and marry Mary. Joe it is not as bad as it looks about right now. Joe I came from Heaven to let you know that your Dollie is not pregnant by another Charlie. Mary was not sleeping around with some soldier. Mary was chosen by God to be impregnated by the Holy Ghost. Mary's name means bitter, but Joe Mary did not cheat on you at all. Mary has the inner strength to deal with the bitterness of life. Mary is faithful to you and Mary is faithful to God. Joe God will bring you through your forward mess. Joe God will bring you through your forward stress. Joe God has given you a forward dream for your inner and outer forward scream. Joe this is a major transition, but Joe God wants you to move forward with meaning.

4.)   THE FORWARD MISSION

21 And she shall bring forth a son, and thou shalt call his name Jesus: for he shall save his people from their sins.

In essence the angel of the Lord said in a nutshell or in street language that Joe the Son of God, the second person of the Trinity, the Redeemer, the Prince of Peace, is moving forward through Mary to make legal entrance into the earth realm to pay the price for the sins of all humanity. Joe the Son of God, the second person of the Trinity, the Redeemer is moving forward through Mary. He will move forward through her birth canal. He will move forward through Mary's womb. Joe the Son of God, the second person of the Trinity, the Redeemer is moving forward through Mary, but Joe the big picture is that Jesus ultimately wants to move forward in you, and all who have and will accept Him, and receive Him as Lord and Savior, in the past, present, and future. Joe Mary cannot, must not, shall not have an abortion. Joe this baby Jesus must not be aborted. Joe, Jesus is moving forward in Mary now so when He gets out of Mary's womb He can grow and move forward in the lives of hurting humanity. Joe this is a major transition, but Joe God wants you to move forward with meaning. Joe, Jesus is moving forward in Mary now so when He gets out of Mary's womb He can grow and move forward in the lives of the broken, the battered, and the bruised worldwide.

Acts 17:28
For <u>in him we live, and move</u>, and have our being;

1 John 4:4
Ye are of God, little children, and have overcome them: because <u>greater is he that is in you</u>, than he that is in the world.

Colossians 1:27
To whom God would make known what is the riches of the glory of this mystery among the Gentiles; which is <u>Christ in you</u>, the hope of glory:

In essence the angel of the Lord said in a nutshell or in street language that, Joe this baby boy is moving forward in and through Mary. Joe you call His name Jesus. Carpenter Joe that is your forward mission. Joe you call His name Jesus. Joe the Savior of all humanity, past, present, and future is literally moving forward through your Bride-to-Be Mary. Joe your Dollie is not pregnant by another Charlie. For Joe, this Jesus, the Son of God, the Messiah, the Redeemer, that is moving forward through Mary will save His people, past, present, and future from their sins. Joe the name Jesus means Savior.

5.) **THE FORWARD PROPHECY**

22 Now all this was done, that it might be fulfilled which was spoken of the Lord by the prophet, saying,

In essence the angel of the Lord was letting Joseph know that, Joe this is bigger than you. Joe you had to go through this forward mess, Joe you had to go through this forward stress to fully embrace God's very best. Joe this is the fulfillment of a forward prophecy given from the Lord Himself to the legendary Prophet of old by the name of Isaiah. Joe the Ultimate Prophetic Word, Jesus, the Savior, the Prince of Peace, is moving forward through your Bride-to-Be.

2 Peter 1:21
For the <u>prophecy</u> came not in old time by the will of man: but holy men of God spake as they were <u>moved by the Holy Ghost</u>.

6.) THE FORWARD MEANING

23 Behold, a virgin shall be with child, and shall bring forth a son, and they shall call his name Emmanuel, which being interpreted is, God with us.

In essence the angel of the Lord said in a nutshell or in street language that, Joe this forward prophecy lets us know that God is with us. Joe this forward prophecy has major forward meaning. Joe I mean that your Bride-to-Be is still a virgin. The baby Jesus will move through her to legally enter the earth realm as fully God and fully man to legally save His people, past, present, and future from their sins. Joe they will call Jesus name Emmanuel. Joe that name has major forward meaning, God with us. Joe God wants you to move forward with meaning.

Dannibelle Hall got it right when she sung those timeless words:

Life full of meaning
Life abundant and free (yeah, yeah, yeah)
Life that opens up the door to all eternity
Yeah, life really begins with Jesus

Isaiah 7:14:
Therefore the Lord himself shall give you a sign; Behold, a virgin shall conceive, and bear a son, and shall call his name Immanuel.

7.) THE FORWARD OBEDIENCE

24 Then Joseph being raised from sleep did as the angel of the Lord had bidden him, and took unto him his wife:

As Joseph came out of his sleep and his highly informative forward dream. Joseph operated in forward obedience and did as the angel of the Lord told him. Joseph moved forward with new meaning in the midst of the transitions of life. Joseph moved forward and overcame his own forward mess. Joseph moved forward and overcame his own forward stress. Joseph's forward dream helped him overcome his very own inner and outer forward scream. Joseph went forth with forward obedience and married Mary. Mr. Joseph moved forward with new meaning and married Miss Mary.

- In forward obedience to the forward dream Joseph moved forward and married Mary in Nazareth as recorded in Matthew 1:24.
- In forward obedience to the forward dream Joseph moved forward and cared, shared, and bared the responsibility to watch out for his wife, Mary, and the baby, Jesus, who was born in a

manager, and wrapped in swaddling clothes, in Bethlehem as recorded in Luke 2:4-7. There was no room for them in the inn.

8.) THE FORWARD DECLARATION

25 And knew her not till she had brought forth her firstborn son: and he called his name Jesus.

DID YOU KNOW? The Carpenter, Joseph, did not move forward sexually with his wife, Mary, until she had her first born son, Jesus, according to Matthew 13:55. Joseph, son of Jacob, went on to have four sons by his beloved wife, Mary. Their names were James, Joses, Simon, and Judas. Matthew 13:56 informs us that Joseph and Mary also had several daughters. These were the half brothers and sisters of Jesus. Joseph, a descendent of the father of the faith - Abraham, King David, and King Solomon, is mentioned 16 times in the biblical books of Matthew, Luke, and John. Joseph's name means increaser and may God add.

- Joseph increased in overcoming forward mess.
- Joseph increased in overcoming forward stress.
- Joseph increased through his God-given forward dream.
- Joseph increased through embracing his God-given forward mission to name Jesus and be His step father.
- Joseph increased through embracing God-given forward prophecy.
- Joseph increased through embracing forward meaning.
- Joseph increased through embracing forward obedience.
- Joseph made a difference.
- Joseph increased through his God-given forward declaration.
- Joseph called His name Jesus.
- Joseph declared His name Jesus as the angel of the Lord said.
- Jesus the Son of God.

- Jesus the Lamb of God.
- Jesus the Lion of the Tribe of Judah.
- Jesus the Deliverer.
- Jesus the Shepherd of the Sheep.
- Jesus the Anchor of the Soul.
- Jesus my Savior.
- Jesus my Redeemer.
- Jesus my Baptizer in the Holy Ghost.
- Jesus my Wounded Healer.
- Jesus my Justifier.
- Jesus my Sanctifier.
- Jesus my Emmanuel.
- Jesus my Lilly of the Valley.
- Jesus my Bright and Morning Star.
- Jesus my Prince of Peace.
- Jesus my All in All.
- Jesus makes the difference.
- Because of Jesus we can move forward with meaning and make a difference.
- Jesus is the living and rising eternal Christ of communion.

CHAPTER THIRTEEN

MOVING FORWARD WITH THE CONVICTION OF COMMUNION – THE 7 PRINCIPLES OF COMMUNION

1 Corinthians 11:27-29:
"Wherefore whosoever shall eat this bread, and drink this cup of the Lord, unworthily, shall be guilty of the body and blood of the Lord. But let a man examine himself, and so let him eat of that bread, and drink of that cup. For he that eateth and drinketh unworthily, eateth and drinketh damnation to himself, not discerning the Lord's body."

The Apostle Paul had enough backbone to move forward and make a difference by educating the corrupt Corinthian church about misusing the Lord's Supper by getting filthy drunk with alcoholic wine instead of utilizing the natural, non-alcoholic, fruit of the vine as the Lord Jesus taught in word and deed. The Apostle Paul was moving forward with the positive and progressive influence, inspiration, and impact of Jesus, the Prince of Peace.

THE 7 PRINCIPLES OF COMMUNION

1.) THE BREAD OF COMMUNION: I Corinthians 11:23-24: "For I have received of the Lord that which also I delivered unto you, that the Lord Jesus the same night in which he was betrayed took bread: And when he had given thanks, he brake it, and said, Take, eat: this is my body, which is broken for you: this do in remembrance of me."

The bread of communion represents the actual body of our Lord Jesus, who died on Calvary's cross for the sin sick souls of all humanity, past, present, and future.

2.) THE CUP OF COMMUNION: I Corinthians 11:25: "After the same manner also he took the cup, when he had supped, saying, this cup is the new testament in my blood: this do ye, as oft as ye drink it, in remembrance of me."

The cup of communion represents the actual blood of our Lord Jesus, who died on Calvary's cross for the sin sick souls of all humanity, past, present, and future.

3.) THE COVENANT OF COMMUNION: "this cup is the new testament (new covenant) in my blood."

The Covenant of Communion is the New Testament, the new covenant, the new agreement, in the soul saving blood of our Lord Jesus. We are no longer in the Old Testament or old covenant today. We are New Testament, new covenant, blood washed believers.

4.) THE CONSISTENCY OF COMMUNION: I Corinthians 11:24-26: "And when he had given thanks, he brake it, and said,

Take, eat: this is my body, which is broken for you: this do in remembrance of me. After the same manner also he took the cup, when he had supped, saying, this cup is the new testament in my blood: this do ye, as oft as ye drink it, in remembrance of me. For as often as ye eat this bread, and drink this cup, ye do shew the Lord's death till he come."

The consistency of communion is absolutely and essentially critical in the powerful process of remembering and reminding ourselves of the precious price that the Lord Jesus paid on the cross for our private and public penalties.

5.) THE CONVICTION OF COMMUNION: I Corinthians 11:27-29: "Wherefore whosoever shall eat this bread, and drink this cup of the Lord, unworthily, shall be guilty of the body and blood of the Lord. But let a man examine himself, and so let him eat of that bread, and drink of that cup. For he that eateth and drinketh unworthily, eateth and drinketh damnation to himself, not discerning the Lord's body."

The conviction of communion is not personal preference. The conviction of communion is Christ-centered and calls for blood-washed believers to boldly move forward and make a difference in this jagged edged world

6.) THE CAUSE AND EFFECT OF COMMUNION: I Corinthians 11:30-31: "For this cause many are weak and sickly among you, and many sleep. For if we would judge ourselves, we should not be judged."

The cause and effect of communion means the Lord's Supper will either be the ministry meal that heals or the ministry meal that kills. We must have some backbone to move forward and make a difference by judging ourselves. We must have some backbone to move forward and make a difference by examining ourselves.

> *It's me. It's me, oh, Lord.*
> *Not my father, not my mother,*
> *not my sisters, or my brothers.*
> *It's me, oh, Lord*
> *standing in the need of prayer.*

MOVING FORWARD FOR THE CAUSE OF COMMUNION – RIGHTLY DISCERNING THE LORD'S BODY

1 Corinthians 11:30:
For this cause many are weak and sickly among you, and many sleep.

When a believer eats the bread that represents Jesus' brutally wounded body, and drinks the cup of the Lord that represents Jesus' life changing blood unworthily, he or she becomes guilty of disrespecting and disregarding the body and blood of the Lord. They have not moved forward and embraced the true cause of communion. Therefore, move forward and let a man examine himself, and so let him eat of that bread that represents the wounded body of Jesus, and drink of that cup that represents the precious blood of Jesus that was shed for you and I. The believer who eats and drinks unworthily is the exact same believer who eats and drinks damnation, not properly discerning the Lord's body. Treating our brother and sister in Christ with malice can be deadly. The cause of communion can be the cause that heals, or sadly, the cause that kills. For this cause, many blood-washed believers are weak and sickly among you, and many have died before their time. For if we would only move forward for this cause and judge ourselves, instead of judging everybody else under the sun, we would not be judged. When we, the blood-washed believers, the church, are judged, we are chastened of the Lord that we should not be condemned to hell with the world, but rather move forward for the cause of the sweet communion of the Holy Ghost. American industrialist, Henry Ford, was right when he wrote,

"If everyone is moving forward together, then success takes care of itself." The spirit of true Christian unity and communion which causes blood washed believers to move forward, onward, and upward is an extremely important catalyst of change that challenges us to be filled with the life changing knowledge of God's will.

7.) THE CHASTENING OF COMMUNION: I Corinthians 11:32-34: "But when we are judged, we are chastened of the Lord, that we should not be condemned with the world. Wherefore, my brethren, when ye come together to eat, tarry one for another. And if any man hunger, let him eat at home; that ye come not together unto condemnation. And the rest will I set in order when I come."

The chastening of communion is the Christ-centered correction that is given for the blood-washed believers' protection from being condemned with the world. Christ gives us the chastening of communion so that we will not end up in the hot and horrific place called hell.

MOVE FORWARD & HAVE SOME BIBLICALLY BASED BACKBONE

Let me share with you a hilarious story of the courageous chicken and the persistent pig. Though the story is humorous, it still has a mighty, meaningful, and motivating message in it. One day, the persistent pig boldly declared to the courageous chicken, "For you to move forward and make a difference by making and hatching eggs is fairly easy. Yet, on the other hand, for me to move forward and make a difference by giving ham absolutely and positively requires total commitment." The courageous chicken paused and then replied, "Yeah, I know because in order for me to move forward and make a difference and give fried chicken it requires the backbone of total commitment."

Yes, my brothers and sisters, in the struggle we must move forward and make a difference with total commitment to effectively reach a generation of youth highly exposed to gang banging, who proudly wear their pants hanging down and publicly show off their own underwear. Yes, my brothers and sisters, in the struggle we must move forward and make a difference with total commitment to more effectively reach our youth and let them know that 'saggin'' is the word 'niggas' spelled backwards. In prison, men could not wear belts and therefore their pants sagged. This made it easier for the men to rape one another.

THE CONVICTION OF COMMUNION THAT BRINGS DEEP SELF-EXAMINATION EVEN FOR THE BELIEVER

Knowledge is power when applied. We must move forward and embrace the conviction of communion that brings deep self-examination.

Move forward and make a difference and pull up your pants, young men. The right to sag your pants is not the modern day civil rights movement. It is disrespectful and indecent exposure. Move forward and make a difference by pulling up your pants. Don't pull down your momma with your gangsta drama. Don't pull your momma down into deep depression. Your father may be there for you or not, but move forward and pull up your pants anyhow, because your brothers, sisters, grandpa, grandma, family, friends, and community need you alive out of jail and not in the grave before your time. Your loved ones truly need you to be more than a mere statistic of a society that does not care.

Move forward and make a difference with total commitment and pull up your pants, young brother, and even sisters, nowadays. Pull up your grades, young man and young woman. Pull up your plans for your future, young brother and young sister. Pull up your God-given purpose, young brother and young sister. Pull up your prayers, young man and young woman. Pull up your patience, young brothers and young sisters. Pull up your persistence, young men and young women. We must move forward and embrace the conviction of communion that brings deep self-examination.

LEGALIZED ABOMINATION BRINGS A NATION BACKWARDS TO TOTAL BETRAYAL OF GOD

Now, our most brilliant and talented politicians and power movers and shakers are so focused on pushing gay marriage and normalizing the gay lifestyle with all their might that they have absolutely failed to see that our young people are totally forgotten and forsaken. The Lord clearly declares in **Leviticus 18:22** that, **"Thou shalt not lie with mankind, as with womankind: it is <u>abomination</u>."** Legalized abomination brings a nation backwards to total betrayal of God who formed the nation in the first place. Our most brilliant and talented politicians who we pray for every day are so dead bent on legalizing gay marriage at any cost, that it does not matter if our youth are totally forgotten and forsaken and even worse, because of this, our top cities are now our top murder capitals. Brown killing brown all over town and pulling the town down, and all the haters and the Ku Klux Klan just love it. To add insult to injury, the powers that be proclaim that crime is down, because it is not happening in their side of town.

Our most historic and our most brilliant minded politicians, even some preachers, and other power movers and shakers, forget and forsake our youth and zero funded youth centers in an effort to be politically correct and push for what they see as the more important gay pride agenda all for acceptance, endorsements, and votes. This is totally phony. This is not true genuine concern. Don't be fooled; this is not true love. This is phony political correctness and the deepest corruption of the soul of a nation at its very worst so far. We can't see the forest for the trees, because the real modern day civil rights movement is being birthed from that very horrifying act of ignoring our children in our governmental budgets and in our time.

Our most powerful politicians are so busy pushing for gay marriage that a bully with a gun shot and killed an unarmed teenager with a bag of Skittles, because the national focus is on issues that totally contradict the teachings of the Bible. Now bullies feel free to shoot and kill young black males at will. Our most talented and well-educated politicians are so busy promoting gay marriage that a bully with a gun shoots ten times into a van filled with black young people killing a young black male teenager who has no weapon because his rap music was too loud. This bully shooter gets away with murder of the 1st degree even though he has taken the innocent life of a young black male. Our top 1% financial experts on Wall Street are so busy wasting big money and getting their financial inductees to dress up in drag that they don't care at all about the plight and poverty of the poor on Main Street, USA.

Our most brilliant politicians need to stop being mere and mundane politicians, and become better public servants who, instead of only focusing on gay marriage so they can be politically correct, begin to fight bullying on every front so the youth of Chicago and the inner cities of the entire nation will know that their lives are just as important to the national agenda, even if they are not old enough to vote. The price that we are paying to be politically correct is way too high when we ignore the pain and plight of our nation's children to win votes from the most influential power groups.

If we move the national agenda forward on bullying, instead of gay marriage, then positive and progressive Christians, Jews, Muslims, and other people of faith, who strongly disagree with gay marriage can fight against the bullying of anyone, hatred of anyone, and abuse of anyone, because they don't have to compromise their faith to stand against bullying. Bullying and negative peer pressure, not gay marriage, is the universal issue, the root issue, the core issue, that we can all march together on. Young people have jumped off of bridges because of bullying and negative peer pressure. People are committing suicide at all ages and stages of life because of bullying and negative peer pressure. This phony political correctness of the season is not moving our nation forward, but backwards to a time where it is open season on killing young black males and cutting back key provisions of the Voter Rights Act with no repercussion. This must come to a stop now. NOW IS THE TIME FOR AMERICA TO MOVE FORWARD AND REPENT BEFORE IT IS TOO LATE. THIS CAN BE OUR GREATEST HOUR IF WE GET RIGHT WITH GOD.

SPEAK THE TRUTH IN LOVE

While the most brilliant and talented movers and shakers see gay marriage as the number one classic civil rights agenda, guns, gangs, and violence are absolutely consuming, yes, literally snuffing out the lives of our youth. Every month there is another mass murder shooting or stabbing. What will it take to be a fool for Christ and admit that the Bible is right, brilliant and most talented politicians? I have the legal right to speak the truth in love. Blacklist me if you want. I love everyone. Never bully anyone and never physically harm anyone just because you don't like what they are doing. I don't hate anyone on God's earth. I don't discriminate against anyone on God's earth, even if I disagree with them. I never disrespect them. I will only speak the truth in love.

Martin Luther King was right when he said "Love is greater than like." God absolutely requires us to love everyone. Brilliant and talented politician, do not spit on God's Holy Word in utter disregard and totally disrespect what He has decreed and declared. Yes, you're my politician and not my pastor. Also remember that you are a public servant to all the people and should not discriminate against any of the people whether you agree or disagree. It takes backbone to be fair and impartial.

God has decreed and declared in His Holy Word, the Bible, that marriage is between a man and woman. Let us not fall into the deep cesspool of sin of discriminating against people, black listing people, and outright ostracizing people from the public square, because their world view is biblically centered with love and not hate. Most brilliant and talented politicians and mover and shakers, if you discriminate biblical world views based in love and not hate, then you do a great injustice to the people. Martin Luther King, Jr. was absolutely right when he wrote in his historic letter from the Birmingham Jail that "injustice anywhere is a threat to justice everywhere."

RESPONSIBLE FREEDOM OF SPEECH

Responsible freedom of speech must be respected and protected under the law and even in the public square. Biblically based critical and crucial world views spoken in pure love and not passionate hate absolutely have the legal right to be spoken in the center of secular society. If no one ever moved forward and made a difference with biblically based world views spoken in pure love and not passionate hate, we would not have the practice of social work. We would not have hospitals with doctors and nurses. We would not have the many colleges and universities started by pioneering, trailblazing Christians who moved forward and made a major difference in the field of education. Love everyone and discriminate against no one on any side of an issue. Most important: remember what God says.

I was in my house with my family when Hurricane Sandy hit. Call it what you want. The insurance people call it an act of God. Some in the church call it the judgment of God. All I know is, the rain falls on the just and the unjust, and I do know beyond a shadow of a doubt that when our most brilliant and talented politicians and movers and shakers push governmental degrees through that contradict the Holy Bible everyone suffers. When there is drought throughout the land everyone suffers. Please, please, please most brilliant and talented politicians and movers and shakers always, always, always remember that there is no one more scientific than God. When He said, "Let there be light" supernatural light moved forward and made a real difference even before God made the sun. That was the true big bang thing moving forward and making a lasting difference. You can't get more scientific than God. We must move forward and embrace the conviction of communion that brings deep self examination. We must move forward and check ourselves, so we won't wreck ourelves.

So most brilliant and talented politicians, movers and shakers, don't be haters or discriminators when someone moves forward and makes a real difference with biblically based backbone speaking the truth in love right in the middle of our public squares, the center of secular society. Most brilliant and talented politicians, movers and shakers, always remember these words also spoken to a brilliant governmental leader, mover and shaker, for the benefit of his entire nation. Most brilliant and talented politicians, movers and shakers, God was right on target when He decreed and declared to brilliant leader, mover and shaker, King Solomon in 2 Chronicles 7:14, "If my people, which are called by my name, shall humble themselves, and pray, and seek my face, and turn from their wicked ways; then will I hear from heaven, and will forgive their sin, and will heal their land."

Please always remember who God is: God is the Prime Mover. Serve God and do only His will in respect of His word even in the public square; even in the center of secular society. So our nation will always be a great nation and not a nation destroyed from within by the cesspool of our own national iniquities.

GET ON THE BALL

In closing, there is the story of the popular politician, the powerful preacher, and the prosperous producer who played golf together one day on one of the most beautiful and plush golf courses in the entire nation. The popular politician ever so carefully chose the perfect golf club to 'seize the moment' as he so proudly swung his golf club and hit the golf ball far away. The popular politician killed a thousand ants in the process. When the powerful preacher pulled out his old and true golf club, he swung it hard in the yard and wiped out five hundred ants instantly. Ashes to ashes and dust to dust and so all those ants were instantly crushed. The powerful preacher proudly picked up his golf bag and moved forward in the game on the glamorous golf course.

The prosperous producer took out his gold golf club and swung it hard in the yard annihilating three hundred ants who would never get a chance to be in the movies. The prosperous producer quickly moved forward to leave the golf course and film his next action picture. There were only now two ants left and they said to themselves, "If we are going to make it, move forward and make a difference, we better have some backbone and <u>get on the ball</u>."

Clearly, this story has a moral and a meaningful message. If the popular nation, powerful church, and the prosperous artistic world are to move forward and make a major difference, we must clearly get on the ball and respect who God is: God is our Creator. God is the Prime Mover. God is the source, and we are resources that must move forward, and be respectful to even biblically based world views, and be resourceful and effective. Never forget, most brilliant politician, mover and shaker, the bridge that brought us over. Never forget or forsake our God, most brilliant politician, mover and shaker, just to win votes, because it is totally possible to win elections and still lose the very heart and soul of our towns, villages, counties, states, and entire nations to the demoralizing spirit of legalized sin. We must move forward and embrace the conviction of communion that brings deep self examination:

THE 7 PRINCIPLES OF COMMUNION

1.) The Bread of Communion
2.) The Cup of Communion
3.) The Covenant of Communion
4.) The Consistency of Communion
5.) The Conviction of Communion
6.) The Cause & Effect of Communion
7.) The Chastening of Communion

THE CHRIST OF COMMUNION MAKES THE DIFFERENCE

The Christ of Communion - 1 Corinthians 10:16: "The cup of blessing which we bless, is it not the communion of the blood of Christ? The bread which we break, is it not the communion of the body of Christ?"

- On Christ not politics. Celebrate the Christ of Communion! Jesus makes the difference!
- On Christ not the Democrats. Celebrate the Christ of Communion! Jesus makes the difference!
- On Christ not the Republicans. Celebrate the Christ of Communion! Jesus makes the difference!
- On Christ not the Independents. Celebrate the Christ of Communion! Jesus makes the difference!

Thank God for all of the various political parties, but we must always remind and remember to celebrate the Christ of Communion! Proudly proclaim that On Christ the Solid Rock we, the church, must have blessed backbone, and must boldly stand, for all other ground is sinking sand.

This gets us to the heart of the matter. Jesus the Christ of communion who moved forward and made a difference. Who showed us in word and deed how to move forward and make a difference.

CHAPTER FOURTEEN

MOVING FORWARD & MAKING A DIFFERENCE – THE MINISTRY OF COMPASSION

Matthew 9:36: "But when he saw the multitudes, he was <u>moved with compassion</u> on them, because they fainted, and were scattered abroad, as sheep having no shepherd."

Jude 1:21-23: "Keep yourselves in the love of God, looking for the mercy of our Lord Jesus Christ unto eternal life. And of <u>some have compassion, making a difference</u>: And others save with fear, pulling them out of the fire; hating even the garment spotted by the flesh."

Our existence is summed up in the eternal truth that we were all created by God to move forward and make a difference in the lives of others.

Rev. Dr. Arthur L. Mackey, Sr., was right when he said, "Watch who you spend your time with." Our job is to get others away from the highly toxic and harmful meetings and get them into the positive and progressive community building meetings through the power of positive and progressive relationships over the long haul. Nelson Mandela stated that, "I am fundamentally an optimist. Whether that comes from nature or nurture, I cannot say. Part of being optimistic is

keeping one's head pointed toward the sun, one's feet <u>moving forward</u>. There were many dark moments when my faith in humanity was sorely tested, but I would not and could not give myself up to despair. That way lays defeat and death." We must realize, however, that we have been chosen to be a soldier fighting the good fight of faith for the very souls of our embattled neighborhoods. The battle is not ours, it is the Lord's, and we know that we have the victory.

Rev. Dr. Arthur L. Mackey, Sr., was also right when he said that "one hand washes the other and both wash the face." Yes, working together has a way of saving lives. Rev. Dr. Arthur L. Mackey, Sr., my father, spiritual father, and major community leader. He made a major difference in the lives so many. My father, Rev. Dr. Arthur L. Mackey, Sr. was born as an incubator baby in Brooklyn, New York. At birth he weighed only two pounds, three ounces. His first bed was a dresser drawer. No one thought he would ever survive, but by the grace of God he moved forward and made a difference.

From a very young age it became apparent that the call of God was upon his life. His father, the Rev. Walter R. Mackey, Sr., my grandfather, moved the family from Brooklyn to Long Island, where he founded Mount Sinai Baptist Church Cathedral, where I now serve as Pastor. He literally built that church with his bare hands, and my father and his brothers and friends were all there supporting the work.

My father, Rev. Dr. Arthur L. Mackey, Sr., my father went to college at Virginia University in Richmond, Virginia, where I also attended. My mother, Rev. Dr. Frances W. Mackey, wanted to go to the jungles of Africa as a missionary, but my father said, "I'm going to bring you back to the jingles of Roosevelt, and you can be a missionary and first lady right there." The Lord tremendously blessed their ministry. Rev. Dr. Arthur L. Mackey, Sr. went on to become a great leader in human rights and civil rights within Nassau County, literally helping to stop riots within the community, and to help people get jobs and housing. On December 26, 1999, in an article appropriately entitled, "A Minister in Many Pulpits", the New York Times said of him: "Dr. Mackey met at the White House with Presidents Johnson, Reagan, Bush, and Clinton. He had a one-on-one relationship with several Nassau County executives – Thomas Gulotta, Francis Purcell and Ralph Caso, as well as well as senator Alfonse D'Amato, his wife said. Nassau's Republican candidates often campaigned at his church. And he was a friend of Martin Luther King Sr., who preached at the Mount Sinai Baptist Church in 1980.

During the 1971 Hempstead riots, his daughter Vivian Mackey-Johnson recalled, the police asked his help in calming the community. He never failed to assist the drug users and the indigent who rang his doorbell seeking help. And every Christmas for more than 20 years, he cooked a giant vat of spaghetti and picked up bags of toys for children of single parents in his congregation." My father, Rev. Dr. Arthur L. Mackey, Sr., did a tremendous work for the Lord because of his availability to God. Rev. Dr. Arthur L. Mackey, Sr. moved forward and made a difference. Ralph Waldo Emerson was right on target when he stated that, "The purpose of life is not to be happy. It is to be useful, to be honorable, to be compassionate, to have it make some difference that you have lived and lived well."

4 STRATEGIES TO MOVE FORWARD & MAKE A DIFFERENCE

1.) MOVING FORWARD AND MAKING A DIFFERENCE WITH LOVE

Yes, yes, yes, I am talking about love again, because enduring love is the most crucial aspect and critical ingredient of the moving forward and making a difference message. The pains and pressures of life will either push and propel you into the necessary shift known as change or it will utterly destroy you. Therefore, move forward with a deeply abiding love for God and the least of these amongst us that makes a lasting difference, and develops a crucial mindset for change.

I John 4:12: "No man hath seen God at any time. If we love one another, God dwelleth in us, and his love is perfected in us."

Always remember that God is constantly calling us to move forward to total commitment so we can learn about His lesson of love.

The late world renown civil and human rights leader, Rev. Dr. Martin Luther King, Jr., who understood the importance of possessing "The Strength To Love" was also an proponent of the moving forward and making a difference message. Dr. King was right when he said, "If you can't fly then run, if you can't run then walk, if you can't walk then crawl, but whatever you do you have to keep moving forward."

John Fitzgerald Kennedy, the 35th President of the United States of America who at the age of 43 was the youngest person to have been elected to the presidency of the United States of America. At that time President Kennedy was the second-youngest president in American history after President Theodore Roosevelt, and the President Kennedy was the very first person born in the 20th century to serve as the United States of America President. President Kennedy was a Catholic. President Kennedy was also the only non-Protestant president in American history, and he was also the only president to have won a Pulitzer Prize. President John Fitzgerald Kennedy said that, "One person can <u>make a difference</u> and every person should try."

2.) MOVING FORWARD AND MAKING A DIFFERENCE WITH MERCY

Move forward and make a difference by sharing the mercy of God in the **seven significant relationship stages**:

1.) Single
2.) Engaged
3.) Married
4.) Separated
5.) Divorced
6.) Remarried
7.) Widowed

If you want mercy in any of the seven significant relationship stages of life, then first show mercy to others. Single people need the mercy of God. Engaged people need the mercy of God. Married people need the mercy of God. Separated people need the mercy of God. Divorced people need the mercy of God. Remarried people need the mercy of God. Widowed people need the mercy of God. Move forward and give mercy. There are many who have been single, engaged, married, separated, divorced, remarried, and widowed all in a lifetime and they need the tender mercy of God to move forward, just like you love to receive the mercy of God. The point here is that everybody's life is important, because God is painting a picture through each and every one of our lives by moving forward with mercy.

Lamentations 3:32: "But though he cause grief, yet will he have compassion according to the multitude of his mercies."

James 5:11: "Behold, we count them happy which endure. Ye have heard of the patience of Job, and have seen the end of the Lord; that the Lord is very pitiful, and of tender mercy."

1 Peter 1:3: "Blessed be the God and Father of our Lord Jesus Christ, which according to his abundant mercy hath begotten us again unto a lively hope by the resurrection of Jesus Christ from the dead."

1 Peter 2:10: "Which in time past were not a people, but are now the people of God: which had not obtained mercy, but now have obtained mercy."

Titus 3:5: "Not by works of righteousness which we have done, but according to his mercy he saved us, by the washing of regeneration, and renewing of the Holy Ghost."

3.) MOVING FORWARD AND MAKING A DIFFERENCE WITH COMPASSION

Jude 1:22: "And of <u>some have compassion, making a difference</u>."

The writer, Jude, is the half brother of Jesus. He certainly knew about the moving forward and making a difference message from behind the scenes, yet, no one except God the Father and the Holy Spirit pushed this message like Jesus, the Prince of Peace. Therefore, modern day Christians must follow Christ's clear example and clarion call to be "moved with compassion."

Matthew 9:36: "But when he saw the multitudes, <u>he was moved with compassion on them</u>, because they fainted, and were scattered abroad, as sheep having no shepherd."

Jesus, the Prince of Peace, moved with compassion, fed 5000 with a little boy's lunch of two fishes and five loaves of bread. Jesus, the Prince of Peace, moved with compassion, healed the leper. Jesus moved with compassion, taught, preached, and healed. Jesus, the Prince of Peace, moved with compassion and made a difference.

Matthew 14:14: "And Jesus went forth, and saw a great multitude, and was <u>moved with compassion toward them</u>, and he healed their sick."

Matthew 18:27: "Then the lord of that servant was <u>moved with compassion</u>, and loosed him, and forgave him the debt."

Mark 1:41: "And Jesus, <u>moved with compassion</u>, put forth his hand, and touched him, and saith unto him, I will; be thou clean."

Mark 6:34: "And Jesus, when he came out, saw much people, and was <u>moved with compassion toward them</u>, because they were as sheep not having a shepherd: and he began to teach them many things."

Today, we are called to move forward and make a difference. Jesus Christ, the Prince of Peace, was clearly the main proponent of the moving forward and making a difference message. Moses and his successor, Joshua, were also strong proponents of the moving forward and making a difference message. In order to effectively move forward and make a difference, we must first stand still and see the salvation of the Lord. As we have seen in previous chapters, standing still and seeing the salvation of the Lord lays the very groundwork to strategically move forward and make a difference.

Even the very best NBA basketball and NFL football teams take a time-out. They get in a huddle to get the most up-to-date strategies and plans from their respective coaches to move forward and make a difference in winning the athletic game. Bus riders must also wait for the bus to arrive before they can get on, pay their bus fare, and move forward riding on the bus to their destination. Isaiah the prophet lets us know in Isaiah 40:31 that in order to move forward and make a difference, we must first wait on the Lord's strategy, then we will mount up with wings like eagles, run and not get weary, walk, and not faint.

I was truly inspired by Malala Yousafzai, the dynamic 15 year old Pakistani young woman who was so tragically shot in the head on October 9, 2012, by the Pakistani Taliban for boldly speaking out for the just cause of women's education. I was praying for her survival as well many other people throughout the entire earth. In her very first interview since the shooting Malala moved forward and made a difference when she boldly said that, "I want every girl, every child, to be educated." In her book appropriately entitled, *I Am Malala: The Girl Who Stood Up for Education and Was Shot by the Taliban*, Malala speaks of her near death experience when she stated that, "I told myself, Malala, you have already faced death. This is your second life. Don't be afraid — if you are afraid, you can't move forward."

Use every single minute to move forward and make a difference.

In his life changing poem titled, "God's Minute," Dr. Benjamin Mays, wrote.

I've only just a minute,
Only sixty seconds in it.
Forced upon me, can't refuse it,
Didn't seek it, didn't choose it,
But it's up to me to use it.
I must suffer if I lose it,
Give an account if I abuse it,
Just a tiny little minute,
 But eternity is in it.

We have to use each minute that God gives us to move forward and make a difference in the lives of the broken, battered, and bruised.

FREE FOOD GIVE-AWAY EVERY MONDAY

Each week we move forward and invite everyone who desires to come to receive a free breakfast and a free bag of groceries every Monday at 9:00 a.m. at Mount Sinai Baptist Church Cathedral, located at 243 Rev. Dr. A. L. Mackey Sr. Avenue, Roosevelt, New York, where I serve as senior pastor. Mary Joesten and Faith Mission Inc. head up the free food give-away every Monday at the church. People come from far and near every Monday for the breakfast and groceries. Catch the vision of victory and never give up. Mother Teresa was right when she stated that, "Let us touch the dying, the poor, the lonely and the unwanted according to the graces we have received and let us not be ashamed or slow to do the humble work."

FREE BREAKFAST EVERY SUNDAY AND THE MISSION

Every Sunday morning, Women's Ministry President and Prayer Partner's Coordinator, Deaconess Ernestine Toliver, moves forward and makes a difference by overseeing the weekly free breakfast open to the community at the church after church school every Sunday. All during the week, Deacon Board Chairman Aaron Scott Jr. and the Co-Chairman of the Deacon Board move forward with the mission to help the homeless, the hungry, and the needy. Also, during the week, Missionary President Doris Amar and Church Missionaries move forward and go where angels fear to tread with aid and support for the broken, the battered, and the bruised. Nelson Mandela stated that, "What counts in life is not the mere fact that we have lived. It is what difference we have made to the lives of others that will determine the significance of the life we lead."

MENTORING AND TRAINING PROGRAM

Monday through Friday, Mr. Dermut Sutherland moves forward and makes a difference by conducting the mentoring and training program at Mt. Sinai in conjunction with Nassau County Department of Social Services. Men and women who are attempting to move forward and get their lives back on track learn highly detailed construction work and trades that will bring beneficial discipline and structure to their life. Mt. Sinai Trustee Board Chairman James Hodges and the Trustees and Deacon Board Chairman Aaron Scott, Jr. work closely with the program.

4.) MOVING FORWARD AND MAKING A DIFFERENCE WITH THE 3 F'S STRATEGY - FEAR, FIRE, & FLESH

Jude 1: 23: "And others save with fear, pulling them out of the fire; hating even the garment spotted by the flesh."

Funerals, funerals, funerals, and more funerals of our own youth snuffed out way before their time, monthly mass murders, and daily drive-by shootings are the demonic order of the day. Love, mercy, and compassion are highly effective methods to move forward and make a difference, but tough love also works. Bishop T. D. Jakes said that, "Moving forward requires three things: preparation, dedication and revelation. To succeed, you must depend upon God for direction daily." We must move forward and make a difference by the clergy and church putting the fear of God back into the Public Square and center of society. We must move forward and make a difference by effective lawyers, elected officials, teachers, concerned residents, and community leaders advocating for the broken, battered, and bruised in our communities. If we move forward and make that difference and work it, we can get the job done by the grace of God. We are soldiers in the army of the Lord. We must fight the good fight of faith. The words of the legendary song entitled "Ain't No Stopping Us Now" speaks to the very heart of the issue when the song declares and degrees "Ain't No Stoppin Us Now! We're on the move!" Nelson Mandela stated that, "Everyone can rise above their circumstances and achieve success if they are dedicated to and passionate about what they do."

I declare and decree that it is high time to turn this tragedy around and take our homes back.

- Take our families back. Move forward and make a difference.

- Take our blocks back. Move forward and make a difference.

- Take our communities back. Move forward and make a difference.

I absolutely love the poem entitled "One" which states that, ONE... One tree can start a forest: One smile can begin a friendship; One hand can lift a soul; One word can frame the goal; One candle can wipe out darkness; One laugh can conquer gloom; One hope can raise your spirits; One touch can show you care; One life can make the difference, be that one today.

FRIDAY NIGHT LIVE & I SUPPORT ROOSEVELT YOUTH CENTER

The Spirit of the Lord laid it on my heart as Chairman of the Board of I Support Roosevelt Youth Center of Long Island, Inc. to move forward and start a youth outreach program to the youth of the community called "Friday Night Live" at I Support Roosevelt Youth Center, 55 Mansfield Avenue Roosevelt, New York, at 7:30 p.m. until 10:40 p.m. This is the same historic facility where my sister's classmate, Eddie Murphy, told his early jokes on the historic stage, shock jock Howard Stern went to school there, Public Enemy did their early raps there, and Julius "Dr. J." Erving played basketball there. Today, the I Support Roosevelt Youth Center is packed with community youth every Friday for a prayer service, basketball, football, and refreshments. Every week, we tell them to **CATCH THE VISION OF VICTORY & NEVER GIVE UP!** Faithful weekly volunteers such as I Support Roosevelt Youth Center Executive Director, Harold Hamilton, Brother Brick, Brother Lee Street, Deacon Aaron Scott Jr., and Deacon Eddie Bryant help me mentor these young people of the community. Rev. Dr. Bernice King was right when she said that "The pride and treasure of our nation is our youth. Any nation that neglects the teaching and the upbringing of its youth is a nation on the decline"

MOVING FORWARD WITH THE SELF DEFENSE CLASS

We also have the very best self defense experts in the community to move forward and make a difference in the precious lives of the children, youth, young adults, and adults by volunteering and conducting self defense classes every Monday and Wednesday at I Support Roosevelt Youth Center at 6.00 p.m. The self defense class is an awesome alternative to being in a gang or any other highly negative and or deadly activities.

MOVING FORWARD WITH THE TUTORING PROGRAM

Our promise is together, we can build change.

Brother Jacob Dixon of Choice For All moves forward and makes a difference by volunteering at I Support Roosevelt Youth Center Monday through Thursday from 2:30 p.m. until 5:30 p.m., and conducts the After School Program with academic support, state test/regents prep, healthy fitness programs, organized group activities, science expeditions, snacks, computer lab, and visual arts. Tutors from the top universities in New York are on hand to help the students Monday through Friday.

When we work together in the trenches, side by side, we can, yes, we can, move forward and make a difference. The mission of Choice for All is to serve as a center of support for youth, family and community development. Choice for All was established in 2011, Choice For All is an emerging, non-profit dedicated to serving as a center of support for youth, family and community development. Our flagship site is in Roosevelt, NY. We focus our efforts on three primary areas: community-based research, advocacy work and supportive services. I Support Roosevelt Youth Center of Long Island, Inc. is proud to have Choice for All as a partner to move forward together for the cause of excellence in education.

MINISTER LARRY MACKEY MOVED FORWARD AND MADE A DIFFERENCE

My uncle, my father's brother, Minister Larry Mackey Sr. recently moved forward, onward, and upward and went home to be with the Lord for eternity. Minister Larry Mackey, Sr. was the last of the seven original charter members of the Mt. Sinai Baptist Church, Inc. of Roosevelt, New York. Minister Larry Mackey, Sr. was ordained as the first deacon of the church in August in the year 1955. He moved forward and made a difference.

Minister Larry Mackey, Sr. was an ordained minister of the Gospel and he loved the Lord. A very devoted man of God who instilled in his family to follow his example. Minister Larry Mackey Sr., Uncle Larry, always said these words of wisdom "Don't spend more than you make in your take home pay." He moved forward and made a difference.

Minister Larry Mackey, Sr. was the son of Mount Sinai Baptist Church Founder, the late Rev. Walter Mackey, Sr. and First Lady Dora Mackey. Uncle Larry, Uncle Walter (who worked for Gruman Aerospace Corporation, which was the leading producer of military and civilian aircraft in the United States, and he help build important parts of the first rocket ship that the United States sent to the moon),

Uncle Johnny (who went to be the founding President of the NFL Union and was the best Tight End in the first 50 years of football), and my father, Rev. Arthur L. Mackey, Sr. (Founder of the I Support Roosevelt Youth Center, former Director of the Nassau County Job Development Center, and former Pastor of Mount Sinai Baptist Church Cathedral in Roosevelt, New York), and Deacon Aaron Scott, Jr. (the current Chairman of the Deacon Board at Mount Sinai, noted artist, former Oceanside, New York Art Teacher, and College of New Rochelle Professor) all helped my grandfather, Rev. Walter R. Mackey, Sr. build Mount Sinai Baptist Church brick by brick. Minister Larry Mackey, Sr. was married to Mrs. Beulah Mackey, Aunt Beulah. Their children are Linda, Elaine, Larry Jr., Bishop J. Raymond, Marilyn, Jerry, Carl, and Ellen.

Minister Larry Mackey, Sr. worked for LILCO for many years. A young man named John who worked with Uncle Larry at LILCO stated that your Uncle's words of wisdom saved my life by the grace of God. Minister Larry Mackey, Sr. wrote a book entitled, "I Did Not Know That – Basic Guidelines To Wholeness". Minister Larry Mackey, Sr. also wrote a song entitled, "Here, Here Comes the Mackeys". We sung it at his funeral as the family marched in Mt. Sinai and we sang it when the family comes together in service. Minister Larry Mackey, Sr., Uncle Larry and Aunt Beulah loved and fully functioned in the sick and shut-in ministry. Many times he would pray for everyone literally on the hospital floor that he was visiting one by one. Minister Larry Mackey, Sr., moved forward and made a difference.

Minister Larry Mackey, Sr. strongly believed in keeping the family together. Minister Larry Mackey loved to show family films and share family history. Minister Larry Mackey, Sr., Uncle Larry loved to take family trips and outings. Minister Larry Mackey, Sr. moved forward and made a difference.

JESUS MOVED FORWARD & MADE A DIFFERENCE

- On Palm Sunday, Jesus moved forward and entered triumphantly into Jerusalem.
- On Monday, Jesus moved forward and cursed the fig tree.
- On Monday, Jesus moved forward and cleansed the temple.
- On Tuesday, Jesus moved forward and His authority was challenged.
- On Tuesday, Jesus moved forward and His feet were anointed.
- On Wednesday, Jesus moved forward and Judas and the chief priests plotted against Him.
- On Thursday, Jesus moved forward and instituted the Lord's Supper and washed the disciples' feet.
- On Thursday, Jesus moved forward and prayed that we might be one, as He and the Father are one.
- On Thursday, Jesus moved forward, "went forward a little," and falling to the ground, prayed "if it were possible, the hour might pass from him" and sweat blood as the angels ministered to Him in the Garden of Gethsemane. Then Jesus continued to move forward and declared "not my will but thine be done." Jesus moved forward to begin to fix in the Garden of Gethsemane what Adam messed up in the Garden of Eden.
- On Friday, Jesus moved forward with determination to die on the cross for the sins of all humanity, past, present, and future.
- On Friday, Jesus moved forward and is betrayed by Judas for thirty pieces of silver and arrested by the Roman soldiers.
- On Friday, Jesus moved forward and was brought before Caiaphas the High Priest.
- On Friday, Jesus moved forward and was brought before the Governor Pontius Pilate.
- On Friday, Jesus moved forward and was brought before King Herod in Galilee.
- On Friday, Jesus moved forward and was brought back

before Governor Pontius Pilate.
- On Friday, Jesus moved forward and the Roman soldiers stripped Jesus of His scarlet robe.
- On Friday, Jesus moved forward and the Roman soldiers put a crown of thorns on His head, mocked Him, and spit on Him.
- On Friday, Jesus moved forward and carried His own cross until a black man named Simon of Cyrene helped to carry His cross to Calvary.
- On Friday, Jesus moved forward with His words while hanging on the cross at Calvary and said, "Father, forgive them, for they know not what they do" (Luke 23:34).
- On Friday, Jesus moved forward with His words while hanging on the cross at Calvary and said, "Verily I say unto thee, today shalt thou be with me in paradise" (Luke 23:43).
- On Friday, Jesus moved forward with His words while hanging on the cross at Calvary and said, "Woman, behold thy son" (to His mother, Mary, in John 19:26); "Behold thy mother" (to John, the beloved apostle, in John 19:27). With these words, Jesus moved forward His request to commend his mother, who was likely a widow, into John's care.
- On Friday, Jesus moved forward with His words while hanging on the cross at Calvary and said, "Eloi Eloi lama sabachthani? My God, My God, why hast thou forsaken me?" (Mark 15:34; also see Matthew 27:46)
- On Friday, Jesus moved forward with His words while hanging on the cross at Calvary and said, "I thirst" (John 19:28).
- On Friday, Jesus moved forward with His words while hanging on the cross at Calvary and said, "It is finished" (John 19:30).
- On Friday, Jesus moved forward with His words while hanging on the cross at Calvary and said, "Father, into thy hands I commend my spirit" (Luke 23:46).
- On Friday, Jesus moved forward in God's perfect plan and He died on the cross at the place of the skull, Golgotha.

- On Friday, Jesus was moved forward and buried in Joseph of Arimathea's borrowed tomb.
- On Saturday, Jesus moved forward conquering death, hell, and the grave, got the keys to the kingdom and gave gifts to men, the five-fold ministry. He did this while His earthly body lay in state.
- On Sunday morning, Jesus moved forward and rose from the dead.
- On Resurrection Sunday, Jesus moved forward and showed Himself alive to Mary Magdalene in the garden.
- On Resurrection Sunday, Jesus moved forward and appeared to the other women.
- On Resurrection Sunday, Jesus moved forward and appeared to two men on the road to Emmaus.
- On Resurrection Sunday, Jesus moved forward and appeared to Peter.
- On the next Sunday, Jesus moved forward and appeared to the disciples in the upper room.
- Jesus moved forward and appeared to seven disciples who were fishing.
- Jesus moved forward and appeared to the eleven disciples on a mountain in Galilee, and commissioned them in Matthew 28:19-20: "Go ye therefore, and teach all nations, baptizing them in the name of the Father, and of the Son, and of the Holy Ghost: Teaching them to observe all things whatsoever I have commanded you: and, lo, I am with you always, even unto the end of the world. Amen."
- Jesus moved forward and appeared to James.
- Jesus moved forward and appeared before His disciples on the Mount of Olives.
- Jesus Christ moved forward and made a difference.

The pains and pressures
of life will either
push and propel you
into the necessary shift
known as change
or it will utterly destroy you.
Therefore, move forward and
make a difference by developing
a mindset for change.

Robert Frost in his classic poem entitled, *The Road Not Taken* states that, "Two roads diverged in a wood, and I,
I took the one less traveled by,
And that has made all the difference."

MOVING FORWARD WITH THE BLOOD OF THE MARTYRS

• Peter moved forward and was crucified upside down on a cross for preaching the Gospel of Jesus Christ, because he did not count himself worthy to die right-side up as the Lord Jesus Christ.

• Matthew moved forward and was stabbed to death with a sword in Ethiopia for preaching the Gospel of Jesus Christ.

• Andrew, Peter's brother, moved forward and was crucified on an X-shaped cross for preaching the Gospel of Jesus Christ.

• Thomas moved forward and was stabbed to death with a spear in India for preaching the Gospel of Jesus Christ.

• Bartholomew, known as Nathanael, moved forward and was whipped to death in Armenia for preaching the Gospel of Jesus

Christ.

- Matthias, who replaced Judas, moved forward and was stoned and beheaded for preaching the Gospel of Jesus Christ.

- John moved forward and was boiled in a pot of oil for preaching the Gospel of Jesus Christ, but survived and died of old age in Ephesus where he took care of Mary, the mother of Jesus.

- James, the brother of Jesus, moved forward and was thrown from the pinnacle of the Temple and survived, but was then beaten to death with a club for preaching the Gospel of Jesus Christ.

- Paul moved forward and was beheaded at Nero's chopping block for preaching the Gospel of Jesus Christ.

The early Christian leaders moved forward and made a difference. Jesus told them in Acts 1:8: "But ye shall receive power, after that the Holy Ghost is come upon you: and ye shall be witnesses unto me both in Jerusalem, and in all Judaea, and in Samaria, and unto the uttermost part of the earth."

The word 'witnesses' in this Scripture in the Greek is the word *martus*, from which we get the word martyr.

If we truly want to move forward and make a difference, we have to cry out in prayer:

> "Father, I stretch my hands to Thee,
> No other help I know;
> If Thou withdraw Thyself from me,
> Ah! whither shall I go?"

- Move forward and make a difference with the spirit of excellence in education.
- Move forward and make a difference with the spirit of excellence in the arts and entertainment.
- Move forward and make a difference with the spirit of excellence in government and politics.
- Move forward and make a difference with the spirit of excellence in the medical field.
- Move forward and make a difference with the spirit of excellence in community outreach.
- Move forward and make a difference with the spirit of excellence in economic development.
- Move forward and make a difference with the spirit of excellence in worship in spirit and in truth.

I love the legendary hymn which states,

> *If I can help somebody, as I pass along,*
> *If I can cheer somebody, with a word or song,*
> *If I can show somebody, how they're travelling wrong,*
> *Then my living shall not be in vain.*

> *Chorus:*
> *My living shall not be in vain,*
> *Then my living shall not be in vain*
> *If I can help somebody, as I pass along,*
> *Then my living shall not be in vain.*

> *If I can do my duty, as a good man ought,*
> *If I can bring back beauty, to a world up wrought,*
> *If I can spread love's message, as the Master taught,*
> *hen my living shall not be in vain.*

CHAPTER FIFTEEN

MOVING FORWARD IN WORSHIP – THE WOMAN, THE WATER, AND THE WELL

In order to truly move forward in worship, you can't be a jack of all trades and a master of none, even if you could do it all. Jesus, the Son of God, the Baptizer with the Holy Ghost and fire, the Prince of Peace, certainly could do it all, yet, to move forward in worship, Jesus gave His disciples authority to baptize. His confidence in them allowed them to baptize even more disciples than John the Baptist who baptized Jesus. Jesus' ability to delegate authority in the baptism ministry allowed Him to move forward from Judea to Galilee.

John 4:1-3: "When therefore the Lord knew how the Pharisees had heard that Jesus made and baptized more disciples than John, (Though Jesus himself baptized not, but his disciples,) He left Judaea, and departed again into Galilee."

MUST NEEDS GO THROUGH SAMARIA

Jesus, a Jew, had to go through Samaria. Jesus, a Jew, had to go through the most racially mixed community that many Jews utterly despised and rejected. The backdrop of this situation is the deep felt hatred that too many Jews and Samaritans had toward one another. The Samaritans responded with anger towards the Jewish people. Most Jews, when moving between Galilee and Judea, would cross the Jordan River two times instead of going through Samaria. Jesus moved forward by going through Samaria. The text declares in **verse**

4, "And he must needs go through Samaria."

WEARIED WITH THE JOURNEY & SITTING ON THE WELL

Samaria means "guardianship." Samaria was a territory in Palestine. Sychar means "drunken." Jesus must needs go through, move forward, and make a difference in a city of Samaria, Sychar, which meant the drunken guardianship. Around twelve noon, Jesus was wearied from His journey and sat on Jacob's well. (Even the very best get weary from the journey. Even the very best have to come to the well to be refreshed, renewed, and revived.) The old Negro spiritual proclaimed: "Sit down servant. Sit down and rest a little while." Read the words of the text in verses five and six: **"Then cometh he to a city of Samaria, which is called Sychar, near to the parcel of ground that Jacob gave to his son Joseph. Now Jacob's well was there. Jesus therefore, being wearied with his journey, sat thus on the well: and it was about the sixth hour."**

THE WOMAN, THE WATER, AND THE WELL

The woman of Samaria, better known in sermons and church services as the woman at the well, was despised, disenfranchised, and downtrodden solely because she was a Samaritan, a racially mixed woman of Palestine. This despised sister of racially ethnic mixture came to Jacob's well to draw water—Jacob's well, the redeemed trickster's well; Jacob's well, the redeemed stealer of his own brother Esau's birthright. Yes, Jacob's well—Jacob who wrestled with the Angel of the Lord all night long until the breaking of day. Jacob's well—Jacob whom the Angel of the Lord touched his hip and left with a limp. Thank God that Jacob's father, Issac, redug the wells of his father, Abraham. That laid the foundation for Jacob to move forward and build his well. Now many, many years later the woman of Samaria comes to Jacob's well to draw water which refreshes, restores, renews, and revives her deep thirst. You can survive without meat, but you will die without water. The earth is made up of 70 percent water and 30 percent land and trees. The human body is 70 percent water and 30 percent flesh and bones.

Jesus asked this thirsty sister of racially ethnic mixture to **"give Me drink."** Jesus, the Prince of Peace, moved forward and engaged true communication with this despised, disenfranchised, and downtrodden sister.

The disciples wanted and went for meat, but Jesus was focused on the woman, the water, and the well as a backdrop to teach about the living water. **"There cometh a woman of Samaria to draw water: Jesus saith unto her, Give me to drink. (For his disciples were gone away unto the city to buy meat.) Then saith the woman of Samaria unto him, How is it that thou, being a Jew, askest drink of me, which am a woman of Samaria? for the Jews have no dealings with the Samaritans. Jesus answered and said unto her, If thou knewest the gift of God, and who it is that saith to thee, Give me to drink; thou wouldest have asked of him, and he would have given thee living water" (verses 7-10).**

THE ETERNAL WELL OF WATER

Jesus, the Prince of Peace, spoke of living water that was deeper than the water in Jacob's well. Jesus stated in **John 7:38: "He that believeth on me, as the scripture hath said, out of his belly shall flow rivers of living water."** Jesus spoke of living water within that quenches thirst for eternity. Jesus was referring to the eternal well of water. **"The woman saith unto him, Sir, thou hast nothing to draw with, and the well is deep: from whence then hast thou that living water? Art thou greater than our father Jacob, which** gave us the well, and drank thereof himself, and his children, and his cattle? Jesus answered and said unto her, Whosoever drinketh of this water shall thirst again: But whosoever drinketh of the water that I shall give him shall never thirst; but the water that I shall give him shall be in him a well of water springing up into everlasting life" (verses 11-14).

The hymn writer, Richard Blancard, was right when he wrote:

> *Like the woman at the well I was seeking*
> *For things that could not satisfy;*
> *And then I heard my Savior speaking:*
> *"Draw from my well that never shall run dry."*
>
> *Fill my cup Lord, I lift it up, Lord!*
> *Come and quench this thirsting of my soul;*
> *Bread of heaven, Feed me till I want no more—*
> *Fill my cup, fill it up and make me whole!*

GIVE ME THIS WATER

The woman of Samaria, the woman at the well, moved forward in her conversation with Jesus and asked Him, **"Sir, give me this water,"** that she would never thirst for relationships that can never fulfill the innermost thirst of her soul. The woman of Samaria, the woman at the well, the sister of racially ethnic mixture had five husbands, but her deep thirst for the living water brought her to the you-ward grace of Jesus Christ. Jesus, the Prince of Peace, is preparing the woman at the well to move forward into prophetic worship—worship that will make the true difference in her life. **"The woman saith unto him, Sir, give me this water, that I thirst not, neither come hither to draw. Jesus saith unto her, Go, call thy husband, and come hither. The woman answered and said, I** have no husband. Jesus said unto her, Thou hast well said, I have no husband: For thou hast had five husbands; and he whom thou now hast is not thy husband: in that saidst thou truly. The woman saith unto him, Sir, I perceive that thou art a prophet" (verses 15-19).

WORSHIP IN SPIRIT & IN TRUTH

John 4:20-24: "Our fathers worshipped in this mountain; and ye say, that in Jerusalem is the place where men ought to worship. Jesus saith unto her, Woman, believe me, the hour cometh, when ye shall neither in this mountain, nor yet at Jerusalem, worship the Father. Ye worship ye know not what: we know what we worship: for salvation is of the Jews. But the hour cometh, and now is, when the true worshippers shall worship the Father in spirit and in truth: for the Father seeketh such to worship him. God is a Spirit: and they that worship him must worship him in spirit and in truth."

The word 'worship' in the Greek is *proskuneo* derived from the meaning to kiss, like a dog licking its master's hand, to move forward in an expression of true reverence, to fall upon our knees and touch the ground with the forehead as an awesome expression of profound reverence, in the New Testament by kneeling or prostration to give homage, whether in order to move forward and boldly express respect or to make supplication.

The classic worship song "Here I Am to Worship" expresses this deep thirst to move forward in worship and make a difference in worship.

Light of the world
You stepped down into darkness.

Opened my eyes, let me see.
Beauty that made this heart adore You
Hope of a life spent with You

Here I am to worship,
Here I am to bow down,
Here I am to say that You're my God
You're altogether lovely
Altogether worthy,
Altogether wonderful to me

The woman of Samaria, the woman at the well, stated in John 4:20, "Our fathers worshiped on this mountain." After the northern kingdom was defeated by the Assyrians in 721 B.C., a major divide came about between the Jewish people in Jerusalem and the Israelite people abiding in Samaria. The Samaritans later went on to build a temple right on Mount Gerizim, which was demolished in 130 B.C. The Samaritans have continued to move forward in worship on Mount Gerizim even in modern day times.

Jesus Christ, the Prince of Peace, boldly declared and decreed in **John 4:23** that, **"the hour is coming, and is now here."** The time was now at hand when the very deepest separation between the Jewish people and Samaritan people will radically change, come to a complete halt, and the temple worship will be superseded. Jesus Christ declared and decreed that the time "is now here," the time is now, because Jesus Christ, the Prime Mover, is here right now and has moved forward and made a difference with the work, which will birth out the major movement of the Holy Spirit in the life of the church regardless of racial ethnicity. The movement of the Holy Spirit is an equal opportunity employer. God is an equal opportunity employer.

The Heavenly Father desires that "true worshippers shall worship the Father in spirit and in truth." Phony worship is not the order of the day. Dead worship is not the order of the day. Dry worship is not the order of the day. Powerfully intimate and passionate worship that moves the church forward into the eternal well springs of spiritual renewal, restoration, revolution, and revival is the order of the day. The time is here. The time is now to worship in spirit and in truth. Radical, yet, responsible. Worship in spirit and in truth.

The Greek word for spirit is *pneuma*, referring to the breath and major movement of the Holy Ghost, the Spirit of God, the Spirit of the Lord, the Spirit of truth, the Spirit of Christ, as well as the human spirit, and even an evil spirit.

The Greek word for truth is *aletheia*, meaning what is true in any matter put under consideration; truly, in truth, according to truth, of a truth, in all reality, in fact, and most certainly.

Move forward and make a difference with what is totally true in matters dealing with God, the Prime Mover, and the responsibilities and duties of man, moral, and spiritual truth in the greatest latitude— the truth as taught in the Christian movement, with respect to God and the execution of His plans and purposes through Jesus Christ, and respecting the duties of man, opposing alike to the superstitions of the Gentiles and the inventions of the Jews, and the corrupt opinions and precepts of false teachers even among Christians; moving forward with truth as a quest for personal excellence; moving forward and making a difference with total clarity of mind, which is completely free from pretense, falsehood, and destructive deceit.

Jesus Christ, the Prince of Peace, made it clear in John 4:24 that true worshipers must worship in spirit and truth. True worship is compared to the dead, dry, and mundane worship controlled and manipulated by the temporary provisions of the law, especially the separation of Jews and Gentiles and the deeply discriminatory segregation requirement of temple worship in Jerusalem at that particular time in history. The ceremonial and animal sacrificial aspects of the law were not falsehoods by any means; they were only temporary and provisional. Worship "in spirit" is worship in the move of the Holy Ghost. The Holy Spirit carries on the marvelous work begun by the earthly ministry of Jesus Christ. This major movement of the Holy Ghost points to the end of dangerous separation and discriminatory segregation amongst the Jews and Gentiles, and the birthing of the Christian movement to worship, not only in beautiful temples made with stone by man, but to worship as blood-washed believers moving about in daily life, for our body is also the temple of God.

LEAVING THE WATERPOT TO BE A WITNESS

"The woman saith unto him, I know that Messias cometh, which is called Christ: when he is come, he will tell us all things. Jesus saith unto her, I that speak unto thee am he. And upon this came his disciples, and marvelled that he talked with the woman: yet no man said, What seekest thou? or, Why talkest thou with her? The woman then left her waterpot, and went her way into the city, and saith to the men, Come, see a man, which told me all things that ever I did: is not this the Christ?" (verses 25-29).

The woman of Samaria, the woman at the well, the sister of mixed ethnic mixture **"left her waterpot."** She left that which keeps her alive naturally to tell, to herald, to proclaim? "Come, see a man" who told me all my personal business, isn't He the Christ? Through a conversation at Jacob's well, Jesus Christ, the Prince of Peace, has completely transformed and totally empowered the woman of Samaria, the woman at the well, the sister of racial ethnic mixture.

She had a new attitude. She had a new function. She had a new gig. She was now a working witness for the Lord. Her time was here. Her time was now, She met a new man, the Son of Man, the Son of God, who totally blew her mind. She is no longer a victim of the system. The woman at the well is now a worshipper in spirit and in truth, excited that Jesus Christ totally changed her life with the living water of the Holy Spirit.

The text states concerning the men of Samaria in **verse 30: "Then they went out of the city, and came unto him."** The woman at the well, the sister of racial ethnic mixture successfully leads the men of Samaria, a large group of racial ethnically mixed brothers, to Jesus Christ.

FINISH HIS WORK

**"In the mean while his disciples prayed him, saying, Master, eat.
But he said unto them, I have meat to eat that ye know not of. Therefore said the disciples one to another, Hath any man brought him ought to eat? Jesus saith unto them, My meat is to do the will of him that sent me, and to finish his work"** (verses 31-34).

The meat that motivated Jesus, the Prince of Peace, pushed Him forward and made a major difference by finishing His Father's work. When Jesus died on the cross, **John 19:30** tells us, **"When Jesus therefore had received the vinegar, he said, It is finished: and he bowed his head, and gave up the ghost."**

Too many churches call it my church, instead of God's church—His church. Too many churches call it my work instead of—His work. **Habakkuk 3:2** states: **"O Lord, I have heard thy speech, and** was afraid: O Lord, revive thy work in the midst of the years, in the midst of the years make known; in wrath remember mercy." God wants His church to finish His work by reaching His harvest of souls.

THE POWER OF A TESTIMONY

"Say not ye, There are yet four months, and then cometh harvest? behold, I say unto you, Lift up your eyes, and look on the fields; for they are white already to harvest. And he that reapeth receiveth wages, and gathereth fruit unto life eternal: that both he that soweth and he that reapeth may rejoice together. And herein is that saying true, One soweth, and another reapeth. I sent you to reap that whereon ye bestowed no labour: other men laboured, and ye are entered into their labours. And many of the Samaritans of that city believed on him for the saying of the woman, which testified, He told me all that ever I did. So when the Samaritans were come unto him, they besought him that he would tarry with them: and he abode there two days" (verses 35-40).

Jesus knew in the natural system, the harvest period that He created would come at the appointed time. Jesus told His disciples to **"Lift up your eyes, and look on the fields"** in preparation for harvest time for the fields are already "white unto harvest."

Jesus, the Prince of Peace, sowed life-changing words of knowledge and wisdom into the spirit of the woman at the well. The woman at the well sowed her new found testimony of personal transformation into the lives of the Samaritan people. That particular day, the twelve disciples were off buying meat and had no part in this impartation of ministry to the woman at the well, yet, they were about to witness and be a part of a reaping of a great harvest. This is just like the few faithful souls who are praying all night and day, witnessing the goodness of the Lord and visiting, calling, checking on the souls all throughout the week, yet, in the church service when many respond to the altar call to repentance, people who were not praying, calling, or visiting witness the great harvest. Many Samaritans believed on Jesus Christ because the empowered woman at the well rose above her own issues and became a highly effective witness for the Lord.

INDEED THE CHRIST

"And many more believed because of his own word; And said unto the woman, Now we believe, not because of thy saying: for we have heard him ourselves, and know that this is indeed the Christ, the Savior of the world. Now after two days he departed thence, and went into Galilee. For Jesus Himself testified that a prophet hath no honor in his own country. Then when he was come into Galilee, the Galileans received him, having seen all the things that he did at Jerusalem at the feast: for they also went unto the feast" (verses 41-45).

Many more Samaritans believed because they heard Jesus' own words. The woman at the well was the witness, but Jesus is the Living Word with the living water of the Holy Ghost. A two day soul winning revival broke out in Samaria. After that two day revival Jesus also testified, "that a prophet hath no honour in his own country." Jesus Christ could relate to the woman at the well for He also understood what it meant to be taken for granted and to be without honor. Thank God that Jesus Christ was directly in touch with His true feelings without demolishing His faith in His Father, because this set the tone for the Samaritans to receive Him. God is calling us to move forward and worship in spirit and in truth.

THE FIRST AFRICAN-AMERICAN COUNCILWOMAN IN AMERICA'S LARGEST TOWNSHIP IS MAKING A DIFFERENCE

Like the woman at the well Town of Hempstead Councilwoman Dorothy L. Goosby moved forward and made a difference. Town of Hempstead Councilwoman Dorothy L. Goosby was elected to the Town Board on November 2, 1999, a few days after the death of my father, Rev. Dr. A. L. Mackey, Sr. She is the first African American woman to serve on the Town Board. The Town of Hempstead, America's largest township, has many historical first. Councilman Curtis Fisher, friend and tennis partner of Republican Party Chairman Joseph Mondello, was the first African-American to be appointed and then elected as Councilman in the entire history of the Town of Hempstead, which was founded in 1644. The Town of Hempstead is actually older than the nation, the United States of America itself. My father, Rev. Dr. Arthur L. Mackey, Sr. and the Nassau Council of Black Clergy fought long and hard for this to happen. Councilwoman Angie M. Cullin of Freeport, New York, was the first woman to be elected to that position. Hempstead Town Supervisor Kate Murray was the first woman elected to the highest ranking position in America's largest township. Town Clerk Mark Bonilla was the first Hispanic American elected as Town Clerk in the Town of Hempstead, and Town Clerk Nasrin Amad was the very first Indian American every elected to that position of governmental leadership. One historical first paved the way for the next. Like the woman at the well Councilwoman Dorothy L. Goosby moved forward and made a difference.

In 1988, Dorothy L. Goosby, filed a class action suit against the Town of Hempstead charging that the Town's at large voting system for the Town Board discriminated against the minority community. In 1997, a federal judge agreed and ruled that the Town of Hempstead's method of voting-at-large was discriminatory and violated the Voting Rights Act. In January 2000, the United States Supreme Court denied review of the Town of Hempstead's appeals. U.S. District Court Judge John Gleeson then ordered that a special election be held for all seats in November 2000. Therefore historically it is because of Councilwoman Dorothy L. Goosby that America's largest township, the Town of Hempstead, has councilmatic districts and Nassau County has legislative districts today. Prior to this court decision every politician ran on an at large system and it was virtually impossible for minorities to win. Republicans, Democrats, and Independents respect Councilwoman Dorothy Goosby today for moving forward and making a difference with such bravery and courage. Today Republicans and Democrats proudly represent their respected councilmatic districts in America's largest township, the Town of Hempstead, as well as County legislators who proudly represent their respective legislative districts in Nassau County, New York. Like the woman at the well Councilwoman Dorothy L. Goosby moved forward and made a difference.

Dorothy L. Goosby is an alumna of Florida A&M University. She received her Masters in Business Administration in Labor Relations/Corporate Finance and Accounting Management from Adelphi University. Councilwoman Goosby is a New York State Certified and Registered Dietitian with more than twenty-five years of exemplary administrative experience in the medical profession. She attended Hofstra University, Hempstead, New York and completed the requirements to obtain certification by the New York State Education Department as a Certified Chemistry teacher. Like the woman at the well Councilwoman Dorothy L. Goosby moved forward and made a difference.

Councilwoman Goosby is the first African-American President of the Association Of Towns of the State of New York, the first to be elected to this position in the history of New York State. She serves on the Executive Committee and the Rules and Resolutions Committee for the organization. Like the woman at the well Councilwoman Dorothy L. Goosby moved forward and made a difference.

While Councilwoman Goosby's accomplishments are noteworthy, she is most recognized for her on-going community efforts in Nassau County and the Town of Hempstead. She has initiated community meetings and Town Board evening meetings that provide access and opportunity for more residents to participate in government than ever before. She has intervened in areas that have resulted in a better life for many. These include repair and renovation of streets that were long neglected, parks that were in total disrepair, vacant lots that were littered and street lights that did not function properly, just to name a few. It is her belief that her election by the people is a mandate to provide equitable representation to all of the residents and that she has a responsibility to make a difference when it is possible and where it is needed. Like the woman at the well Councilwoman Dorothy L. Goosby moved forward and made a difference.

Councilwoman Goosby lives in Hempstead. She cherishes the memory of her late husband, Anderson Jay Goosby. They are the proud parents of Alcina and Cassandra Goosby. The Goosbys are long time members of the historic, Union Baptist Church in Hempstead.

Councilwoman Dorothy L. Goosby's First Councilmatic District of the Town of Hempstead includes: Hempstead, Lakeview, Roosevelt and Uniondale, as well as portions of Baldwin, Freeport, Garden City, Lynbrook, Rockville Centre, West Hempstead and Westbury. Like the woman at the well Councilwoman Dorothy L. Goosby moved forward and made a difference. She truly made a shout out for the shut-out.

Part 4

MOVING FORWARD WITH PRACTICAL TEACHING

CHAPTER SIXTEEN

MOVING FORWARD WITH YOU-WARD GRACE— SHOUTOUT FOR THE SHUTOUT

Ephesians 3:1-7:
"For this cause I Paul, the prisoner of Jesus Christ for you Gentiles, If ye have heard of the dispensation of the grace of God which is given me to <u>you-ward</u>: How that by revelation he made known unto me the mystery; (as I wrote afore in few words, Whereby, when ye read, ye may understand my knowledge in the mystery of Christ) Which in other ages was not made known unto the sons of men, as it is now revealed unto his holy apostles and prophets by the Spirit; That the Gentiles should be fellow heirs, and of the same body, and partakers of his promise in Christ by the gospel: Whereof I was made a minister, according to the gift of the grace of God given unto me by the effectual working of his power."

Book of Ephesians Brief Outline

I. The blood washed believer's position in Jesus Christ. (1:1-3:21)
II. The blood washed believer's condition in the world. (4:1-6:24.)

2 Corinthians 1:12: "For our rejoicing is this, the testimony of our conscience, that in simplicity and godly sincerity, not with fleshly wisdom, but by the grace of God, we have had our conversation in the world, and more abundantly to <u>you-ward</u>."

Condition of Existence – We all need you-ward grace in order to live, to move, to function, and operate in this world

Acts 17:28: "For in him we live, and <u>move</u>, and have our being; as certain also of your own poets have said, For we are also his offspring."

When God gave you air to breathe, that is you-ward grace, because I would die without it.
When God woke you up this morning that is an example of you-ward grace, because God kept the death angel away from you.
When God gave you a song to sing and strength for the journey of life, that was you-ward grace for you to be an overcomer.

Yes, you-ward grace is God's shout-out for the shut-out. That does not mean that God embraces and okays every single lifestyle under the sun, but it does mean that God still loves us all. Clearly, God hates sin, but clearly, God loves the sinner. Clearly, Jesus Christ hates sin, but clearly, Jesus Christ loves the sinner.

- With you-ward grace, Richard Allen became the Founder of the African Methodist Episcopal church.
- With you-ward grace, Harriet Tubman became the "Moses" of her People.
- With you-ward grace, Sojourner Truth became an abolitionist and women's rights advocate.
- With you-ward grace, Rosa Parks refused to sit in the back of the bus and became the mother of the Civil Rights Movement.
- With you-ward grace, Rev. Dr. Martin Luther King, Jr., led marches for jobs, equality, and freedom, put his very life on the line for the cause of justice in a hostile and racist system, and became the foremost leader of the civil rights movement.
- With you-ward grace, Barack Obama became the first black man to be elected twice as President of the United States of America.

- With you-ward grace, Michelle Obama became the first black woman to be First Lady of the United States of America.

WHAT IS YOU-WARD GRACE?

- You-ward Grace – "the grace of God which is given me to you-ward"
- You-ward Grace, not hyper grace, is God's good grace to reach the rejected, to reach the disgraced, to reach the misplaced, and even to reach the replaced. You-ward Grace is God's eternal shout-out to the shut-out showing that God cares for the shut-out.
- You-ward Grace, not hyper grace, is the supernatural empowerment of the Holy Spirit to move the disgraced, despised, and downtrodden forward into the full plan, power, and purpose of God.
- You-ward Grace, not hyper grace, empowers us to embrace grace (God's unmerited favor) in our private and public personal pain.

Augustine stated that "Nothing whatever pertaining to godliness and real holiness can be accomplished without grace."

PEOPLE WHO MOVE FORWARD TO YOU-WARD GRACE LITERALLY EMBRACE THE CAUSE OF CHRIST

"For this cause I Paul, the prisoner of Jesus Christ for you Gentiles,"

People Who Move Forward To You-Ward Grace Literally Embrace The Despised and Rejected

"the prisoner of Jesus Christ for you Gentiles"

PEOPLE WHO MOVE FORWARD TO YOU-WARD GRACE LITERALLY EMBRACE SHOUT-OUTS FOR THE SHUT-OUT

"the prisoner of Jesus Christ for you Gentiles"

CORRECT INFORMATION CONCERNING THE DISPENSATION

"If ye have heard of the dispensation of the grace of God which is given me to you-ward"

Don't Live Your Life In The Wrong Dispensation

THE SEVEN DISPENSATIONS IN THE BIBLE

- One - The Dispensation of Innocence (Genesis 1:28)
- Two – The Dispensation of Conscience (Genesis 3:7)
- Three – The Dispensation of Human Government (Genesis 8:15)
- Four – The Dispensation of Promise (Genesis 12:1)
- Five – The Dispensation of Law (Exodus 19:1)
- Six – The Dispensation of Grace (Ephesians 3:2)
- Seven – The Dispensation of The Kingdom (Revelation 20:4)

Move Forward and Live Your Life In The Dispensation of The Grace of God
The Grace of God Given To You – You-ward Grace.

1.) REVELATION TO UNDERSTAND THE MYSTERY OF YOU-WARD GRACE

"How that by revelation he made known unto me the mystery; (as I wrote afore in few words,"

2.) KNOWLEDGE IN THE MYSTERY OF CHRIST

"Whereby, when ye read, ye may understand my knowledge in the mystery of Christ"

- The Mystery of Christ Revealed As You-Ward Grace
- Moving Forward To You-ward Grace, The Grace of God, For The Shutout!
- Moving Forward To You-ward Grace, The Grace of God, For The Down and Out!
- Moving Forward To You-ward Grace, The Grace of God, For The Up and Out!

Rev. Dr. Martin Luther King, Jr., declared, "If you can't fly then run, if you can't run then walk, if you can't walk then crawl, but whatever you do you have to keep moving forward."

3.) YOU-WARD GRACE NOW REVEALED BY THE SPIRIT

"Which in other ages was not made known unto the sons of men, as it is now revealed unto his holy apostles and prophets by the Spirit."

The shutouts are part of the same-body because they are somebody! The put-down and the put-out become partakers of the promise%"That the Gentiles should be fellow heirs, and of the same body, and partakers of his promise in Christ by the Gospel."

4.) PAUL'S PERSONAL TESTIMONY OF YOU-WARD GRACE

"Whereof I was made a minister, according to the gift of the grace of God given unto me by the effectual working of his power."

MADE A MINISTER
According To The Gift of the Grace of God
By The Effectual Working of His Power

I rise today
    with the power of God to pilot me,
God's strength to sustain me,
God's wisdom to guide me,
God's eye to look ahead for me,
God's ear to hear me,
God's word to speak for me,
God's hand to protect me,
God's way before me,
God's shield to defend me,
God's host to deliver me,
    from snares of devils,
    from evil temptations,
    from nature's failings,
    from all who wish to harm me,
    far or near,
    alone and in a crowd.

—"Saint Patrick's Breastplate,"
Old Irish, eighth-century prayer

5.) YOU-WARD GRACE, THE GRACE OF GOD, HELPS US SEE OURSELVES IN OTHERS

"Unto me, who am less than the least of all saints, is this grace given, that I should preach among the Gentiles the unsearchable riches of Christ..."

- You-ward grace, the grace of God makes us remember – "Unto me."
- You-ward grace, the grace of God keeps us balanced and focused to fulfillment – "who am less than the least of all saints." (A true candidate for grace.)
- You-ward grace, the grace of God is a gift - "is this grace given?"
- You-ward grace, the grace of God must be proclaimed to the shut-out. "That I should preach among the Gentiles the unsearchable riches of Christ."

YOU-WARD GRACE, THE GRACE OF GOD, IS AMAZING GRACE

The classic Christian Hymn "Amazing Grace" has touched and moved the hearts of millions of people worldwide with life changing inspiration.

Amazing grace! How sweet the sound
That saved a wretch like me!
I once was lost, but now am found;
Was blind, but now I see.

'Twas grace that taught my heart to fear,
And grace my fears relieved;
How precious did that grace appear
The hour I first believed!

God wants us to move forward for this cause with some stability in our Christian walk, and not only in our Christian talk.

CHAPTER SEVENTEEN

MOVING FORWARD FOR THIS CAUSE – BEAR WITNESS TO THE TRUTH

The meaningful and moving statement "for this cause" is creatively utilized in the Scripture, the holy writ, both in the Old and New Testaments, ever so effectively and ever so strategically by the inspiration of the Holy Spirit as a major catalyst of change. To literally move forward, the powerful precepts, plans and purposes of the Creator in the journey of His new creation in our Lord and Savior, Jesus Christ, who is the mediator between God and man.

Hebrews 9:15 states:
And <u>for this cause</u> he is the mediator of the New Testament that by means of death, for the redemption of the transgressions that were under the first testament, they which are called might receive the promise of eternal inheritance.

RAISED UP FOR THIS CAUSE

Exodus 9:16:
And in very deed <u>for this cause</u> have I raised thee up, for to shew in thee my power; and that my name may be declared throughout all the earth.

For example, the Book of Exodus reveals to the reader that God literally raised up Pharaoh to teach people what not to do % such as Pharaoh supporting the 400 year Egyptian practice of enslaving the Israelites when God clearly said to Pharaoh through, the deliverer, Moses, "Let my people Go." Good, bad, or indifferent, God can utilize a teaching moment of correction "for this cause" even when powerful people and powerful politics of the day are dead wrong as in this particular case. Pharaoh did not free the children of Israel from 400 years of enslavement in Egypt even after God sent the first nine of ten plagues upon Egypt. It was the tenth plague of the death angel passing over all of Egypt and every first born child in a home without blood over the doorpost died. Pharaoh and the Egyptians did not have the blood of the lamb (which foreshadowed and pointed to the Blood of Jesus Christ) on their doorpost, and all their firstborn children died. Only after this tenth deadly plague did Pharaoh let the Israelites go. Moses led the newly freed Israelite slaves to the Red Sea. Pharaoh discovered that the freed Israelites did not go out empty. They left out with the gross national product of Egypt, gold and silver, for their captors. Long before Rev. Dr. Martin Luther King, Jr., preached about moving forward, long before the wonderful new moving forward worship and praise songs were ever written and sung by Israel Houghton or ministered by Bishop Hezekiah Walker, the Lord told stuttering Moses thousands of years ago to stop crying and speak directly to the children of Israel that they may "go forward'. From the very lips of the Lord, a major life-changing movement of deliverance was motivated for this cause. Let's go back and review this important information so we can continue to move forward.

Exodus 14:13-16
And Moses said unto the people, Fear ye not, stand still, and see the salvation of the LORD, which he will shew to you to day: for the Egyptians whom ye have seen to day, ye shall see them again no more for ever. The LORD shall fight for you, and ye shall hold your peace. And the LORD said unto Moses, Wherefore criest thou unto me? speak unto the children of Israel, that they go forward: But lift thou up thy rod, and stretch out thine hand over the sea, and divide it: and the children of Israel shall go on

dry ground through the midst of the sea.

When the children of Israel saw Moses divide the Red Sea by the power of God. They followed Moses forward that day and crossed the Red Sea on dry ground. Pharaoh sent his army to get the children of Israel and Egypt's riches back. Well, like the world-renown song clearly says:

> *O, Mary, Don't You Weep*
> *O, Mary, don't you weep*
> *Tell Martha not to moan*
> *Pharaoh's army drowned in the Red Sea*
> *O Mary don't you weep*
> *Tell Martha not to moan*
> *If I could I surely would*
> *Stand on the rock where Moses stood*
> *Pharaoh's army drowned in the Red Sea*
> *O, Mary, don't you weep*
> *Tell Martha not to moan*

Pharaoh's army was drowned in the Red Sea. Showing people that it does not pay to go against the God of Israel. Thereby literally moving forward God's divine precepts, plans and purposes for this cause so His **name may be declared throughout all the earth.** Like Mothers Against Drunk Driving displaying large signs of horrifying youthful driver crash scenes just to ever so effectively and strategically show people what not to do. Good, bad, or indifferent God will use us all "for this cause" either to show people what to do, or what not to do. So His **name may be declared throughout all the earth.** The choice is ours concerning exactly how our life will make a difference.

THE CAUSE OF BEING THE PRISONER OF JESUS CHRIST

Ephesians 3:1:
<u>**For this cause**</u> **I Paul, the prisoner of Jesus Christ for you Gentiles,**

Moving forward for this cause in the Lord Jesus Christ, in whom the whole true church, the blood washed body of Christ, is the building fitly framed together to move forward, onward, and upward, yes to grow up unto an holy temple in the Lord, for our very bodies are the temple of God.

Moving forward for this cause in the Lord Jesus Christ, in whom we also are builded together for an habitation of God through the Spirit. Always remember that God inhabits the praises of His people and never does God ever inhabit the complaints of His people. Moving forward for this cause in the Lord Jesus Christ, as voluntary prisoner of Jesus Christ for the Gentiles, the shut-out, to reach and teach the shut-out, the deprived of today's society throughout the world.

- Moving forward for this cause as the passionate prisoner of Jesus Christ to reach and teach the shut-out, the downtrodden of today's society throughout the world.

- Moving forward for this cause as the powerful prisoner of praise to reach and teach the shut-out, the despised of today's society throughout the world.

- Moving forward for this cause as a passionate prisoner of the persistent prisoner of prayer to reach and teach the shut-out, the disinherited of today's society throughout the world.

- Moving forward for this cause as the prepared prisoner of planning to reach and teach the shut-out, the discriminated within today's society throughout the world.

- Moving forward for this cause as the purpose driven prisoner of patience to reach and teach the shut-out, the disgraced within today's society throughout the world.

- Moving forward for this cause as the peculiar prisoner of persistence to reach and teach the shut-out, the downright dangerous, desperate, and dirty within today's society throughout the world.

- Moving forward for this cause as the prisoner of Jesus Christ into the dispensation of the grace of God, you-ward grace, which is amazing grace that saved a wretch like me.

THE CAUSE OF KNEELOGY

Ephesians 3:14
<u>**For this cause**</u> **I bow my knees unto the Father of our Lord Jesus Christ,**

- Moving forward for the cause of kneelogy leads the blood washed believer right to the Heavenly Father of our Lord Jesus Christ of whom the entire family, both in heaven and in earth is named.

- Moving forward for the cause of kneelogy leads the blood washed believer to earnestly pray in Jesus mighty name that God the Father would grant the believer, according to the riches of His awesome glory, to be literally strengthened with matchless might by His Holy Spirit in the inner man.

- Moving forward for the cause of kneelogy leads the blood washed believer to stand in the gap in deep intercessory prayer so that Jesus Christ may dwell in the hearts of true believers by faith. That the believers, being rooted and grounded in true love, may be able to comprehend with all saints, all the blood washed believers, what is the five dimensions of the Christian faith,

    1.) The Dimension of Breadth
    2.) The Dimension of Length
    3.) The Dimension of Depth
    4.) The Dimension of Height
    5.) The Dimension of Knowing the Love of Christ,

Which passeth knowledge, that the true blood washed believer might be filled with all the awesome fullness of God. There we should have a burden for this cause that literally drives us to bust a move on our knees in intercessory prayer.

J. Hudson Taylor stated, "Brother, if you would enter that Province, you must go forward on your knees."

- Will the monthly mass murders drive us to bow our knees for this cause? Will the weekly senseless gang related drive by shootings drive us to bow our knees for this cause?

- Will killing of innocent children by lovers of violence drive us to bow our knees for this cause?

Yes, now is the time to be driven to our knees for this cause? So we will cry to the our Creator as in the classic words of the hymnologist, Charles Wesley:

Father, I stretch my hands to thee,
No other help I know;
If thou withdraw thyself from me,
Ah! whither shall I go?

- Dr. Martin Luther King, Jr., moved forward and bowed his knees in prayer for this cause long before he led any civil rights protest march or told the entire world of his now famous dream. Steve Harrison says that, "As you get moving you get more clarity." Mr. Harrison goes on to state that, "Sometimes we have to <u>stumble forward</u>. But keep stumbling. <u>Keep moving forward</u>."

- The Apostle Paul moved forward and bowed his knees in prayer for this cause long before he reached the ends of the earth of his day and was literally beheaded for the cause of Christ as a Christian martyr in Rome.

- The Lord and Savior, Jesus Christ, moved forward and bowed His knees in prayer for this cause before He was brutally tortured and died on the cross for all of our sins and rose again to give us new life. Frederick Douglass hit nail on the head when he stated "If there is no struggle, there is no progress."

MOVING FORWARD FOR THE CAUSE OF MARRIAGE BETWEEN A MAN AND A WOMAN

Ephesians 5:31:
<u>For this cause</u> **shall a man leave his father and mother, and shall be joined unto his wife, and they two shall be one flesh.**

Matthew 19:5:
And said, <u>For this cause</u> shall a man leave father and mother, and shall cleave to his wife: and they twain shall be one flesh?

Mark 10:7
<u>For this cause</u> shall a man leave his father and mother, and cleave to his wife.

Romans 1:26
<u>For this cause</u> God gave them up unto vile affections: for even their women did change the natural use into that which is against nature:

These scriptures clearly shows that with no hatred in their heart that the Lord Jesus Christ, Himself, and His chosen Apostle to the Gentiles, Paul, clearly taught through the inspiration of the Holy Spirit that **true marriage is only between a man or a woman.** It totally breaks my heart to see how so many elected officials utterly disrespect and totally disregard the truth of God's holy word. In fact the very first, the initial "cause" scripture is literally moved forward for this cause in the book of beginnings, the book of Genesis.

Genesis 2:21-25:
And the LORD God <u>caused</u> a deep sleep to fall upon Adam, and he slept: and he took one of his ribs, and closed up the flesh instead thereof; And the rib, which the LORD God had taken from man, made he a woman, and brought her unto the man. And Adam said, This is now bone of my bones, and flesh of my flesh: she shall be called Woman, because she was taken out of Man. Therefore shall a man leave his father and his mother, and shall cleave unto his wife: and they shall be one flesh. And they were both naked, the man and his wife, and were not ashamed.

It is so sad that many only quote the Holy Scripture after a major disaster or tragic mass murder. Yet, these powerful and thought provoking passages of scripture are totally ignored by too many elected officials in today's politically correct world and even banned in the minds of many. It is way past time to move forward for this cause of truly loving all people, but yet, not agreeing with all people whose opinions, decisions, statements, and votes totally contradict the Bible, and blame it on civil rights. If the Bible is worthy to hold ones hand on and take the oath of office. Then it is worthy enough to follow its mandates in governing. Yes, it is possible to disagree, and yet never discriminate. Martin Luther King worked with all people and loved all people. We must work with all people, and love all people. Yet, Rev. Dr. Martin Luther King, Jr., never ever pushed for gay marriage. He just fought the good fight of faith for jobs, justice, equality, and freedom for all. In fact, in 1958 Rev. Dr. Martin Luther King, Jr.'s only writing on the subject of homosexuality in his Ebony Magazine column clearly confirms that he did not embrace the lifestyle. King spoke the truth in love as a caring Pastor compassionately without any condemnation. Here is the boy's question and King's answer.

Question: "My problem is different from the ones most people have. I am a boy, but I feel about boys the way I ought to feel about girls. I don't want my parents to know about me. What can I do? Is there any place where I can go for help?"

Answer: "Your problem is not at all an uncommon one. However, it does require careful attention. The type of feeling that you have toward boys is probably not an innate tendency, but something that has been culturally acquired. Your reasons for adopting this habit have now been consciously suppressed or unconsciously repressed. Therefore, it is necessary to deal with this problem by getting back to some of the experiences and circumstances that led to the habit.

In order to do this I would suggest that you see a good psychiatrist who can assist you in bringing to the forefront of conscience all of those experiences and circumstances that led to the habit. You are already on the right road toward a solution, since you honestly recognize the problem and have a desire to solve it."

- Rev. Dr. Martin Luther King, Jr. clearly calls homosexuality a problem three times.
- Rev. Dr. Martin Luther King, Jr. clearly calls homosexuality a habit three times.
- Rev. Dr. Martin Luther King, Jr. clearly calls homosexuality a problem or habit that is "culturally acquired."
- Rev. Dr. Martin Luther King, Jr. clearly calls homosexuality a problem or habit that a person can "honestly recognize the problem and have a desire to solve it."
- Rev. Dr. Martin Luther King, Jr. clearly supported Bertrand Rustin as the main organizer of the March on Washington. Rev. Dr. Martin Luther King, Jr. never ever discriminated against Bertrand Rustin, and Rev. Dr. Martin Luther King, Jr. never supported the gay agenda. Rev. Dr. Martin Luther King, Jr. clearly fought for jobs, justice, and freedom for all, but never supported the gay agenda. That is the historical truth.
- Rev. Dr. Martin Luther King, Jr. clearly teaches us that it possible to disagree without discriminating against anyone. Rev. Dr. Martin Luther King, Jr. clearly teaches us that it possible to disagree without disrespecting anyone. Rev. Dr. Martin Luther King, Jr. clearly teaches us that it possible to disagree with a person and still work with them on the issues that you do agree on.
- We must move forward learning in the public square not to use bullying and black listing tactics, because a person believes marriage is only between a man and a woman in the sight of

God.
- We must move forward learning in the center of public society not to use bullying and black listing tactics blocking honest people from praying or singing at high profile public events, because a person believes marriage is only between a man and a woman in the sight of God.
- Those modern day bullying and black listing tactics are not godly, and they are unjust.
- Just imagine if Rev. Dr. Martin King, Jr. was told that you cannot make your "I have A Dream" speech, because you don't support gay marriage. Well that type of bullying and blacklisting tactic is currently happening to many Ministers of the Gospel today, and that is pure discrimination.

We need to speak the truth in love without any condemnation. We need more leaders with a firmly solid biblical worldview backbone like Rev. Dr. Martin Luther King, Jr. today who will move forward and fight for jobs, justice, and freedom for all without compromising the eternal truth of God's word to please the powers that be. Why compromise the truth for votes and popularity polls of the day. Why compromise the truth for a false sense of self esteem and still be broken, battered, and bruised. Compromising eternal truth will only force God to remove His Hands of protection. Move forward for this cause and boldly declare no compromise. Love every one. Hate no one. Get right with God. Run, rush, and roll right into the eternal loving arms of the Wounded Healer, Jesus Christ. Jesus' bloody, nailed, scarred hands are waiting to hold and heal you, my dear broken, battered, and bruised brothers and sisters of humanity and make you whole.

Whatever the case may be, let us all move forward for this cause, and always speak the truth in love, and never in hatred. Yes, God surely does hate all sin, but God truly loves all sinners to salvation through our Lord and Savior Jesus Christ's precious blood. Therefore, yes, blood-washed believers in Jesus Christ must hate sin, but we must never hate a human being. Always love the sinner; yes, love all sinners to the true place of repentance at the bloody cross of Christ. The truth will always be the truth even in times like these.

In times like these, you need a Savior
In times like these, you need an anchor;
Be very sure, be very sure
Your anchor holds and grips the Solid Rock!

MOVING FORWARD FOR THE CAUSE OF MEETING THE MIRACLE WORKER

John 12:18:
<u>For this cause</u> **the people also met him, for that they heard that he had done this miracle.**

The people moved forward and met Jesus for this cause. That cause being that Jesus had raised Lazarus from the dead. You know the story: Jesus showed up on the scene late after Lazarus had been dead for four days. Jesus moved forward and spoke directly to the Father saying, "I know that You hear me always: but because of the people which stand by, I said it, that they may believe that thou hast sent me." When Jesus spoke those words, Jesus cried out with a loud voice, "Lazarus, come forth." If Jesus had not called Lazarus by name everyone who was dead would have move forward from the dead. Since Jesus called Lazarus by name, Lazarus moved forward from the grave. Lazarus came forth, bound hand and foot with his grave clothes, and Lazarus' face was bound about with a napkin. Jesus said, "Loose him, and let him go". We too need to move forward for this cause to meet the miracle worker, Jesus, in a fresh, new, and intimate manner as never before. Jesus is ready to raise us and loose us for this cause % the cause of Christ. Move forward and meet the Miracle Worker, Jesus. Move forward and spend time with the Miracle Worker, Jesus. Spend time with Jesus through Bible study, prayer, and praise.

MOVING FORWARD FOR THE CAUSE OF FUNCTIONING IN THIS HOUR

John 12:27:
Now is my soul troubled; and what shall I say? Father, save me from this hour: but <u>for this cause</u> came I unto this hour.

Jesus' very own soul was deeply troubled and Jesus felt speechless in the depth of His soul. Even Jesus wanted the Heavenly Father to save Him and spare Him from His treacherous hour of hatred, horror, and humiliation for all humanity. Yet, Jesus moved forward and declared and decreed that for this cause He came to this torturous hour of hatred, horror, and humiliation for the salvation of all humanity who will accept the finished work of Christ on the cross of Calvary. Spiritual or physical suicide was not and is the answer.

MOVING FORWARD FOR THE CAUSE OF BEARING WITNESS TO THE TRUTH

John 18:37:
Pilate therefore said unto him, Art thou a king then? Jesus answered, Thou sayest that I am a king. To this end was I born, and <u>for this cause</u> came I into the world, that I should bear witness unto the truth. Every one that is of the truth heareth my voice.

Judea's Governor Pontius Pilate's question to Jesus concerning whether He is a King brought about an awesome answer from Jesus, whose message, ministry, and mission are moved forward for this cause to bear witness to the truth. Jesus' birth and physical bodily entrance into this world through the birth canal and womb of Mary was only to bear witness to the truth % that He is the King of Kings, the Son of God, the Savior of the world. Only the truthful believer can tune in and clearly hear God's voice speak in spite of the pain of persecution for this cause. President Theodore Roosevelt was totally right when he stated:

"No man is worth his salt who is not ready at all times to risk his well-being, to risk his body, to risk his life, in a great cause."

MOVING FORWARD FOR THE CAUSE OF HOPE

Acts 28:20:
For this cause therefore have I called for you, to see you, and to speak with you: because that for the hope of Israel I am bound with this chain.

When you move forward for this cause, the cause of Christ, you must make things crystal clear and call those who you have been assigned to minister to as a hostage of hope.

When you move forward for this cause, the cause of Christ, you must make things crystal clear and see, face to face, in person, to those that you have been created to minister to be a hostage of hope.

When you move forward for this cause, the cause of Christ, you must make things crystal clear and speak with, communicate with, and spiritually connect with those that you have been burdened to never forget to be a hostage of hope.

For the hope of home base, for this cause, the cause of Christ, we must make things crystal clear and be bound with this particular positive and progressive type of chain of total commitment to make a real difference to be a hostage of hope. Paul was chosen by God as an Apostle to the Gentiles, but he stayed connected to the hope of Israel. Even when he was arrested and seen as a reckless jail bird, Paul made it clear to the folks at home that it was for this cause, the cause of the cross of Christ, that we was in chains. Nelson Mandela said it this way, "Difficulties break some men but make others. No axe is sharp enough to cut the soul of a sinner who keeps on trying, one armed with the hope that he will rise even in the end."

Move forward for this cause of caring, sharing, and bearing the heavy burdens of the broken, battered, and bruised by being a hostage of hope. Hold on to your hope. Don't let go of your hope. Move forward for this cause and keep hope alive, my brother and my sister, because you can make a difference. Rev. Dr. Martin Luther King, Jr., was right when he said, "If you lose hope, somehow you lose the vitality that keeps life moving, you lose that courage to be, that quality that helps you to go on in spite of all. And so today I still have a dream."

MOVING FORWARD FOR THE CAUSE OF SLAYING YOUR GIANTS

Before the young shepherd boy, David took down his sling shot which he had five smooth stones, one for Goliath (and four more for his giant brothers if they showed up); before the young shepherd boy, David cut off the head of the Philistine giant of Gath, Goliath, the uncircumcised Philistine who wanted to destroy Israel, young David asked his oldest brother, Eliab, who wanted young David to stay home and off the battlefield, **"Is there not a cause?"** God wants some modern day Davids to commune with Him in order to move forward for this cause to demolish, destroy, and dismantle the giants of poverty, hunger, joblessness, and deep social-political corruption.

Let us move forward for this cause and pay attention to the details. All the men of Israel, when they saw the Philistine giant, Goliath of Gath, ran fast, fled from the giant from Gath, and the men of Israel were totally afraid. They moved backward instead of forward. The men of Israel said, Have you seen this man, this giant from Gath, Goliath, that is come up? Surely to defy Israel is Goliath come up: and it shall be, that the man who moves forward and kills him, the king will enrich that man with great riches, and will give that man his daughter, and make that man's father's house free in Israel. The young shepherd boy, David, moved forward for this cause and spoke to the men of Israel that stood by him, saying, "What shall be done to the man that kills this Philistine giant from Gath, Goliath, and takes away the reproach from Israel? Who is this uncircumcised Philistine, that he should defy, disregard, disrespect the armies of the living God?" The people answered young David after this manner, saying, "So shall it be done to the man that kills the Philistine giant, Goliath of Gath." Eliab, who was David's oldest brother heard when young David moved forward and spoke boldly unto the men of Israel; and Eliab's anger was kindled against young David, and Eliab said, "Why do you come here? and with whom have you left those few sheep in the wilderness? I know your pride, and the naughtiness of your heart; for you are come down that you might see the battle."

IS THERE NOT A CAUSE?

David said, What have I now done? Is there not a cause? Gang members are killing our children at younger and younger ages and developmental stages. Is there not a cause? Democrats and Republicans don't work together in bipartisanship for the benefit of the people. Is there not a cause? Racism is running rampant in the land. Is there not a cause? Hardly anyone cares about the pain of the people. Is there not a cause?

The young shepherd boy David turned from Eliab toward another, and spake after the same manner, "Is there not a cause?" And the people answered him again after the former manner, "Is there not a cause?" Young David moved the agenda of heaven and the agenda of God forward. When the words were heard which the young shepherd boy, David so boldly moved forward to speak for this cause, they rehearsed them before Saul, "Is there not a cause?" And King Saul sent for the young shepherd boy, David.

Young David said to King Saul, "Let no man's heart fail because of the giant, Goliath of Gath; your servant will go, will move forward for this cause and fight with this Philistine." King Saul said to the young shepherd boy, David, "You are not able to go against this Philistine to fight with him: for you are but a youth, and Goliath a man of war from his youth."

Young David said unto King Saul, "your servant kept his father's sheep, and there came a lion, and a bear, and took a lamb out of the flock." Young David said, "I went and I moved forward for this cause out after him, and smote him, and delivered it out of the lion's mouth: and when the lion arose against me, I caught him by his beard, and smote him, and slew the lion."

Young David went on to say "your servant moved forward for this cause and slew both the lion and the bear: and this uncircumcised Philistine shall be as one of them, seeing he hath defied the armies of the living God."

Young David said, "moreover, the LORD that delivered me out of the paw of the lion, and out of the paw of the bear, he will deliver me out of the hand of this Philistine." And King Saul said unto the young shepherd boy. David, "Go, move forward, and the LORD be with you, young David."

USE THAT WHICH IS PROVEN

King Saul armed the young shepherd boy David with his armour, and King Saul put an helmet of brass upon young David's head and he armed David with a coat of mail. The young shepherd boy, David girded Saul's sword upon his armour, and he prepared to go; but he had not proved the armor. And young David said unto King Saul, "I cannot go with these"; I can not move forward with Saul's stuff, for I have not proved them. And young David put them off him.

The young shepherd boy David took his staff in his hand, and chose him five smooth stones (one for Goliath and four more for his four giant brothers if they showed up) out of the brook, and put them in a shepherd's bag which he had, even in a scrip; and his sling was in his hand: and he drew near, moved forward for this cause, to the Philistine giant, Goliath of Gath.

The Philistine came on and drew near, moved forward, unto young David; and the man that bear the shield went before him. When the Philistine looked about and saw young David, Goliath disdained him: for he was but a youth, ruddy, and of a fair countenance. The Philistine giant, Goliath of Gath, said unto young David, "Am I a dog, that you come to me with staves?" And the Philistine giant cursed the young shepherd boy David by his gods. Goliath the Philistine giant said to young David, "Come to me, and I will give your flesh unto the fowls of the air, and to the beasts of the field."

THE BATTLE IS THE LORD'S

Then said young David to the Philistine, Goliath, "you come to me with a sword, and with a spear, and with a shield: but I come, I move forward for this cause, to you in the name of the LORD of hosts, the God of the armies of Israel, whom you have defied. This day will the LORD deliver you, Goliath of Gath, into mine hand; and I will smite you, and take your head from you; and I will give the carcases of the host of the Philistines this day unto the fowls of the air, and to the wild beasts of the earth; that all the earth may know that there is a God in Israel. And all this assembly shall know that the LORD saves not with sword and spear: for the battle is the LORD's, and he will give you, Goliath of Gath, into our hands."

When the Philistine arose, and came, and drew nigh to meet young shepherd boy David, that David moved forward, and ran toward the army to meet the Philistine giant.

Young David put his hand in his bag, and took out a stone, and slang it, and smote the Philistine Goliath in his forehead, that the stone sunk into his forehead; and he fell upon his face to the earth. Young David prevailed over the Philistine with a sling and with a stone, and smote the Philistine Goliath, and slew him; but there was no sword in the hand of young David.

Therefore, young David ran, moved forward, and stood upon the Philistine, Goliath of Gath, and took Goliath's sword, and drew it out of the sheath thereof, and slew the Philistine giant, Goliath of Gath, and cut off his head with his own sword. And when the Philistines saw that their champion Goliath of Gath, the great was dead, they ran, they fled for their very lives.

MOVING FORWARD FOR THE CAUSE OF THE KNOWLEDGE OF GOD'S WILL

Colossians 1:9:
<u>For this cause</u> we also, since the day we heard it, do not cease to pray for you, and to desire that ye might be filled with the knowledge of his will in all wisdom and spiritual understanding;

Knowledge is power when applied. Moving forward for this cause challenges the blood washed believer to pray without ceasing for the broken, battered, and bruised, that they may be filled with the powerful knowledge of God's perfect will for our daily lives, all the wisdom and all the spiritual understanding needed in this life to be an overcomer. In life and in death, the safest place in the whole wide world is in the will of God. Move forward for this cause and discover the knowledge of His will with all wisdom and spiritual understanding.

MOVING FORWARD FOR THE CAUSE OF RECEIVING THE WORD OF GOD IN TRUTH

1 Thessalonians 2:13
<u>For this cause</u> also thank we God without ceasing, because, when ye received the word of God which ye heard of us, ye received it not as the word of men, but as it is in truth, the word of God, which effectually worketh also in you that believe.

When blood-washed believers move forward for this cause, the cause of Christ, there is an overwhelming spirit of thanksgiving, a truly continuous flow of praise and worship, moving forward as the wind of the Holy Spirit, that sets the tone to hear and receive the word of God not as the word of mere men, but rather as crystal clear divine truth inspired by God to effectively work in the life of the believer. Many people need to know their faith, to move forward for this cause, so the tempter, satan, will not destroy you and your testimony. The cause of knowing your faith is extremely important so our labor will not be in vain.

The Apostle Paul in **1 Thessalonians 3:5** declares:
<u>For this cause</u>, **when I could no longer forbear, I sent to know your faith, lest by some means the tempter have tempted you, and our labour be in vain.**

MOVING FORWARD FOR THE CAUSE OF LONGSUFFERING

1 Timothy 1:16:
Howbeit for this cause I obtained mercy, that in me first Jesus Christ might shew forth all longsuffering, for a pattern to them which should hereafter believe on him to life everlasting.

The Apostle Paul moved forward and wrote to his beloved son in the ministry, Timothy, for this cause for which Paul received the magnificent mercy of the Master, that Jesus Christ display every angle of long suffering through Paul's testimony, trails, tribulations, and triumphs. As an example, as a pattern, as a blueprint, and as a crystal clear road map, to others in the future to believe on Christ as the compass, the GPS system, the only way to the life that will never ever end.

THE PHYSICALLY CHALLENGED MOVING FORWARD FOR THIS CAUSE

Recently, there has been an effort to revise the icon that has for so long been the symbol of accessibility for the physically challenged within New York City, which recently decided to adopt the fresh, new, and cutting edge icon with the positive and progressive moving forward theme. New York City Mayor's Office for People With Disabilities Commissioner Victor Calise stated in a recent interview with The Chronicle of Higher Education that "It's such a forward-moving thing."

New York City, America's largest city, plans to adopt this new and freshly updated version of the old blue and white "handicapped" icon which will soon be placed throughout New York City. Rather than showing a stale and motionless person in a wheelchair, the new icon portrays an active, physically challenged person moving forward and leaning forward in the wheelchair ready to go and make a difference for this cause.

MOVING FORWARD FOR THIS CAUSE BY OCCUPYING UNTIL JESUS COMES

Long before the Disney Company purchased *Star Wars*, *The Power Rangers*, Marvel Comics, and ABC (The American Broadcasting Company). Long before Disney teamed up with Dream Works Studios to make modern movie classics for children of all ages and stages. Long before the Disney Channel, any kind of cable television, or Dish Network and Direct TV ever existed the founder Walt Disney moved forward a cause that he deeply believed in and said that, "We keep moving forward, opening new doors, and doing new things, because we're curious and curiosity keeps leading us down new paths." Disney Land and Disney World and all of the other Disney brands only exist today because a business man utilized biblical principles of moving forward for the cause that he was born for. Stir up the gift within you and move forward for this cause. Remember what Jesus Christ said in **Luke 19:13** before He triumphantly entered in Jerusalem, before His passion, crucifixion, resurrection, and ascension, Jesus said **"Occupy till I come."**

The Complete Jewish Bible translates Jesus' words in **Luke 19:13** as **'Do business with this while I'm away.'** Well, it seems like Mickey Mouse is doing more to occupy and to do business, than many Christians. Now is the time to move forward for this cause so serious Christians will also sit down at the table of influence and impact the newspapers, magazines, comics, music, sports, movies, television shows, radio programs, and internet content in a positive and progressive manner. Bible prophecy is so extremely important, especially in today's world as never ever before, but the Lord Jesus Christ does not want blood washed believers to just sit idly around on our seats of do nothing, on a lonesome mountain and bury His investment until He comes. The Lord Jesus Christ wants us, the redeemed, blood washed believers, to move forward for this cause by occupying, literally doing business until He comes. Albert Einstein stated "Life is like riding a bicycle. To keep your balance you must keep moving." For we serve God, the Creator of every living thing that moves upon the earth. **Acts 17:28** states, **"For in him we live, and <u>move</u>, and have our being."**

CHAPTER EIGHTEEN

MOVING FORWARD WITH LOVE – PROVE THE SINCERITY OF YOUR LOVE

2 Corinthians 8:7-9: "Therefore, as ye abound in every thing, in faith, and utterance, and knowledge, and in all diligence, and in your love to us, see that ye abound in this grace also. I speak not by commandment, but by occasion of the <u>forwardness</u> of others, and to prove the sincerity of your love. For ye know the grace of our Lord Jesus Christ, that, though he was rich, yet for your sakes he became poor, that ye through his poverty might be rich."

Condition of Existence -- Every single one of us is required by God to prove the sincerity of our love. Every single one of us will be required by God to prove with our own life, time, tithe, and talent whether or not our love is real. Mother Theresa was correct when she said, "Spread love everywhere you go. Let no one ever come to you without leaving happier."

DID YOU KNOW? - Titus, the young Pastor and faithful co-laborer in Christ of the Apostle Paul had traveled to Corinth when the Apostle's first letter was delivered to the Corinthian church. Pastor Titus had begun the offering collection which was commanded by Paul in 1 Corinthians 16:1. Now Apostle Paul directs Pastor Titus to return and complete the collection before his arrival. Instead of the faithful Macedonian church setting the example for the Corinthian church, the latter ought to have led the way in the grace of giving. The Corinthian church was rich in gifts. The Apostle Paul applies no pressure concerning the gift of giving by command. The gift giving must be totally freewill in nature with a cheerful heart in order to be blessed of God. In order to prove the sincerity of their love, the Apostle Paul encourages the Corinthian church by the forwardness of others; namely, the good example of the faithful Macedonian believers, and by the ultimate example of the major sacrifice by Jesus Christ through His life, His bloody and brutal death, and His resurrection from the grave.

During the time of this letter written by the Apostle Paul to the Corinthian church, the temple of Aphrodite Pandemos was standing, "the Venus Temple of all the people," which had one thousand consecrated priestesses. Every single priestess was completely dedicated to the service of Aphrodite, or in plain words, to prostitution and harlotry. The Corinthian temple of worship was a huge house of prostitution! Corinth had such a horrible reputation that the very words "to Corinthianize" had become synonymous with an absolutely corrupt lifestyle. With this raunchy backdrop, some of the Gentiles who had become new converts to Christianity and members of the Corinthian Church manifested the negative influence of their old ways.

SEVEN SCRIPTURAL STRATEGIES TO MOVE FORWARD & ABOUND

1.) MOVE FORWARD, ABOUND IN EVERY AREA OF LIFE

"Therefore, as ye abound in every thing," Move Forward, Abound Holistically.

2.) MOVE FORWARD, ABOUND IN FAITH

"in faith,"

William H. Bathurst wrote in Psalms and Hymns in 1831:

> *O, for a faith that will not shrink,*
> *Though pressed by every foe,*
> *That will not tremble on the brink*
> *Of any earthly woe!*

3.) MOVE FORWARD, ABOUND IN UTTERANCE

"and utterance,"

Move Forward, Abound In Utterance -- **Ephesians 6:19: "And for me, that utterance may be given unto me, that I may open my mouth boldly, to make known the mystery of the gospel."**

Move Forward, Abound In Utterance -- **Colossians 4:3: "Withal praying also for us, that God would open unto us a door of utterance, to speak the mystery of Christ, for which I am also in bonds."**

4.) MOVE FORWARD, ABOUND IN KNOWLEDGE

"and knowledge,"

Move Forward, Abound In Knowledge -- Sir Frances Bacon said that "Knowledge is power."

Move Forward, Abound In Knowledge -- Hosea 4:6: "My people are destroyed for lack of knowledge: because thou hast rejected knowledge."

5.) MOVE FORWARD, ABOUND IN ALL DILIGENCE

"and in all diligence,"

Proverbs 4:23: "Keep thy heart with all diligence; for out of it are the issues of life."

2 Peter 1:10: "Wherefore the rather, brethren, give diligence to make your calling and election sure: for if ye do these things, ye shall never fall."

6.) MOVE FORWARD, ABOUND IN LOVE

"and in your love to us,"

Move Forward, Abound In Love -- Romans 5:5: "And hope maketh not ashamed; because the love of God is shed abroad in our hearts by the Holy Ghost which is given unto us."

Move Forward, Abound In Love -- Kirk Franklin wrote:

"Patient love, kind love, sweet love, kind love."

Verse 1

Love a word that comes and goes
But few people really know what it means to really love somebody
Love though the tears may fade away
I'm so glad your love will stay
'cause I love you and you show me
Jesus what it really means to love."

Move Forward, Abound In Love -- The Message Bible says in **I Corinthians 13:**

Love never gives up.

Love cares more for others than for self.
Love doesn't want what it doesn't have.
Love doesn't strut,
Doesn't have a swelled head,
Doesn't force itself on others,
Isn't always "me first,"
Doesn't fly off the handle,
Doesn't keep score of the sins of others,
Doesn't revel when others grovel,
Takes pleasure in the flowering of truth,
Puts up with anything,
Trusts God always,
Always looks for the best,
Never looks back,
But keeps going to the end.
Love never dies.

Song of Solomon 8:6: "Love is strong as death."

7.) MOVE FORWARD, ABOUND IN GRACE

"see that ye abound in this grace also."

Move Forward, Abound In Grace -- Grace is the super natural empowerment of the Holy Spirit to move the disgraced, despised, and downtrodden soul forward into the full plan, power, and purpose of God.

2 Corinthians 13:14: "The grace of the Lord Jesus Christ, and the love of God, and the communion of the Holy Ghost, be with you all. Amen."

8.) IT IS BETTER TO ASK PEOPLE TO DO THAN TO

COMMAND PEOPLE TO DO

"I speak not by commandment." You get better results asking, 'Would you please make me a sandwich?' than saying 'I command you to make me a sandwich.'

9.) LEARN FROM THOSE WHO MOVE FORWARD

"but by occasion of the forwardness of others."

The Macedonian Church Moved Forward With Love and Gave of Their Time, Tithe, and Talent. Move Forward with Love, Abound Like the Macedonians and Help Spread the Gospel of Jesus Christ Through Your Support.

JESUS MOVED FORWARD WITH LOVE -- Mark 14:34-36: "And saith unto them, My soul is exceeding sorrowful unto death: tarry ye here, and watch. And he went <u>forward</u> a little, and fell on the ground, and prayed that, if it were possible, the hour might pass from him. And he said, Abba, Father, all things are possible unto thee; take away this cup from me: nevertheless not what I will, but what thou wilt."

Move forward like Jesus in the Garden of Gethsemane. Move forward just a little, that is all you have to do. Even if you fall down in agony to the ground; even if you sweat blood; even if you pray for the cup of pain to be taken away—move forward in prayer just like Jesus. Even when you can't move your painful bleeding body, move forward in your deepest pain; move forward in your most heartfelt soul wrenching prayer to the Father and say, "Not my will, but thine be done." What the first Adam messed up in the Garden of Eden, Jesus, the last Adam, fixed in the Garden of Gethsemane.

10.) PROVE THE SINCERITY OF YOUR LOVE

"and to prove the sincerity of your love."

Deuteronomy 13:3: "Thou shalt not hearken unto the words of that prophet, or that dreamer of dreams: for the Lord your God proveth you, to know whether ye love the Lord your God with all your heart and with all your soul."

True love that is deeply rooted and grounded in the love of God can heal and make whole the broken, battered, and bruised.

Ephesians 5:25: "Husbands, love your wives, even as Christ also loved the church, and gave himself for it."

Colossians 3:19: "Husbands, love your wives, and be not bitter against them."

John 13:34: "A new commandment I give unto you, That ye love one another; as I have loved you, that ye also love one another."

- Prove the sincerity of your love and wash the dishes.
- Prove the sincerity of your love and clean the room.
- Prove the sincerity of your love and shovel the snow.
- Prove the sincerity of your love and walk together.
- Prove the sincerity of your love and talk together.
- Prove the sincerity of your love and work together.
- Prove the sincerity of your love and take the pain.
- Prove the sincerity of your love and pay the price
- Prove the sincerity of your love and be a carer, sharer, and heavy load bearer.
- Prove the sincerity of your love and do more than buy your

love a box of chocolate, a nice card, and roses on Valentine's Day.
- Prove the sincerity of your love and give your love a back rub and foot rub.

You have got to prove your love. You have got to show your love. **II Corinthians 8: 24: "Wherefore shew ye to them, and before the churches, the proof of your love."**

11.) THE LORD JESUS CHRIST PROVED THE SINCERITY OF HIS LOVE

2 Corinthians 8:9: "For ye know the grace of our Lord Jesus Christ, that, though he was rich, yet for your sakes he became poor, that ye through his poverty might be rich."

John 15:13: "Greater love hath no man than this, that a man lay down his life for his friends."

No Greater Love
Jesus went to Calvary
to save a wretch,
like you and me;
that's love, that's love.

They hung Him wide,
they stretched Him wide.
He hung His head, and then He died;
that's love, that's love.

That's not how the story ends,
three days later He rose again;
that's love, that's love.

On August 20, 2013, Book Keeper Antoinette Tuff moved forward and made a major difference at Ronald E. McNair Discovery Learning Academy near Atlanta. Antoinette Tuff's actions on that day literally redefined how to approach the national and international conversation concerning gun violence. Antoinette Tuff would go on to declare and degree that "God had been preparing me for this moment."

Antoinette Tuff stated that, "I got up that morning just as normal, went in to have my prayer time and spend some time with the Lord, talking to him and listening to him, but unfortunately during that time he didn't tell me that I was going to be meeting Michael Hill later that day,...."

Antoinette Tuff made her way to work as she would any other workday at the front desk of Ronald E. McNair Discovery Learning Academy near Atlanta. Later on that day, Antoinette saw 20 year old, Michael Hill, who got in the school with 500 rounds of ammunition and an assault rifle. On the now famous 911 call Antoinette Tuff stated that, "I'm on Second Avenue in the school and the gentleman said tell them to hold down the police officer coming and he said he going to start shooting so tell them to back off."

25 minutes into the now legendary 911 call Antoinette Tuff begins to literally bond with Michael Hill, Tuff stated that, "He said he should've just went to the mental hospital instead of doing this because he's not on his medication. But do you want me to try - I can help you. Let's see if we can work it out so that you don't have to go away with them for a long time." Antoinette Tuff, who clearly understood what it is to be broken, battered, and bruised by the vicious pains and plight of life, was able to connect with and reach the young 20 year-old, Michael Hill, as she prayerfully talked Hill down from murdering innocent people and from committing suicide, and Tuff convinced Hill to actually surrender himself to the authorities. When Michael Hill mentions suicide Antoinette Hill quickly responded by saying, "No. You don't want that. You gonna be okay. I thought the same thing. You know, I tried to commit suicide last year after my husband left me, but look at me now. I'm still working and everything is okay." Antoinette Tuff continued to move forward with the sincerity of love and made a major difference with her powerful words of wisdom that literally prevented another mass school slaughter when she said to Michael Hill those know famous words that touched Hill and touched the nation, "It's gonna be all right, sweetheart. I just want you to know that I love you, though, okay? And I'm proud of you. That's a good thing that you're just giving up and don't worry about it. We all go through something in life."

The police officers immediately rushed into Ronald E. McNair Discovery Learning Academy near Atlanta. Antoinette Tuff told the 911 Dispatcher Kendra McCray that, "I'm gonna tell you something, baby, I ain't never been so scared in all the days of my life." The 911 Dispatcher Kendra McCray told Antoinette Tuff that, "But you did great." Antoinette Tuff said, "Oh, Jesus." The 911 Dispatcher said again, "You did great." Antoinette Tuff said" Oh, God." Antoinette Tuff moved forward with the sincerity of love and made a major difference. Antoinette Tuff recently wrote an outstanding book appropriately entitled, *Prepared for a Purpose: The Inspiring True Story of How One Woman Saved an Atlanta School Under Siege*. I strongly encouraged every one ever where to pick up a copy of this awesome book. I hope it becomes a movie. Pablo Picasso was right on target when he stated that, "The meaning of life is to FIND your GIFT! The purpose of life is to GIVE it AWAY!"

- Love is what love does.
- Jesus proved the sincerity of His love when He left His throne in Heaven to come down to earth and die on a cross for sinful humanity.
- Jesus proved the sincerity of His love when He left streets paved with gold to come down to earth and die on an old rugged cross for all of our sins.
- Jesus proved the sincerity of His love when He could have called down a legion of angels to stop the crucifixion, but He gave His life for our sins.
- Jesus proved the sincerity of His love when He became poor so that through His poverty we might be rich.
- Jesus proved the sincerity of His love when He saved my sin-sick soul.
- Jesus proved the sincerity of His love when He was buried in a borrowed tomb and after that He rose from the dead, ascended to the Father and is preparing us mansions in Heaven.

Winston Churchill said, "The farther backward you can look, the farther forward you are likely to see." Therefore, look farther back to the bloody and brutal cross of Jesus Christ at Calvary, and learn to look farther forward with a vision of victory into our God given purpose and divine destiny.

II Corinthians 5:21: "For he hath made him to be sin for us, who knew no sin; that we might be made the righteousness of God in him."

James Rowe wrote:

> *I was sinking deep in sin, far from the peaceful shore,*
> *Very deeply stained within, sinking to rise no more,*
> *But the Master of the sea, heard my despairing cry,*
> *From the waters lifted me, now safe am I.*
>
> *Refrain:*
> *Love lifted me!*
> *Love lifted me!*
> *When nothing else could help*
> *Love lifted me!*

CHAPTER NINETEEN

MOVING FORWARD FOR THE HEALTH OF THE CHURCH – OVERCOMING SPIRITUAL ILLNESSES, INJURIES, INSTABILITIES, & IMPAIRMENTS

There are too many horrible abuses and misuses in the church. Jesus Christ is coming back for a church without spot or wrinkle. Daily change must occur. We must move forward with the 7R's%renewal, rebuilding, restoration, repentance, revelation, revolution, and revival for the very health of the church. We don't need only one of these seven words working in our lives; we need them all and even more to move forward for the health of the church so that the church can be delivered from lethal religious sickness, deadly spiritual weakness, and devilish wickedness in high places, to recommit our lives to helping the poor and the oppressed.

The Apostle Paul clearly understood the moving forward and making a difference for the health of the church message when he wrote in Galatians 2:10, "Only they would that we should remember the poor; the same which I also was forward to do." The Apostle Paul clearly admonished the Christian church to move forward and to "remember the poor," just as he and even Jesus Christ, the Head of the church, Himself, had moved forward and remembered the poor.

Ephesians 1:22-23 states, **"And He put all things under His feet, and gave Him to be head over all things to the church, Which is the body, the fullness of Him that filleth all in all."**

Now, if Christ is head over all things to the church, then Jesus Christ is the head of the church, and the church is His body, the fullness of Him that filleth all in all. Christ desires for the modern day church to move forward and be whole and healthy because the Head of the church, Jesus Christ, is whole and healthy, and He would deeply desire for wholeness and for health to be in His body, the church. Don't give Jesus Christ, the Head of the church, who died on Calvary's cross for the remission of our sins, a constant torturing headache and massive migraine by being a disrespectful and disobedient body, an ungrateful and unhealthy church. Don't take the Lord Jesus Christ for granted.

DID YOU KNOW? The Apostle Paul moved forward with his God-given purpose and made a major difference on his second missionary journey when he visited Ephesus leaving Priscilla and Aquila to lead that fine church. Acts 18:19-21 lets us know that the Apostle Paul really helped to get this church of Ephesus strong and healthy. The Apostle Paul returned two years later and he ministered there for about three years reaching that whole province of Asia with the Gospel of Jesus Christ. It was some time later that Paul was a prisoner in Rome. Later, he was martyred by having his head chopped off at Nero's chopping block. It was before then that he wrote his epistle to the Ephesians.

Now, one of the major themes of this book of Ephesians is God's work through the ministry of His church. Although the book of Ephesians was written initially to the people at Ephesus, it was also a popular circular letter that went to all the churches in the region. Ephesus was a very important city that boasted worship to the goddess Diana. It included the extremely well-known temple of Diana, one of the seven great wonders of the ancient world. It was completely devoted to idol worship. This is why Paul was deeply concerned about the spiritual health and well-being of the local church. Paul had so much to say about moving forward for the health of the church, the heritage of the church, the heart of the church, the hope of the church, the help of the church, and the Head of the church, Jesus Christ. The Ephesian church had to worship Jesus Christ in the midst of a people who were constantly worshipping idols. No wonder the Apostle Paul talks to the church at Ephesus about putting on the whole armor of God. The Book of Revelation lets us know that the Church at Ephesus lost her first love, Jesus Christ, and could only become healthy by repenting and returning to her first works. If you want to have a strong church that moves forward putting on the whole armor of God, you're going to have to be spiritually healthy soldiers. You don't want to have a Christian soldier going off in war who can barely stand up even before getting to the battlefield. We need a healthy church which embraces its heritage, heart, hope, help and Head, Jesus Christ, so it can march forward, move forward, move onward, and move upward as a strong Christian soldier of the Lord in holiness and make a difference. To God be the glory, to God be the honor, and to God be the praise for moving forward for the health of the church.

WHAT IS THE HEALTH OF THE CHURCH? WHY DO WE NEED TO MOVE IT FORWARD?

To begin with, we must ask ourselves the important question: what is health? Well, health is the overall general physical and emotional condition of the human body and mind, especially regarding the overall manifestation or absence of the four I's, which are illnesses, injuries, instabilities, or impairments. So as we look at health in the human body, we have to look at the 4 I's: illnesses, injuries, instabilities, or impairments.

Now what is the health of the church? First, Jesus Christ wants His body, His church, to be healthy. Second, most people call the church, "my church," and that's exactly why the church gets unhealthy. The church is Jesus Christ's church. The church is His body. The building is not the church. The people of God are the church. The blood-washed believers in the Lord Jesus Christ are the church. Jesus said "Upon this rock will I build My church and the gates of hell shall not prevail against it." What was that rock that Jesus was building it on? It was the prophetic proclamation that Peter made, "Thou art the Christ, the Son of the living God." Upon this prophetic proclamation from the mouth of Peter, Jesus said, "I'll build My church and the gates of hell shall not prevail against it."

The church has only one foundation to heal the spiritual four I's: illnesses, injuries, instabilities, and/or impairments.

The church's one foundation is Jesus Christ the Lord; she is His new creation by water and the Word. From Heaven, He came and sought her to be His holy bride, and with His own blood, He bought her, and for her life, He died.

The New Testament Greek word for 'church' is the word *Ekklesia*. The definition of this word is: an assembly, a gathering of citizens who are called out from their homes. The *Ekklesia* is the called out ones. If we are to be a healthy church we must be the called out ones—called out of the darkness into the marvelous light to move forward with impact and make a major difference in the culture. We are called to commitment, called to minister to the broken, the battered and the bruised, and called to bring inner healing, essential wholeness and real revival.

Proverbs 13:17 states:

"A wicked messenger falleth into mischief: but a faithful ambassador is health."

Rev. Dr. Martin Luther King, Jr., in his classic book, *Strength to Love*, wrote: "The church must be reminded that it is not the master or the servant of the state, but rather the conscience of the state. It must be the guide and the critic of the state, and never its tool. If the church does not recapture its prophetic zeal, it will become an irrelevant social club without moral or spiritual authority." This statement is extremely critical for today's culture. This subject matter must be revisited in order for the modern day church to move forward and make a lasting difference.

We are the church. We are the body of Christ. Like Peter, we must daily preach the eternal truth that Jesus is the Christ, the Son of the living God. If He is the Christ, the Son of the living God in our hearts and in our souls, then we must impact our culture, our communities, our society, our block, our homes, and our neighborhoods with the Gospel that is meaningful, that is relevant, and that will bring positive and progressive change and transformation.

Remember again that **Matthew 16:18** says, **"And I say unto thee, thou art Peter and upon this rock I will build My church, and the gates of hell shall not prevail against it."** Now, a healthy church is a church that is moving forward by being filled with the fullness of Jesus Christ who fills all in all. Money and bling-bling cannot fill our all in all. You can have billions of dollars, but you cannot take it with you when you die. Fame and fortune cannot fill your all in all. Who is the one who fills your all in all? Who scratches your itch? Who pulls you out of the ditch? Who are we full of? Are we full of the devil? Is his fatal, foolish, fake and phony fullness filling our all in all?

On the other hand, is the church full of Jesus Christ, a friend who sticks closer than a brother, a father to the fatherless, and a judge to the widow. Jesus Christ can and He will truly and fully fill our all and all.

Again and again, I think of the song by Ken Blanchard titled, "Fill My Cup, Lord." It says:

Like the woman at the well, I was seeking
For things that could not satisfy.
And then I heard my Savior speaking—
"Draw from My well that never shall run dry."

Fill my cup, Lord;
I lift it up Lord;
Come and quench this thirsting of my soul.
Bread of Heaven, feed me till I want no more.
Fill my cup, fill it up and make me whole.

This song helps to keep me moving forward.

MOVING FORWARD AND MAKING A DIFFERENCE FOR THE HERITAGE OF THE CHURCH

As we discuss moving forward for the health of the church, let us look at the heritage of the church. In order to understand the health of the church, we must embrace the heritage of the church. **Ephesians 1:14** (King James Version) says, **"Which is the earnest of our inheritance until the redemption of the purchased possession, unto the praise of His glory."**

Ephesians 1:14 (Amplified Version) says, **"That Spirit is the guarantee of our inheritance, the first fruits, the pledge and foretaste, the down payment on our heritage and anticipation of its full redemption of our acquiring complete possession of**

it to the praise of His glory."

As we look at the words "purchased possession," we find that these words in the Greek are *Peripoiesis*. It means to obtain, obtaining, and has to do with preservation, possession, preserving and obtaining. This particular word has everything to do with moving forward with our heritage in God, the down payment that Jesus put upon it. In other words, the purchased possession is about our deep abiding Christian heritage that we must preserve, which was obtained by Jesus Christ's life, death, and resurrection.

In his famous letter from the Birmingham Jail written in April of 1963, Rev. Dr. Martin Luther King, Jr., stated concerning moving forward with the heritage of the Church: "There was a time when the church was very powerful. It was during that period that the early Christians rejoiced when they were deemed worthy to suffer for what they believed. In those days the church was not merely a thermometer that recorded the ideas and principles of popular opinion; it was the thermostat that transformed the mores of society. Wherever the early Christians entered a town the power structure got disturbed and immediately sought to convict them for being 'disturbers of the peace' and 'outside agitators.' But they went on with the conviction that they were 'a colony of heaven' and had to obey God rather than man. They were small in number but big in commitment. They were too God-intoxicated to be 'astronomically intimidated.' They brought an end to such ancient evils as infanticide and gladiatorial contests..."

The church must move forward and completely embrace her rich heritage and history such as the blood of the martyrs, the suffering of the early saints, and the slain overcomers in order to be an effectively whole and healthy church serving in this present age. Dr. King went on to write, "We will win our freedom because the sacred heritage of our nation and the eternal will of God are embodied in our echoing demands. One day, the South will know that when these disinherited children of God sat down at lunch counters they were in reality standing up for the best in the American dream and the most sacred values in our Judeo-Christian heritage, and thus, carrying our whole nation back to those great wells of democracy which were dug deep by the founding fathers in the formulation of the Constitution and the Declaration of Independence."

I think of that great song by Charles Wesley:

A charge to keep I have to keep,
A God to glorify,
A never dying soul to save,
And fitted for the sky.

We have a sacred charge to keep.

MOVING FORWARD AND MAKING A DIFFERENCE FOR THE HEART OF THE CHURCH

As we talk about the heritage of the church in reference to this overall theme of the health of the church, that brings us over to this issue of the heart of the church. We really can't tell about the health of the church and the heritage of the church without getting into the heart of the church.

Ephesians 1:17 says, "that the God of our Lord Jesus Christ, the Father of glory, may give unto you the spirit [the spirit, the heart, the very essence] of wisdom and revelation in the knowledge of Him." The church must have a heart, a spirit for hurting humanity, the spirit of wisdom that the Apostle Paul wrote about in his prayer to and for the Ephesian church, to make a lasting difference, to have a positive and progressive impact, to bring about change in order to be a healthy church. So come and join us as we delve into this, as we try to get a better understanding, because just like we need a healthy body, because the body is the temple of God, we need a healthy church. A healthy church is a praying church. When we pray in the Spirit, get into the service, and open our mouths, the power of God will flow powerfully in the service, will shake the place, and will revolutionize the lives of the people. So, in order to have a healthy church, you have to have a healthy spiritual heart.

Proverbs 4:23: "Keep thy heart with all diligence; for out of it are the issues of life."

The Book of Revelation makes it even more overwhelmingly clear that the heart of the church most definitely impacts the overall health of the church.

Revelation 2:23: "And I will kill her children with death; and all the churches shall know that I am he which searcheth the reins and hearts: and I will give unto every one of you according to your works."

That Scripture verse certainly brings a fresh perspective and a sense of urgency to the subject. If there is a spiritual heart attack within the church, if the church goes into spiritual cardiac arrest, then things are shut down, are inoperable, and cannot function or flow. God wants to clear the arteries and the veins of the heart of the church. If anything has collapsed, He wants to reconnect to it so His blood will flow in. The Father, Son, and Holy Ghost want to perform a triple by-pass surgery. So where His covering will flow in, the church can make a difference. God is going to heal churches of heart attacks.

God is going to heal churches of cardiac arrest and raise up a church without a spot or a wrinkle in this last day. This will be done for those who are willing to lean on, depend on, and be covered by the blood of Jesus and know that He will lead, guide, and direct their lives in the right way.

The Apostle John, the author of the Gospel of John, Revelation, 1st, 2nd, and 3rd John, the only one of Jesus' twelve disciples who did not deny nor forsake Him, understood the importance of believers moving forward and making a difference as did Moses, Joshua, Jesus Christ, and the Apostle Paul. The Apostle John encourages us to be faithful in our doings with believers and even with total strangers who are also watching us. Third John 1:6 further states, "Which have borne witness of thy charity before the church: whom if thou bring forward on their journey after a godly sort, thou shalt do well." Yes, we need to bring brothers, sisters, and strangers forward on their journey to come closer to Jesus.

MOVING FORWARD AND MAKING A DIFFERENCE FOR THE HOPE OF THE CHURCH

As we address the serious subject matter of moving forward for the health of the church via the heritage of the church, and the heart of the church, we can't ignore the crucial issue of hope, yes, the blessed hope, the hope of the church.

Psalm 31:24 says: **"Be of good courage, and he shall strengthen your heart, all ye that hope in the LORD."**

In our key Scripture verse for this book, **Ephesians 1:18** says, **"The eyes of your understanding be enlightened that ye may know what is the hope of His calling and what is the riches of the glory of His inheritance in the saints."**

The church must move forward and embrace hope, even in hopeless times, in order to be a healthy church. Romans chapter 5 verse 5 says, **"And hope maketh not ashamed because the love of God is shed abroad in our hearts by the Holy Ghost which is given unto us."**

Our hope has to be built on Jesus Christ. I think of the song "The Solid Rock" by Edward Mote, which goes like this:

My hope is built on nothing less
than Jesus' blood and righteousness,
I dare not trust the sweetest frame
but wholly lean on Jesus' name.

On Christ the solid rock I stand,
all other ground is sinking sand,
all other ground is sinking sand.

So the bottom line is, we have to move forward and learn to look to the hope of the church, which is the Lord Jesus Christ.

Hebrews 6:19 states: **"Which hope we have as an anchor of the soul, both sure and stedfast, and which entereth into that within the veil."**

So we have to move forward and make a difference by praying for our president. We have to move forward and make a difference and also pray for our senators, for our congressmen, for our elected officials, our state governors, our county executives, and our town supervisors and council members, because Christ is the hope of the church and His Word tells us to pray for those in authority that we might live a quiet and a peaceable life. There is still hope. Stay involved. Your voice counts.

Zechariah 9:12 says: **"Turn you to the strong hold, ye prisoners of hope: even to day do I declare that I will render double unto thee."**

So we, the prisoners of hope, must look and move forward to the eternal hope of the church, our strong hold, the Lord and Savior Jesus Christ who can render double for our trouble.

Psalm 43:5 states: **"Why art thou cast down, O my soul? and why art thou disquieted within me? hope in God: for I shall yet praise him, who is the health of my countenance, and my God.**

MOVING FORWARD AND MAKING A DIFFERENCE FOR THE HELP OF THE CHURCH

Then we've got to look at the help of the church. There's not just a heritage of the church; there's not just the heart of the church; there's not just the hope of the church as we look at this bigger issue of moving forward for the health of the church. We need all of these things. But then there's the crucial issue of moving forward for the help of the church.

Ephesians 1:20 says: "Which He wrought in Christ when He raised Him from the dead, and set Him at His own right hand in heavenly places." We have literal, awesome, and powerful help from the right hand in heavenly places for earthly problems. **"I look to the hills from which cometh my help, my help cometh from the Lord."**

The church needs consistent help from heavenly places in order to be a healthy church moving forward, onward, and upward. We so desperately need the awesome presence of the Holy Spirit—the Holy Spirit who is called alongside to help us. When Jesus was on the earth He was our comforter, our advocate, the One called alongside to help us, but now the Holy Spirit is the comforter, our advocate on earth, and Jesus is our advocate in Heaven.

Hebrews 13:6 says: **"So that we may boldly say, The Lord is my helper, and I will not fear what man shall do unto me."**

So we have help in Heaven, and we have help on earth.

God the Father has blessed us with double help. We can triple our trouble and get the victory because we have the help of Christ and we have the help of the Holy Spirit. With access to the Heavenly Father in Jesus name we have triple help.

Hebrews 4:16 tells us: **"Let us therefore come boldly unto the throne of grace, that we may obtain mercy, and find grace to help in time of need."**

MOVING FORWARD AND MAKING A DIFFERENCE WITH THE HEAD OF THE CHURCH

Even when we talk about the moving forward for the health of the church, and as we look at the heritage of the church in this conversation concerning the health of the church, the heritage of the church, the heart of the church, the hope of the church, and the help of the church, that brings us to something that is even of more importance. All these things point to the Head of the church which is Jesus Christ our Lord. Of course, the Head of the church is expressed in the hope of the church. Jesus is the Head of the church and this is the reason why the body of Christ needs to be healthy. This is the reason why the church needs to be healthy because we represent Jesus Christ, and if we represent Him in a sloppy manner then we bring shame to His name.

Ephesians 1:22 states**, "And He put all things under His feet and gave Him to be the head over all things to the church which is His body the fullness of Him that filleth all in all."**

Now, Charles Wesley wrote, Head of thy church triumphant, we joyfully adore thee, till thou appear, thy members here shall sing like those in glory. We lift our hearts and voices with blessed anticipation and cry aloud and give to God the praise of our salvation.

Yes, the church needs the Head of the church, the fullness and the filler of all in all, the Lord and Savior, Jesus Christ Himself in order to be the healthy church. Yes, we can have all of these other things: the heritage of the church, the heart of the church, the help and the hope of the church, but the bottom line is, Jesus is the head of the church.

Colossians 1:18 states**, "And he is the head of the body, the church: who is the beginning, the firstborn from the dead; that in all things he might have the preeminence."**

Jesus deserves that respect, glory, and honor. I think of that song that says:

I need thee every hour most gracious Lord,
no tender voice like thine can peace afford.

I need thee, oh, I need thee,
every hour I need thee
oh, bless me now my Savior,
I come to thee.

This is the type of moving forward and making a difference mentality that we must have, realizing that Christ is the head of the church, and realizing that Christ is the fullness that fills all and all, and when we realize this, we can embrace the message of the health of the church.

Ephesians 5:23 tells us: **"For the husband is the head of the wife, even as Christ is the head of the church: and he is the Saviour of the body."**

God's prescription and remedy for the overall health and total well-being of His church is celebrating the rich heritage of the church, taking proper care of the church, boldly proclaiming the hope of the church, utilizing the help of the church, and of course, serving the Lord and Savior Jesus Christ, who is the head of the church. That prescription and remedy sent from the very throne of God will help us move forward and make a difference in being the healthy church with a lasting impact. Luke hit it on the head concerning the church moving forward with the Head of the church, Jesus Christ, in **Acts 17:28** which declares and decrees, **"For in him we live, and move, and have our being; as certain also of your own poets have said, For we are also his offspring."**

MOVING FORWARD AND MAKING A DIFFERENCE FOR THE HOLINESS OF THE CHURCH

In too many cases, the church is not holy or even whole. This must change. When we look at all of these areas of importance that the church must move forward in daily, the health of the church, the heritage of the church, the heart of the church, the hope of the church, the help of the church, and Jesus Christ as the head of the church, it should birth something within us. It should bring a transformation, a call to commitment, a mindset for change, a real revival, an inner healing, essential wholeness, and a real breakthrough in our lives. The classic Old Testament verse in Chronicles 7:14 hits the nail directly on the head in this discussion of the overall spiritual health of the church and how to get there through holiness, by turning from our wicked ways.

2 Chronicles 7:14:
"If my people, which are called by my name, shall humble themselves, and pray, and seek my face, and turn from their wicked ways; then will I hear from heaven, and will forgive their sin, and will heal their land."

What should the health of the church, the heritage of the church, the heart of the church, the hope of the church, the help of the church, and most of all, Jesus Christ, the Head of the church birth in our life? God said, "Be ye holy because I am holy." And we can be. In order to be a healthy church, we need to be a holy church so that we can follow in Jesus' footsteps. We could speak of the hurt and the hypocrisy of the church, for there is no hurt like church hurt. There is no hurt like being wounded in the house of your own friends. But thank God for Jesus, the Head of the church, who is a wound Healer. Jesus knows how to heal us and make us a healthy and holy church. Without true scriptural Bible-based holiness it is totally impossible to be a healthy church.

We see this in **Hebrews 12:14:**
"Follow peace with all men, and holiness, without which no man shall see the Lord."

We would never move forward and see Jesus Christ, the Head of the church, face-to-face without holiness. This is an extremely important point that can't be ignored. If we do it in the philosophy of me, myself and I we're going to mess it up. Please always remember that holiness and holier than thou are two different things. The Bible clearly encourages believers to be holy, but absolutely speaks out against anyone being holier than thou. God literally hates it, because it is phony. It is absolutely 100% hypocrisy in its purest form. That is the reason many Christians never move forward and make a difference, because they are holier than thou.

Isaiah 65:5 says:
"Which say, Stand by thyself, come not near to me; for I am holier than thou. These are a smoke in my nose, a fire that burneth all the day."

We can't be holy in and of ourselves, but God's Word declares: "Be holy for I am holy." Those who are "holier than thou" stand by themselves and do not stand with God, because they are phony. If we would be truthful, we would admit that the vessel God used to write that famous quote denied Jesus Christ three times and had a major cussing and anger management problem prior to being baptized with the Holy Spirit. This vessel of God was the Apostle Peter. Remember, as long as Peter kept his eyes on Jesus he actually moved forward and walked on water, but as soon as he took his eyes off Jesus he began to sink.

1 Peter 1:16:
"Because it is written, Be ye holy; for I am holy."

If we just move forward and follow Jesus Christ we're going to make it. If we stand alone as an island thinking we are better than everyone else, thinking we are holier than thou, we are in deep trouble. That is unhealthy, that is selfish, because God is a social being. God is not a selfish being.

THE CHURCHES MOVING FORWARD AND MAKING A DIFFERENCE AT THE CONVOY OF HOPE

One of the most powerful examples of the church coming together, crossing all racial, social, and economic barriers, and literally moving forward and making a difference was the Convoy of Hope Long Island at Mitchel Athletic Complex in 2012 after Hurricane Irene and in 2012 after Hurricane Sandy. Being Hurricane Sandy survivors ourselves Brenda and I where supportive of this highly effective outreach. Church volunteers from every denomination and independent congregation were out in full force greeting the long lines of people. The people saw the love of Jesus in full effect as Convoy of Hope volunteers from the local churches prayed for them, washed their feet like Jesus did in the Bible, and gave them a pair of brand new sneakers. As the people moved forward at the Mitchel Field Complex, they received free professional hair cuts from Christians in Action for Christ who were making a difference one hair cut at a time. As the people moved on, they discovered families taking free family portraits and receiving the professional picture the same day. The people received a free meal, live entertainment, help preparing their resumes at the job fair and medical information at the health fair while the children enjoyed the kid's zone. As the people left out they all received a bag of free groceries from church volunteers of all racial and ethnic backgrounds. Yes, it is possible for the church to come together on a massive scale and move forward and make a major difference in the lives of the people.

I think of that song by Kenneth Morris titled, "Christ is All." He said:

Well, I don't possess houses or land
Fine clothes or jewelry, sorrows and cares
In this whole word my life seems to me
But I have a Christ who paid the price
Way back on Cavalry, and oh
He is all, all and all this world to me.

Christ is all
Well, he's everything to me
Don't you know that he's all
Well, just 'ruse the land and see
He's all, he's all, he's all
All and all this world to me.

Part 5

MOVING FORWARD WITH PASSION

CHAPTER TWENTY

MAKING A DIFFERENCE BY HOW WE WALK, STAND, AND SIT – MOVING FORWARD INSPITE OF NEGATIVITY

Psalm 1:1: Blessed is the man that walketh not in the counsel of the ungodly, nor standeth in the way of sinners, nor sitteth in the seat of the scornful.

Blessed and highly favored is the positive and progressive person in God's will who moves forward and does not walk according to faulty advice. Blessed and highly favored is the positive and progressive person in God's will who moves forward and does not walk according to extremely poor guidance that totally eliminates God's perspective from the entire picture. This positive and progressive person is on the move for God. We must all examine ourselves by looking deeply inward and asking ourselves, Are you a man on the move for God? Are you a woman on the move for God?

Blessed and highly favored is the positive and progressive person in God's will that does not stand in the unhealthy lifestyle of sin. Sin means to miss the mark. The wages of sin is always death via demonic deception. This positive and progressive person does not stand in the unhealthy lifestyle of sin and is on the move for God. We must all examine ourselves by looking deeply inward and asking ourselves, Are you a man on the move for God? Are you a woman on the move for God? We move forward and make a difference by how we walk, stand, and sit every single day. Nelson Mandela was right when he stated that, "Where you stand depends on where you sit." We move forward and make a difference by watching who we spend our time with.

Blessed and highly favored is the positive and progressive person in God's will who does not sit in the dangerous seat of haters, discriminators, and deadly eliminators. This positive and progressive person is on the move for God. We must all examine ourselves by looking deeply inward and asking ourselves, Are you a man on the move for God? Are you a woman on the move for God? We move forward and make a difference by how we walk, stand, and sit every single day. We move forward and make a difference by watching who we spend our time with.

DIANE ROBINSON, THE TERRIFIC TEACHER, THE TALENTED TUTOR, AND THE TIMELESS TROUBLE SHOOTER

Diane Robinson moved forward and made a major difference as a local Roosevelt High School graduate in 1974. Diane Robinson moved forward and received her undergraduate degree from Florida A&M in Tallahassee, and she continued to move forward and obtained her Master's degree from Marquette University in Milwaukee. Diane returned home and made a major difference as a 31-year veteran high school teacher in Roosevelt. She died of a heart attack recently at Mercy Medical Center in Rockville Centre at the young age of 58. Five meaning the number of grace and eight meaning a new day. I presided over her funeral and preached the eulogy at Mount Sinai

Baptist Church Cathedral in Roosevelt, New York. Diane Robinson moved forward with a positive and progressive passion to teach and reach the poor, the economically oppressed, and the underprivileged.

Thank God for the positive and progressive teachers and youth center volunteers like my Roosevelt High School History Teacher, the late, the great, Diane Robinson, who moved forward daily and made a difference by staying divinely committed to educating the despised, disinherited, and downtrodden. The terrific teacher, the talented tutor, and the timeless trouble shooter % they're the true heroes and heroines who move forward and make a major difference every day by educating the poor, the economically oppressed, and the underprivileged.

Thank God for the positive and progressive teachers and youth center volunteers who moved forward daily and made a difference by staying divinely committed to teaching, reaching, and preaching truth to power by continuing to enlighten, enrich, and empower the broken, the battered, and the bruised. Former U.S. President Jimmy Carter once stated that, "I have one life and one chance to make it count for something... My faith demands that I do whatever I can, wherever I am, whenever I can, for as long as I can with whatever I have to try to make a difference."

MOVING FORWARD THROUGH MEDITATION

Psalm 1:2: But his delight is in the law of the Lord; and in his law doth he meditate day and night.

This positive and progressive person's greatest joy is in the Word of

God, because it proclaims the will of God. Like a cow chewing on its cud, this person swallows it and brings it up, only to chew the cud again and again. This is how the positive and progressive person in the will of God constantly meditates on God's Word in the brightest day and in the darkest night. Godly advice moves forward from daily meditation on the Word of God and through actually practicing those living principles. The best way to move forward in finding out who we are in Christ, and what rightfully belongs to us as believers is through meditation on the Word. Meditation is a time to be quiet and let the Holy Spirit move and minister to your heart through the Scripture. Meditation is the continual study of the Bible. Meditation means those precious moments of pondering, thinking about, and studying the Bible. Words that once were meaningless come to life through quiet time and prayer. Without meditation on God's Word, it is impossible to grow spiritually. This positive and progressive person who meditates day and night on the Word of God is on the move for God. We must all examine ourselves by looking deeply inward and asking ourselves, are you a man on the move for God? Are you a woman on the move for God? We move forward and make a difference by how we walk, stand, and sit every single day. We move forward and make a difference by watching who we spend our time with.

WHEN THE ROOTS AND THE RIVERS COME TOGETHER

Psalm 1:3: And he shall be like a tree planted by the rivers of water, that bringeth forth his fruit in his season; his leaf also shall not wither; and whatsoever he doeth shall prosper.

This positive and progressive person in God's will is just like a tree planted by the rivers of water. Under the anointing of the Holy

Spirit, the psalmist David, in the first psalm, painted a vivid picture of a believer who is fixed firmly by a mighty rushing stream of water. Trees are important to the environment because trees add oxygen to the air and help purify it. Believers are called by the Creator to be like a tree and help to purify the sinful environment in which we live. The tree's deepest roots have resolved to reach the deep rushing waters by any means necessary in order to live. The roots and the rivers of water must come together to save the trees. The roots and the rivers of water must come together to rescue and revive the righteous. The roots and the rivers of water must come together to nourish the babes in Christ so they won't spiritually die. This positive and progressive person in the will of God is on the move for God. We must all examine ourselves by looking deeply inward and asking ourselves, Are you a man on the move for God? Are you a woman on the move for God? We move forward and make a difference by how we walk, stand, and sit every single day. We move forward and make a difference by watching who we spend our time with.

THE UNGODLY & UNREPENTANT HATER, DISCRIMINATOR, AND DEADLY ELIMINATOR

Psalm 1:4: The ungodly are not so: but are like the chaff which the wind driveth away.

The ungodly, the spiritual terrorist, and the unholy hater is just like the dried up chaff on a dead tree whose roots never reached the rivers of water. The contrast revealed here is extremely powerful. The ungodly are literally compared to dry and dead chaff of plants without roots. The wind gusts blow the chaff away. The ungodly and unrepentant hater, discriminator, and deadly eliminator are on the move for the wrong cause and will be driven away by the wind of time.

Psalm 1:5: Therefore the ungodly shall not stand in the judgment, nor sinners in the congregation of the righteous.

The ungodly, the spiritual terrorist, and the unholy hater cannot stand before God in the judgment because they did not stand up for Jesus when they had the chance, they did not repent when they had a chance, they did not stand up for truth when they had the chance. If you did not roll righteously down here on earth or even at least truly repent during your very last breathe on earth, then you will not roll righteously in Heaven. True righteousness is only found in Jesus Christ. The unrepentant hater, discriminator, and deadly eliminator are on the move for the wrong cause.

Psalm 1:6: "For the Lord knoweth the way of the righteous: but the way of the ungodly shall perish."

For the Lord who searches the reins of the hearts knows beyond a shadow of a doubt who is really righteous and who is all about mere outward show and possesses no inward Christ-centered growth. The destructive way of the ungodly, the deadly way of the spiritual terrorist, and the deceptive way of the unholy hater will utterly perish because it has no long-term Christ-centered vision to move forward and make a positive and progressive difference. The unrepentant hater, discriminator, and deadly eliminator are on the move for the wrong cause.

The ungodly, the spiritual terrorist, and the unholy hater are always connected to death and destruction because the true love of Christ was totally left out of the picture. The dangerous haters, demonic discriminators, and deadly eliminators are on the move for the wrong cause. We must fight for the souls of communities. We must take action now and move forward and make a difference. We move forward and make a difference by how we walk, stand, and sit every single day. We move forward and make a difference by watching who we spend our time with. Too many people are spending their time with the wrong, violent people and taking innocent lives.

THE SENSELESS KILLING OF 15-YEAR-OLD HADIYA PENDLETON

The tragic death of the young, black, bright, and beautiful 15-year-old girl from Chicago, Illinois, Hadiya Pendleton, happened on January 29, 2013. Pendleton was shot in her back and killed while she was innocently standing with her friends at Harsh Park in Chicago after finishing her final exams at school. Hadiya Pendleton was a student at King College Prep High School. Hadiya Pendleton was killed only one week after she had performed for President Barack Obama's second inauguration celebration event. Our hearts and souls deeply mourned as our First Lady Michelle Obama attended the funeral for Hadiya Pendleton in Chicago, Illinois. First Lady Michelle Obama clearly saw herself in Hadiya Pendleton. Gang members literally kill, steal, and destroy our children and our communities by being deeply deceived by the devil. We must take action now and move forward and make a difference by caring, sharing, and bearing the burdens of the massive multitude of our hurting humanity.

THE BOSTON MARATHON BOMBING

The Boston Marathon Bombing on Patriot's Day, April 15, 2013, occurred when two pressure cooker bombs exploded, near the finish

 line stealing, killing, and destroying the lives of three precious and innocent people: 8-year-old Martin Richard (who had just hugged his father after he crossed the finish line); 29-year-old Krystle Campbell, a restaurant worker; and 23-year-old Lingzi Lu, a Boston University graduate student and Chinese national.

The bombs injuring almost 200 more precious and innocent individuals. The deadly bombs had been placed near the world renowned Boston Marathon finish line along Boylston Street. The bombs exploded at 2:49 p.m. The twin deadly explosions were twelve seconds apart. Boston faced the deep darkness of despair head on in their hour of personal and public pain as the whole world watched in horror. Yet, the police, firemen, physicians, nurses, EMS workers, volunteers, and many other modern day Good Samaritans moved forward and made a difference as first responders who medically cared, shared, and bore the burdens of a broken, battered, and bruised humanity in Boston. Many terrorists have been taught that they are on the move for God, but they are not for terrorists literally kill, steal, and destroy by being deeply deceived by the devil. We must take action now and move forward and make a difference by caring, sharing, and bearing the burdens of the massive multitude of our hurting humanity.

THE WEST TEXAS FERTILIZER PLANT EXPLOSION

On April 17, 2013, the West Texas Fertilizer Plant Explosion occurred about twenty miles away from Waco, Texas at 7:50 p.m. 2,600 residents were forced to evacuate. 75 homes were damaged from the explosion. A 50-unit apartment building was destroyed by the explosion. The blast area resembled a war zone. Many people said that the blast resembled a nuclear explosion. The first responders moved forward towards the fire in spite of the pain and possibility of losing their lives. We must take action now and move forward and make a difference by caring, sharing, and bearing the burdens of the massive multitude of our hurting humanity.

RICIN LACED LETTERS SENT TO SENATOR AND PRESIDENT

A lethal ricin laced letter was sent to Mississippi Senator Roger Wicker and United States President Barack Obama. On April 16, 2013, an envelope that preliminarily tested positive for the deadly substance known as ricin was intercepted at the U.S. Capitol's off-site mail facility in Washington, D.C. According to reports, the envelope was addressed to the office of United States Senator Roger Wicker, a Republican from Mississippi.

On the very next day, April 17, 2013, an envelope was addressed to United States President Barack Obama and it also preliminarily tested positive for the deadly substance known as ricin. Both of these letters were mailed from Memphis, Tennessee and both letters contained the statements: "to see a wrong and not expose it, is to become a silent partner to its continuance" and "I am KC and I approve this message." This was an act of bioterrorism and an attempted assassination through poisoning. Thank God it did not succeed. We must take action now and move forward and make a difference by caring, sharing, and bearing the burdens of the massive multitude of our hurting humanity.

MASS SHOOTING AT SANDY HOOK SCHOOL

On December 14, 2012, twenty-year-old Adam Lanza fatally shot twenty precious innocent children and six innocent adult school staff members in a mass murder at Sandy Hook Elementary School in Newtown, Connecticut. Prior to the Sandy Hook School shooting, Lanza had fatally shot and murdered his own mother, Nancy, at their home on in Newtown, Connecticut. When first responders moved forward on the scene of the mass shooting at Sandy Hook, Adam Lanza committed suicide as he shot himself in the head. Many terrorists have been taught that they are on the move for God, but they are not for terrorists literally kill, steal, and destroy by being deeply deceived by the thief, that old serpent. We must take action now and move forward and make a difference by caring, sharing, and bearing the burdens of the massive multitude of our hurting humanity.

MOVING FORWARD INSPITE OF NEGATIVITY

- In spite of the increase of violent gun use, we will move forward.
- In spite of the increase in crime, we will move forward.
- In spite of the rapid spread of drugs, we will move forward.
- In spite of the pain of peer pressure, we will move forward.
- In spite of violent gangs, we will move forward.
- In spite of the budget deficit, we will move forward.
- In spite of poor economic conditions, we will move forward.
- In spite of racial hatred and strife, we will move forward.

- In spite of abortion and AIDS, we will move forward.

We will still move forward and let the whole world know that there is hope for the hopeless. Yes there is hope even in the valley of decision. John 10:10 says, "The thief cometh not, but for to steal, and to kill, and to destroy: I am come that they might have life, and that they might have it more abundantly."

Now the powerful passage of Scripture in John 10:10 clearly shows us that the devil is doing his job as the leader of a massive worldwide terrorism movement that literally steals, kills, and destroys the lives of innocent individuals as clearly stated in the holy writ.

Now if satan, lucifer, the devil is strategically doing his job non-stop every single day, 24/7 around the clock, then concerned Christians, blood-washed believers in our Wounded Healer, the Lord and Savior, Jesus Christ, and all people of good will worldwide must positively and progressively move forward strategically, and make a major difference by being proactive and not only reactive on a consistent, non-stop basis every single day, 24/7 around the clock. Intercessory prayer meetings, rap sessions, and informative community town hall meetings need to be done in a positive, progressive, and proactive manner before a disaster hits. Powerfully pray before the problem hits and receive the righteous resolve to move forward and make a difference. Righteously rap long before the crap hits and receive the righteous resolve to move forward and make a difference. Clearly communicate before the unholy hate hits and receive the righteous resolve to move forward and make a difference. Speak long before the lethal leak catches on fire and receive the righteous resolve to move forward and make a difference. We move forward and make a difference by how we walk, stand, and sit every single day. We move forward and make a difference by watching who we spend our time with.

THE SEVENFOLD VISION FOR THE CHURCH TO MOVE FORWARD

1.) Worshiping Church - Receive the righteous resolve to move forward and make a major difference by becoming the worshiping church according to I Chronicles 16:29.

1 Chronicles 16:29: Give unto the Lord the glory due unto his name: bring an offering, and come before him: worship the Lord in the beauty of holiness.

2.) Word Church - Receive the righteous resolve to move forward and make a major difference by becoming the word church according to Psalm 119:11.

Psalm 119:11: Thy word have I hid in mine heart, that I might not sin against thee.

3.) Warrior Church - Receive the righteous resolve to move forward and make a major difference by becoming the warrior church according to 2 Corinthians 10:4.

2 Corinthians 10:4: (For the weapons of our warfare are not carnal, but mighty through God to the pulling down of strong holds.)

4.) Witnessing Church - Receive the righteous resolve to move forward and make a major difference by becoming the witnessing church according to Proverbs 14:25.

Proverbs 14:25: A true witness delivereth souls: but a deceitful witness speaketh lies.

5.) Working Church - Receive the righteous resolve to move forward and make a major difference by becoming the working church according to John 9:4.

John 9:4: I must work the works of him that sent me, while it is day: the night cometh, when no man can work.

6.) Wisdom Church - Receive the righteous resolve to move forward and make a major difference by becoming the wisdom church according to Psalm 111:10.

Psalm 111:10: The fear of the Lord is the beginning of wisdom: a good understanding have all they that do his commandments: his praise endureth for ever.

7.) Whole Church - Receive the righteous resolve to move forward and make a major difference by becoming the whole church according to I Thessalonians 5:23.

1 Thessalonians 5:23: And the very God of peace sanctify you wholly; and I pray God your whole spirit and soul and body be preserved blameless unto the coming of our Lord Jesus Christ.

MOVE FORWARD AND EMBRACE YOUR DELIVERENCE FROM SLAVERY

Exodus 14:13-16: "And Moses said unto the people, Fear ye not, stand still, and see the salvation of the Lord, which he will shew to you to day: for the Egyptians whom ye have seen to day, ye shall see them again no more for ever. The Lord shall fight for you, and ye shall hold your peace. And the Lord said unto Moses, Wherefore criest thou unto me? speak unto the children of Israel, that they <u>go forward</u>: But lift thou up thy rod, and stretch out thine hand over the sea, and divide it: and the children of Israel shall go on dry ground through the midst of the sea."

- Move forward and embrace our new season.
- Move forward and embrace our deliverance from the brutal bondage of seemingly endless enslavement.
- Move forward and embrace our deliverance from the brutal bondage of the slave mentality.
- Move forward and embrace our Jesus as Savior.

Matthew 1:21: "And she shall bring forth a son, and thou shalt call his name Jesus: for he shall save his people from their sins."

Move forward and embrace our Jesus as Lord.

Acts 2:36: "Therefore let all the house of Israel know assuredly, that God hath made the same Jesus, whom ye have crucified, both Lord and Christ."

- Move forward and embrace our Jesus as the Baptizer with the Holy Ghost.

Matthew 3:11: "I indeed baptize you with water unto repentance. but he that cometh after me is mightier than I, whose shoes I am not worthy to bear: he shall baptize you with the Holy Ghost, and with fire."

- Move forward and embrace our Jesus' name as Wonderful, Counselor, The Mighty God, The Everlasting Father, and The Prince of Peace.

- Move forward and embrace the government of God.

Isaiah 9:6-7:

"For unto us a child is born, unto us a son is given: and the government shall be upon his shoulder: and his name shall be called Wonderful, Counsellor, The mighty God, The everlasting Father, The Prince of Peace. Of the increase of his government and peace there shall be no end, upon the throne of David, and upon his kingdom, to order it, and to establish it with judgment and with justice from henceforth even for ever. The zeal of the Lord of hosts will perform this."

- Move forward and embrace His increase.

John 3:30: "He must increase, but I must decrease."

Luke 2:52: "And Jesus increased in wisdom and stature, and in favour with God and man."

1 Corinthians 3:6: "I have planted, Apollos watered; but God gave the increase."

- Move forward and embrace the kingdom of God.

Acts 14:22: "Confirming the souls of the disciples, and exhorting them to continue in the faith, and that we must through much tribulation enter into the kingdom of God."

We must all examine ourselves by looking deeply inward and asking ourselves, Are you a man on the move for God? Are you a woman on the move for God? We move forward and make a difference by how we walk, stand, and sit every single day. We move forward and make a difference by watching who we spend our time with.

Exodus 14:13-16 gives us some highly critical and extremely crucial information to utilize in this journey called life filled with great peer pressure, gangster style drive by shootings, mass murders, and terrorist activities in the homeland and abroad. At this point in his life, Moses decided not to walk in the council of the ungodly. First of all, this wise statement spoken by **Moses, "Fear ye not, stand still, and see the salvation of the Lord"** is extremely important, because this makes a direct crystal clear connection between Moses' "stand still" statement, and God's moving forward and making a difference strategy. Red seas are only divided when you stand still and hear directly from God and speak to the people, speak to the nation, speak to the business, speak to the church, speak to the family concerning moving forward from a long dreadful and demoralizing life of deep bondage. This makes a direct connection between the "I Shall Not Be Moved" non-violent strategy, and birthing a God ordained movement like the Civil Rights Movement, that most clearly moves forward boldly fighting for equality, freedom, and justice.

- Positively and progressively proclaiming, "I shall not be moved, I will not take drugs," and you take crystal clear corresponding action by not taking highly addictive drugs, the dope, the crack, the cocaine, and/or your favorite get high choice ever again, that is the act of literally birthing a drug free movement both in word and deed.

- Positively and progressively proclaiming, "I shall not be moved, I will not be violently controlled by hate," and you take crystal clear corresponding action by eliminating the spirit of hate forever in your life, that is the act of literally of birthing a hate free movement both in word and deed.

- Positively and progressively proclaiming, "I shall not be moved, I will not be in the gang," and you take crystal clear corresponding action by staying out of the gang forever, that is the act of literally birthing an anti gang violence movement both in word and deed.

Pure, plain, and simple we must always move forward with the strategy of the 4P's of prayer, planning, patience, and persistence. We must all examine ourselves by looking deeply inward and asking ourselves, Am I a man on the move for God? Am I a woman on the move for God? We move forward and make a difference by how we walk, stand, and sit every single day. We move forward and make a difference by watching who we spend our time with.

CHAPTER TWENTY-ONE

MOVING FORWARD IN OPERATION EVANGELISM

EQUIPPING THE CHURCH TO CARRY OUT CHRIST'S COMMISSION

Matthew 28:18-20 (King James Version):
"And Jesus came and spake unto them, saying, All power is given unto me in heaven and in earth. Go ye therefore, and teach all nations, baptizing them in the name of the Father, and of the Son, and of the Holy Ghost: Teaching them to observe all things whatsoever I have commanded you: and, lo, I am with you always, even unto the end of the world. Amen."

DEFINITION OF EVANGELISM

1.) The winning or revival of personal commitments to Christ

1.) Mission Get Away, a.k.a., Steal Away to Jesus - If you're gonna stay, you must get away. One must spend time with Jesus in order to effectively evangelize. Don't miss your appointment with Jesus.

Matthew 28:16: "Then the eleven disciples went away into Galilee, into a mountain where Jesus had appointed them."

2.) MOVING FORWARD IN MISSION WORSHIP -- WORSHIP DESTROYS THE DOUBT

Matthew 28:17: "And when they saw him, they worshipped him:

but some doubted."

We know historically that true worship destroys the doubt because the large majority of Jesus' original disciples died as martyrs for the cause of Christ. Ten out of twelve disciples all died as martyrs for the cause of Christ. Their true worship destroys doubt.

7 WORDS OF WORSHIP

1. YADAH - ידא

Definition: *Yadah* is a verb with a root meaning, "the extended hand, to throw out the hand, therefore to worship with extended hand." According to the Lexicon, the opposite meaning is, "to bemoan, the wringing of hands."

Example: **Psalm 63:4: "Thus I will bless Thee while I live, I will (YADAH) lift up my hands in Thy name."**

2. TOWDAH - תודא

Definition: *Towdah* comes from the same principal root word as Yadah but is used more specifically. Towdah literally means, "an extension of the hand in adoration, avowal, or acceptance." By way of application, it is apparent in the Psalms and elsewhere that it is used for thanking God for "things not yet received" as well as things already at hand.

Example: **Psalm 50:14: "Offer unto God praise (TOWDAH) and pay thy vows unto the Most High."**

"What I want from you is your true thanks. I want your promises fulfilled."

3. HALAL - حلال

Definition: *Halal* is a primary Hebrew word for praise. Our word "hallelujah" comes from this base. It means, "to be clear, to shine, to boast, to show, to rave, to celebrate, to be clamorously foolish."

Example: Psalm 113:1: "Praise (HALAL) ye the Lord, Praise (HALAL) O ye servants of the Lord, praise (HALAL) the name of the Lord."

4. SHABACH - شباخ

Definition: *Shabach* means, "to address in a loud tone, to commend, to triumph, to exclaim, glory, shout."

Example: **Psalm 145:4: "One generation shall praise (SHABACH) thy works to another and declare Thy mighty acts."**

5. BARAK - براك

Definition: *Barak* means, "to kneel down, to bless God as an act of adoration." When used in the Scripture it implies, "expecting to receive a blessing from the Lord."

Example: Psalm 95:6: "O come let us worship and bow down; let us kneel (BARAK) before the Lord our maker."

"Come let us throw ourselves at His feet in homage." [NEB] "Let us bend the knee in the presence of Jehovah our Creator." [Spurrel]

6. ZAMAR - ذمار

Definition: *Zamar* means, "to touch the strings" and is used concordantly with instrumental worship. Psalm 150 is a perfect example of this kind of praise. David said, "Awake my glory; awake harp and lyre, I will awaken the dawn!"

"I will give thanks to Thee, O Lord, among the peoples; I will sing praises (ZAMAR) to Thee among the nations."

Example: Psalm 21:13: "Be Thou exalted O Lord, in Thine own strength, so will we sing and praise (ZAMAR) Thy power." "We sing and strike the harp to Thy power." [DeWitt] "With song and with string we will sound forth Thy power." [RHM]

7. TEHILLAH - تحيلا

Definition: *Tehillah* simply means, "to sing, to laud." "God is enthroned on the praises (TEHILLAH) of Israel" (Psalm 22:3). This is the kind of praise that God dwells in. Any form of singing can be praise, but one of the higher forms was the Dorean mode which was neither western major nor oriental minor. It was sort of chanting whereby the words of HALAL were melodiously chanted. This is the expression of praise the Psalmist said God inhabited.

Examples: Psalm 33:1: "Rejoice in the Lord, O ye righteous; for praise (TEHILLAH) is comely for the upright."

Psalm 34:1: "...His praise (TEHILLAH) shall continually be

in my mouth."

3.) MOVING FORWARD IN MISSION - Matthew 28:18: "And Jesus came and spake unto them, saying, All power is given unto me in heaven and in earth."

Jesus came and said He has "all power" in Heaven and on earth. Operation Evangelism only works effectively when we listen to Jesus. Jesus has a very specific assignment for us. To move forward with a positive and progressive passion to teach and reach the broken, the battered, and the bruised with the Gospel of Jesus Christ.

4.) MOVING FORWARD IN MISSION TEACHES & REACHES - Matthew 28:19: "Go ye therefore, and teach all nations, baptizing them in the name of the Father, and of the Son, and of the Holy Ghost."

Two thirds of God's name is GO. Operation Evangelism as spoken by Jesus requires us to "Go." If you don't go you won't grow, so go and grow. Teach all nationalities, cultures, and races of people. Reach out and baptize them in the name of the Father -- He is a father to the fatherless; in the name of the Son -- He is a friend that sticketh closer than a brother; in the name of the Holy Ghost -- He is the Comforter Who will lead and guide you into all truth.

5.) MOVING FORWARD IN MISSION EQUIPS - Matthew 28:20: "Teaching them to observe all things whatsoever I have commanded you: and, lo, I am with you always, even unto the end of the world. Amen."

Teach to observe. Watch as well as pray. Be observant concerning the commands of Christ. Christians can get lonely, but thank God we are never alone. Christ is with us always, even to the end of the age. To move forward with a positive and progressive passion to teach and reach the broken, the battered, and the bruised with the Gospel of Jesus Christ.

6.) MOVING FORWARD IN MISSION EVANGELISTIC EMPOWERMENT

Acts 1:8: "But you will receive power when the Holy Spirit comes on you; and you will be my witnesses in Jerusalem, and in all Judea and Samaria, and to the ends of the earth."

The power for Operation Evangelism only is received when the Holy Spirit comes on you. True witnessing always starts at home and then spreads abroad. One cannot reach the ends of the earth without caring and sharing first in their own Jerusalem.

7.) MOVING FORWARD IN MISSION EVANGELISTIC ENLIGHTENMENT

Proverbs 11:30: "The fruit of the righteous is a tree of life; and he that winneth souls is wise."

DEFINITION OF EVANGELISM:

1. The winning or revival of personal commitments to Christ
2. Militant or crusading zeal

DETAILED OUTLINE OF THE BOOK OF ACTS BASED ON ACTS 1:8

1. Sharing the Gospel, Operation Evangelism in Jerusalem (Acts 1:12-8:3)
2. Sharing the Gospel, Operation Evangelism throughout Palestine (Acts 8:4-11:18)
   a. Caring and Sharing the Gospel, Operation Evangelism In Samaria

    b. Caring and Sharing the Gospel, Operation Evangelism In Judea
 3. Sharing the Gospel, Operation Evangelism to the Gentile World (Acts 11:19-21:14) Antioch, Syria
 4. Sharing the Gospel, Operation Evangelism to Rome (Acts 21:15-28:31)

GENERAL OUTLINE OF THE BOOK OF ACTS:

A. Caring and Sharing the Gospel, Operation Evangelism in Jerusalem: Evangelistic Origins (Acts 1-7)
B. Caring and Sharing the Gospel, Operation Evangelism in Samaria and Judea: Evangelistic Transition (Acts 8-10)
C. Caring and Sharing the Gospel, Operation Evangelism in the Uttermost Parts: Evangelistic Expansion (Acts 11-28)

8.) MOVING FORWARD IN MISSION EVANGELISTIC ENCOURAGEMENT

Acts 4:36: "And Joses, who by the apostles was surnamed Barnabas, (which is, being interpreted, The son of consolation,) a Levite, and of the country of Cyprus."

Deuteronomy 1:38:
"But Joshua the son of Nun, which standeth before thee, he shall go in thither: encourage him: for he shall cause Israel to inherit it."

Deuteronomy 3:28:
"But charge Joshua, and encourage him, and strengthen him: for he shall go over before this people, and he shall cause them to inherit the land which thou shalt see."

Judges 20:22:
"And the people the men of Israel encouraged themselves, and set their battle again in array in the place where they put themselves in array the first day."

1 Samuel 30:6:
"And David was greatly distressed; for the people spake of stoning him, because the soul of all the people was grieved, every man for his sons and for his daughters: but David encouraged himself in the LORD his God."

Be equipped, empowered, enlightened, and encouraged for moving forward in operation evangelism. To move forward with a positive and progressive passion to teach and reach the broken, the battered, and the bruised with the Gospel of Jesus Christ.

Move Forward & Make A Difference: Win Souls to Christ

I love the hymn "Lift Him Up" written by Johnson Oatman, Jr. It goes like this:

Stanza 1:
How to reach the masses, men of every birth,
For an answer, Jesus gave the key:
"And I, if I be lifted up from the earth,
Will draw all men unto Me."

Refrain:
Lift Him up, Lift Him up,
Still He speaks from eternity:
"And I, if I be lifted up from the earth,
Will draw all men unto Me."

Stanza 2:
Oh! the world is hungry for the Living Bread,
Lift the Savior up for them to see;
Trust Him, and do not doubt the words that He said,
"I'll draw all men unto Me."

Refrain:
Lift Him up, Lift Him up,
Still He speaks from eternity:
"And I, if I be lifted up from the earth,
Will draw all men unto Me."

- Lift Him up!
- Lift Jesus up!
- Move forward and make a difference: Win souls to Christ.
- Move forward and make a difference: Clothe the naked.
- Move forward and make a difference: Rescue the perishing.
- Move forward and make a difference: Care for the dying.
- Move forward and make a difference: Feed the hungry.
- Move forward and make a difference: Love, care, share, and bear the burdens of the broken, battered, and bruised.

CHAPTER TWENTY-TWO

THE FORWARD JOURNEY – LEARNING FROM THE ELDER, THE ENCOURAGER, THE EGO MANIAC, AND THE EXCELLENT EXAMPLE

3 John 1:6: "Which have borne witness of thy charity before the church: whom if thou <u>bring forward on their journey</u> after a godly sort, thou shalt do well:"

A.) THE FORWARD JOURNEY AS AN ENCOURAGING EXHORTER

1.) REMEMBER TO ENCOURAGE THE ENCOURAGER - The Forward Journey teaches us to remember the wise lover of the truth, Gaius. Exhort the exhorter of truth. Encourage the encourager of truth. The Forward Journey teaches us through the text about appreciating the encouraging exhorter of truth, Gaius, whose name means "rejoice."

3 John 1:1: "The elder unto the well beloved Gaius, whom I love in the truth." Today we should also be on the forward journey to show our deep appreciation for those faithful leaders, movers and shakers, who we love in the truth. The Apostle John, the Elder, the cousin of John the Baptist, the disciple whom Jesus loved, the only disciple to stayed with Jesus until He died on the cross, clearly identifies himself as "The elder." John, who personally took care of Jesus' mother Mary until the day she died, writes to his highly regarded and deeply respected friend Gaius to clearly commend him for welcoming the missionaries on the move with open arms and to discuss in detail with Gaius the troubling state of the church of which Gaius is a faithful member. The Apostle, the Elder, John prays for the total well-being of Gaius in three dimensions of life which is most moving in this epistle.

2.) **PUSH FORTH ON THE FORWARD JOURNEY IN THREE DIMENSIONS** -- Forward Journey teaches us to be truly concerned about the financial and physical well-being of others. Gaius, the encouraging exhorter, clearly had a prosperous soul. Yet John yearned that the Elder Gaius' financial status and health would move forward in reaching the great heights of his soul's deepest blessings and benefits. **"Beloved, I wish above all things that thou mayest prosper and be in health, even as thy soul prospereth."**

  A.) Push forth on the forward journey spiritually
  B.) Push forth on the forward journey physically
  C.) Push forth on the forward journey financially

3.) **THE TESTIMONY OF TRUTH** --The Forward Journey exhorts us too truly rejoice over the testimony of truth. There are way to many testimonies of lies. Not only was the truth in the encouraging exhorter, Gaius, but he walked in the truth. Gaius preached and taught the truth, but more importantly he lived it daily. For that cause John, the writer of St. John, 1st John, 2nd John, and 3rd John, as well as the Book of Revelation, greatly rejoiced. **"For I rejoiced greatly, when the brethren came and testified of the truth that is in thee, even as thou walkest in the truth.."**

4.) **MOVING FORWARD TO BE JOYFUL ABOUT SOMEONE ELSE OTHER THAN YOURSELF--** The Forward Journey teaches us the joy of hearing our seed, our children walk in truth. We should have no greater joy in this forward journey than hearing that the next generation is walking in truth. That is a most worthy cause absolutely worth giving one's life for. **"I have no greater joy than to hear that my children walk in truth."**

5.) **TREAT PEOPLE RIGHT**--The Forward Journey encourages us to faithfully treat people right. **Hebrews 13:2** states, **"Be not forgetful to entertain strangers: for thereby some have entertained angels unawares."** Whether a well known fellow believer, or a total stranger who got saved in the street-- faithfully treat people right. **"Beloved, thou doest faithfully whatsoever thou doest to the brethren, and to strangers."**

6.) **DO WELL WITH OUR WITNESS** -- The Forward Journey exhorts us to do well with our witness. Are ordinary people bearing witness of extraordinary love in our lives? Are we bringing people on the forward journey after a godly manner? How well is our witness? We must bring babes in Christ forward and not backwards on their journey in Jesus. **"Which have borne witness of thy charity before the church: whom if thou bring forward on their journey after a godly sort, thou shalt do well..."**

7.) **BE A MISSIONARY ON THE MOVE** -- The Forward Journey encourages us to be missionaries on the move for the Master. We go forth as witnesses for the Word for His name's sake. We go forth as positive and progressive missionaries on the move for His name's sake. We help the helpless for Christ Jesus name's sake. **"Because that for his name's sake they went forth, taking nothing of the Gentiles.**

8.) **BE A FELLOWHELPER TO THE TRUTH** --The Forward Journey exhorts us to be Fellowhelpers to the truth. True fellowhelpers of the truth ought to receive true missionaries on the move to support this forward journey for the cause of Christ. Help the mission minded bearers of truth; don't hurt the bearers of truth. "We therefore ought to receive such, that we might be fellowhelpers to the truth."

B.) DON'T TRAVEL THE BACKWARDS JOURNEY OF THE EGO MANAIC
3 John 1:9-11

DON'T LET EGOTISTICAL FOLK BRING YOU BACKWARDS -- The Apostle John wrote to the church: but an evil ego maniac, named, Diotrephes, who loved to have the preeminence, all the praise himself in the church, did not receive the Apostle John and the brothers in Christ with open arms. He was clearly threatened by the truth.

The genuine concern that should exist between blood washed believers had been destroyed by the evil actions of Diotrephes, who absolutely abused his position in the local church by rebelling against and totally resisting the ministering missionaries on the move for the Master. **Don't Travel The Backwards Journey of The Ego Maniac.**

DON'T LET SLANDER BRING YOU BACKWARDS -- The Apostle John, the Elder, knew if he came, he would remember the ego maniac, named, Diotrephe and his deeds which he did, prating against the believers with malicious words. The ego maniac was not being content with receiving the brothers in Christ himself, and forbidding, threatening those that would by casting them out of the church. **Don't Travel The Backwards Journey of The Ego Maniac.**

DON'T LET EVIL BRING YOU BACKWARDS -- John, the Elder, emphasized that the beloved, follow not that which is evil, but keep moving forward, follow that which is good. He that does good is of God: but he that does evil has not seen God. **Don't Travel The Backwards Journey of The Ego Maniac.**

Like the song says,

> *I'm not going back, I'm moving ahead.*
> *Here to declare to You my past is over in You,*
> *All things are made new, surrendered my life to Christ.*
> *I'm moving, moving forward*

C.) TRAVEL THE FORWARD JOURNEY OF THE EXCELLENT EXAMPLE
3 John 1:12-14

LET OUR LIVES PRODUCE A GOOD REPORT CONSISTENTLY -- The Apostle John clearly saw Demetrius as an excellent example who had a good report of all men. John and his brothers in Christ knew the truth itself, yes, indeed, and they bore record for the record was true. **Travel The Forward Journey of The Excellent Example**

DON'T EVER LET THERE BE ENOUGH INK, PEN AND PAPER TO EVER WRITE ALL ABOUT THE EXCELLENCE IN YOU -- Concerning Demetrius' excellent example, John had many things to write, but he could not write it all with ink and pen. **Travel The Forward Journey of The Excellent Example.**

SOME THINGS MUST BE SAID FACE TO FACE -- The

Apostle John trusted that he would shortly see the encouraging exhorter of truth, Gaius, to speak face to face concerning Demetrius' excellent example. **Travel The Forward Journey of The Excellent Example.** The Apostle John would render this short benediction, "Peace be to thee". He would tell the Elder of Encouraging Exhorter, Gaius, "Our friends salute you. Greet the friends by name."

- **CLEARLY COMMEND THE ENCOURAGING EXHORTER --** On The Forward Journey, John clearly Commends the Encouraging Exhorter, Gaius, whose name means "rejoice." John expressed his deep appreciation with the dynamic duo of prayer and praise for the faithfulness of Gaius to the testimony of truth and the testifiers of truth.

- **CLEARLY CONDEMN EVIL AND EGOTISTICAL EFFORTS --** On the Forward Journey, John clearly condemns the evil ego maniac, named, Diotrephes. Diotrephes names means "nurtured by Zeus." Diotrephes was an evil man with an evil attitude who sadly had a position of influence in the church. Diotrephes was a rebellious and ungodly leader in the church.

- **CLEARLY CELEBRATE EXCELLENT EXAMPLES -- On The Forward Journey, John Celebrates Demetrius' excellent example. Demetrius was the bearer of the epistle, the bearer of the letter. Demetrius was respected for his good report. Demetrius was respected for his commitment to truth. John could clearly verify Demetrius' record was true.**

- On our forward journey we have discovered in scripture an encouraging exhorter named Gaius.
- On our forward journey we have discovered in scripture an

- evil ego maniac named Diotrephes.
- On our forward journey we have discovered in scripture an excellent example named Demetrius.

1 Corinthians 11:28:
But let a man examine himself, and so let him eat of that bread, and drink of that cup.

Let's examine our hearts deeply before moving forward and ever eating again of that bread and drinking of that cup of communion.

Move forward and examine ourselves by asking the crucial question, "Am I an encouraging exhorter moving on the forward journey for the cause of Christ?"

Move forward and examine ourselves by asking the critical question, "Am I an evil ego maniac?"

Let us all move forward to learn from this most moving and life changing epistle written by the elder through the inspiration of the Holy Spirit to the encouraging exhorter concerning the ego maniac and the excellent example.

Move forward and examine ourselves by asking the crystal clear question, "Am I an excellent example moving on the forward journey for the cause of Christ? Is my flesh on the cross? Is my all on the altar?

Moving forward, examine ourselves, and learn from the elder, the encouraging exhorter, the ego maniac, and the excellent example in the timeless text of 3 John for it points us with precision to the Eternal and Everlasting God who is totally committed to our forward journey even through our very own good, bad, and indifferent experiences of real life.

MY FORWARD JOURNEY IN THE WORKING WORLD

I recently had the distinct honor of being recognized by Town of Hempstead Supervisor Kate Murray (right) and Councilwoman Dorothy L. Goosby (left) for working 25 years at the Town of Hempstead, America's largest township, as a Community Research Assistant in the Office of Communications and Public Affairs. My lovely wife, Elder Brenda Jackson Mackey (2nd left), was also honored for singing on the Town of Hempstead African-American History Month Celebration Program where this took place in the Nathan L. H. Bennett Pavilion at town hall in Hempstead, N.Y. My forward journey in the working world started early at the age 14 when I first got my working papers. My first job on my forward journey in the working world was mopping floors and cleaning up at Miss Shelly's Nursery School in Roosevelt, New York. Then my forward journey in the working world took me to the EOC Feeding Program where I received the lunches at 6:00a.m. Mondays through Friday in the summer and loaded the refrigerator fully with sandwiches, snacks, juices, and milk at the church. Then my forward journey in the working world took me to the world's famous, Jones Beach, where I cleaned bathroom toilets, mopped floors, cut grass, and cleaned out dumpsters. After doing a good job I was asked the following year to work in the Financial Office at Jones Beach. Where the financial staff counted and accurately recorded every single financial medium of exchange that came into Jones Beach in Long Island, New York. Then my forward journey took me to the Town of Hempstead, America's largest township, where I worked at town hall starting off in the mail room as a seasonal worker, and years later moved on to the Office of Communications and Public Affairs as a fulltime employee. Over the last 25 years in the Office of Communications and Public Affairs I have written short stories for the town that were submitted to newspapers featuring Town of Hempstead, Nassau County, New York State, and United States of America elected officials including Town of Hempstead Supervisors Thomas S. Gulotta, Joseph Mondello, Gregory Peterson, Richard Guardino, and Kate Murray; former New York Senator Alfonse Damato (a former Hempstead Town Clerk), former New York Senator Hilary Clinton, Congressman Peter King, Presidents Ronald Reagan and George Bush. Just to name a few. In fact it was writing short stories for elected officials that moved me in the direction of writing books. On my forward journey I had to and I still must always develop a positive and progressive mindset to move forward with purpose and be ready to walk through the different doors of opportunity in the midst of the years full of the good, bad, and indifferent jagged edged realities of life.

Part 6

MOVING FORWARD WITH PURPOSE

CHAPTER TWENTY-THREE

THE FORWARD MINDSET -- BE READY

2 Corinthians 9:1-3:

1 For as touching the ministering to the saints, it is superfluous for me to write to you:

2 For I know the forwardness of your mind, for which I boast of you to them of Macedonia, that Achaia was ready a year ago; and your zeal hath provoked very many.

3 Yet have I sent the brethren, lest our boasting of you should be in vain in this behalf; that, as I said, ye may be ready:

DID YOU KNOW? 2 Corinthians was written somewhere around 55-56 A.D. in Macedonia, one year after the writing of 1 Corinthians by the Apostle Paul. This epistle was written to the church at Corinth and the house churches in Achaia. The main people mentioned in 2 Corinthians are Paul, Timothy, Titus, and the Corinthian church.

2 Corinthians is a highly intense epistle, an in your face letter from the Apostle Paul, written to the complex issue church he had started in Corinth. The backdrop behind this epistle shows how hard the jagged edge realities of ministry were. The Apostle Paul shows the reader his wounded heart as a pastor reaching out to broken, battered and bruised parishioners.

1 Corinthians reveals that the church at Corinth was spiritually sick and not unified. Apostle Paul's leadership had been belittled by a phony teacher that divided and deceived the people with false doctrine.

In an effort to rectify the trouble, the Apostle Paul went back to Corinth. The young Corinthian church thought that their stuff did not stick. They were above the law. The Apostle Paul went back to Ephesus and he wrote once more to the Corinthian church. Paul pleaded with the Corinthian Church to truly repent so they would not experience God's wrath and God's judgment. Pastor Titus contacted founding pastor, Paul the Apostle, and informed him that many members in the Corinthian church had repented of their sins, but a little clique, a small group remained to be sinful trouble makers. The faithful in the Corinthian church now longed deeply to see their founding pastor again.

In 2 Corinthians, founding Pastor Paul comes out against false teachers. Paul encourages the truly faithful members of the Corinthian church to stay totally committed and reassures the congregation at Corinth that he loves them. Paul moved forward with purpose.

2 Corinthians is extremely applicable to today's modern church, and its leadership. 2 Corinthians teaches about the responsibilities and benefits of servant leadership. 2 Corinthians also teaches the blood-washed believer that Christ-centered suffering, such as Paul's thorn in the flesh, discipline, hope, giving, and sound doctrine are an integral ingredient to move forward more effectively in our Christian journey.

1.) A MINDSET FOR MINISTRY

Paul had bragging rights to commend the faithful, the newly repented parishioners in the Corinthian church, for lifting an offering for the poor brothers and sisters in Christ. In essence, he was saying that I can't touch this when it came to **"…as touching the ministering to the saints."** Paul bragged about the faithful who embraced the grace of giving for they possessed a mindset for ministry. True blood-washed believers must possess a mindset for ministry to overcome the jagged edged issues of satanic oppression and possession. Without a solid Bible-based mindset for ministry, you will fail. And failure is not an option. Therefore, the blood-washed believer must possess the forward mindset in a backwards world. So we will also move forward with purpose.

2.) THE FORWARD MINDSET

For I know the forwardness of your mind, for which I boast of you to them of Macedonia, that Achaia was ready a year ago; and your zeal hath provoked very many.

Founding Pastor Paul boasted of the members of the Corinthian church who now possessed a forward mindset to make a major difference through the grace of giving to the saints in Jerusalem. The eagerness, the zeal to be ready to move forward and make a difference a year in advance was a major motivating factor that provoked other believers to do the right thing. Is our zeal, is our eagerness provoking others to stay with God? Is our zeal, is our eagerness provoking others to move forward and make a difference?

As a young man, my father's brother, my Uncle John Mackey, had a forward mindset and a passion for playing football. My Grandfather, the late Rev. Walter R. Mackey, Sr., would tell him, "If you make a touchdown, I will give you $5. Uncle Johnny told me that, "In those days, the 1950's, $5 was a lot of money for a teenager". Also, during those days, his mother, my grandmother, Ma Mack, the late

Mrs. Dora Mackey, gave her son some sound advice that changed the course of his life.

She said, "John, if you want to be a football player, be the best player you can be." So Uncle Johnny decided to move forward, to have a forward mindset, to be the best football player he could be, a focused desire deep within his heart that drove him to "maximize his fullest potential.

With the help of "the four P's," prayer, planning, patience, and persistence, while Uncle Johnny was still a student at Hempstead High School in 1958, he continued to move forward and won the prestigious Thorp Award as the most outstanding football player in Nassau County, Long Island.

At the same time, Uncle Johnny also took to heart the sound advice of his father, my Grand Father, Big Daddy, who told him to "always keep your feet planted firmly on God's good earth and keep your head out of the clouds."

Therefore, my Uncle Johnny, never got into ride and saw himself as a hero. Most of all, Uncle Johnny moved forward and made a difference. Uncle Johnny caught the vision of victory and never gave up. His decision to be a man of vision took him to Baltimore. There he became a member of the Colts' team.

From there, Uncle Johnny's decision to move forward to be a man of vision who remembered the sound advice of his parents, bought these results:

- John Mackey was voted the NFL's Best Tightend by a group of noted sports writers in 1969. John Mackey moved forward with purpose.

- John Mackey caught a deflected pass in Super Bowl IV and ran 75 yards to score in the Colts' 16 – 13 win against the Dallas Cowboys in 1971.

- John Mackey was inducted into the NFL's Hall of Fame in Canton, Ohio, August 1, 1992, the payoff of having a forward mindset and making a decision as a young man in Roosevelt, New York.

- John Mackey was born on September 24, 1941 and passed on July 6, 2011 in Baltimore, Maryland at the age 69. John Mackey moved forward with purpose. John Mackey moved forward and made a difference.

- John Mackey's hindsight is our foresight to move forward and actually learn with a positive and progressive mindset from the good, bad, and indifferent jagged edged realities of life.

- The church today needs a forward mindset to help the helpless.
- The church today needs a forward mindset to bear, care, and share the burden of the broken, battered, and bruised.
- The church today needs a forward mindset to remember the widows.
- The church today needs a forward mindset to remember the orphans.
- The church today needs a forward mindset to fight for our families.
- The church today needs a forward mindset to fight for the jobless.
- The church today needs a forward mindset to fight for the forgotten.

3.) BE READY, BE READY, BE READY

Now is the time to move forward and be ready. Tomorrow is not promised to us. Now is the time to be ready. As in rapture ready. As in, if I died today would I make it in to heaven? Is my heart right with God right now? Is my soul right with God right now? Is my life right with God right now?

- Get a forward mindset and be ready to stand against the attack of the enemy on every side, economically, mentally, physically, politically, psychologically, socially, and spiritually.
- Get a forward mindset and be ready to lose some friends.
- Get a forward mindset and be ready to be talked about like a low down dirty dog.
- Get a forward mindset and be ready to die to self.
- Get a forward mindset and be ready to grow in grace.
- Get a forward mindset and be ready to laugh, learn, and love again.
- Get a forward mindset and be ready to embrace the grace of giving.

Be ready to review the importance of having a mindset for ministry, and not a dropout spirit every single time a major problem arises. Be ready to have rock solid spiritual backbone.

Be ready to solve problems. Be ready to deal with real people with real issues. It's called ministry. True leaders solve problems. If you complain about problems and never move to solve them, then you are showing that you are not a leader at all. Be ready to solve problems if you really love Jesus. Bust a move with a forward mindset for Jesus and be part of the solution and not part of the problem.

2 Corinthians 9:6-12 lets us know to:

- Possess a forward mindset and be ready for**, "He which soweth sparingly shall reap also sparingly; and he which soweth bountifully shall reap also bountifully."**

- Possess a forward mindset and be ready **"…for God loveth a cheerful giver."**

- Possess a forward mindset and be ready for **"…God is able to make all grace abound toward you…"**

- Possess a forward mindset and be ready for **"…he hath given to the poor: his righteousness remaineth for ever."**

- Possess a forward mindset and be ready for **"he that ministereth seed to the sower both minister bread for your food, and multiply your seed sown, and increase the fruits of your righteousness."**

- Possess a forward mindset and be ready for **"Being enriched in every thing to all bountifulness, which causeth through us thanksgiving to God."**

- Possess a forward mindset and be ready **"For the administration of this service not only supplieth the want of the saints, but is abundant also by many thanksgivings unto God."**

Be Ready, Be Ready, Be Ready

- Be ready with a forward mindset for Isaac showed us how to move forward and tap into the year of influence.
- Be ready with a forward mindset for Noah showed us how to be moved with the fear of God.

- Be ready with a forward mindset for Moses showed us how to go forward together in inter-generational ministry, march through the wilderness, and set forward and raise the standard.
- Be ready with a forward mindset for Joshua showed us how to be leaders, learners, and Levites who go after their goals.
- Be ready with a forward mindset for Rahab and the scarlet thread of redemption showed us how to move forward from prostitution to proclamation.
- Be ready with a forward mindset for Ruth taught us about moving forward in the power of friendship and the true test of friendship.
- Be ready with a forward mindset for Job taught us about moving forward in a backwards world and life on the left hand of God.
- Be ready with a forward mindset for John taught us about the forward journey – learning from the elder, the encourager, the ego maniac, and the excellent example.
- Be ready with a forward mindset for Paul taught us about the conviction of communion and how to move forward and have some biblically based backbone.
- Be ready with a forward mindset for Jesus taught about moving forward and making a difference.
- Be ready with a forward mindset for Jesus and the woman at the well taught us about moving forward in worship.
- Be ready with a forward mindset for Jesus taught us about moving forward for this cause.
- Be ready with a forward mindset for Paul taught us about you-ward grace; a shout-out for the shutout.
- Be ready with a forward mindset for Paul taught about proving the sincerity of your love % learn from those who move forward.
- Be ready with a forward mindset for Paul showed us about moving forward for the health of the church.

- Be ready with a forward mindset for the psalmist asked us are you on the move for God?
- Be ready with a forward mindset for Jesus ministered concerning moving forward in operation evangelism and equipping the church to carry out Christ's commission.
- Be ready with a forward mindset for Deacon Eddie Bryant taught us to not give up when things get rough. Just hold on. That's all you have to do.
- Be ready with a forward mindset for Rev. Dr. Frances W. Mackey taught us to bloom where we are planted.
- Be ready with a forward mindset for I taught you to catch the vision of victory and never give up.

BE READY WHEN HE COMES AGAIN

Be ready when He comes again,
Be ready when He comes again;
Be ready when He comes again—
He is coming again so soon.
Don't let Him catch you with your work undone,
Don't let Him catch you with your work undone,
Don't let Him catch you with your work undone,
He is coming again so soon.

Be praying when He comes again,
Be praying when He comes again,
Be praying when He comes again,
He is coming again so soon.

Be watching when He comes again,
Be watching when He comes again,
Be watching when He comes again,
He is coming again so soon.

Oh Lord, when He comes again,
Oh Lord, when He comes again,
Oh Lord, when He comes again,
　He is coming again so soon.

Don't let Him catch you on the ballroom floor,
Don't let Him catch you on the ballroom floor,
Don't let Him catch you on the ballroom floor,
　He is coming again so soon.

Don't let Him catch you with a lying tongue,
Don't let Him catch you with a lying tongue,
Don't let Him catch you with a lying tongue,
　He is coming again so soon.

Oh Lord, when He comes again,
Oh Lord, when He comes again,
Oh Lord, when He comes again,
　He is coming again so soon.

CHAPTER TWENTY-FOUR

THE FORWARD DRIVE—IT IS WELL

2 Kings 4:22-26

And she called unto her husband, and said, Send me, I pray thee, one of the young men, and one of the asses, that I may run to the man of God, and come again.

And he said, Wherefore wilt thou go to him to day? it is neither new moon, nor sabbath. And she said, It shall be well.

Then she saddled an ass, and said to her servant, Drive, and go forward; slack not thy riding for me, except I bid thee.

So she went and came unto the man of God to mount Carmel. And it came to pass, when the man of God saw her afar off, that he said to Gehazi his servant, Behold, yonder is that Shunammite:

Run now, I pray thee, to meet her, and say unto her, Is it well with thee? is it well with thy husband? is it well with the child? And she answered, It is well.

Have you ever had an emergency situation with your beloved family member and you got in the passenger's seat of the car and said to the driver, "Drive! Go forward. Get me to the hospital right now. Get me to the emergency room, right now. Don't slack up, don't slow down, get me to the doctor right now. Get me to a place where I can get help for my loved one!"? Have you ever been on a forward drive in the time of trouble with an overwhelming sense of urgency?

There was a day when the Shunammite woman's son—the son, the miracle baby that the Prophet Elisha, whose name means, God is Savior; Elisha, the successor of Elijah, who prophesied that the Shunammite woman's son would be conceived and born according to the time of life—went to work with his elderly father in the field of the reapers. This was probably one of the proudest days of this son's life—to go to work with his father. On this most momentous and meaningful day, the son's head begins to hurt. It may have been a sudden migraine headache. The text does not say. The son goes to his elderly, hard working father and says, "My head, my head." The father says to one of the young workers, "Carry him to his mother."

The young worker brought the son of the Shunammite woman to her, and the son sat on her knees till noon, and then died. Death at noon. The day should be moving forward with full force, and now everything is falling apart and going wrong at noon. She had no time to get on her knees, even in prayer, which is extremely important. The Shunammite woman, the mother, went up; she moved forward, she went up and laid her dead son on the bed of the man of God, Elisha, in the room that she and her husband had made for the Prophet Elisha, and shut the door and went out of the room. In the time of trouble the Shunammite woman went up and went out with wisdom from above. She moved forward and called her husband and said, "Send me one of your young workers and one donkey that I may run to the man of God and come again." Her husband said in essence, why go to him today? There is no new moon, this is not the Sabbath. No church services are going on. No miracle meetings are going on. The Shunammite woman whose son died right on her knees says to her husband, "It shall be well." The Shunammite woman moved forward with purpose.

IT SHALL BE WELL

"It shall be well." That was the positive and progressive confession that the Shunammite woman declared and decreed to her elderly husband. "It shall be well." The Shunammite woman, this great woman, boldly declared and decreed "It shall be well" when her miracle son was lifeless and dead. After thirty years of ministry, I have seen both sides of the "It shall be well" experience.

One day, when I was a young teenage preacher, there was a knock on the church parsonage door where my two sisters, Frances and Vivian and I lived with my father/Pastor, the Rev. Dr. Arthur L. Mackey, Sr., and mother/First Lady, the Rev. Dr. Frances W. Mackey. The parsonage was located right next door to the church. I answered the door and one of the church ushers said, "Please rush right over to the church; our oldest usher passed out at the altar." I rushed right over and held the elderly usher's hand and prayed as the Nurses Unit of the Usher Board worked with her until the paramedics arrived. The elderly usher died at the altar saying, "Jesus, Jesus, Jesus," as I held her hand. "It shall be well." Her spirit and soul was absent from the body, but present with the Lord. "It shall be well."

One day, many years later, after my father's death, when I was in the early years of my pastorate at Mt. Sinai, one of our beloved deacons began to die right before our eyes. He was on the front row in Sunday morning service, slumped over while life was quickly leaving his body. I went over to him and began to pray in tongues and the congregation began to pray as well. As we prayed and spoke the Word over him, the elderly deacon began to respond. His life came back to him and he and his family continued on. "It shall be well."

One day, many years prior to this time, my mother had a life threatening medical matter. The whole family went with her to the hospital. She was dressed for surgery, and the doctors came in and said, "Rev. Dr. Frances W. Mackey, we cannot find anything. You are free to go home." "It shall be well." One day, fourteen years ago, on October 29, 1999, after a long fight of faith with cancer which spread from my father's liver to his colon, he went home to glory. After 35 years of pastoring and advocating for jobs, justice, and social-economic freedom, the angels came for him and released him from his earthly pain. "It shall be well."

Yes, the Shunammite woman, this great woman, boldly moved forward when she declared and decreed "It shall be well." She boldly made a confession of faith even when her miracle son was now completely lifeless and dead. Her miracle became a mess. After thirty years of ministry I have seen both sides of the "It shall be well" experience—the side where there is healing on this side of glory called earth, and the side on the other side of glory called Heaven where there are no more tears. Whether you get a right now miracle on this side, or the comfort that you will see your loved one totally well onward and upward in Heaven, "It shall be well." No matter what, keep moving forward.

THE FORWARD DRIVE

The Shunammite woman, the resourceful wife and mother, in 2 Kings 4:24, saddled a donkey and told her worker to drive and go forward. Rev. Willie R. Reid, the renowned Head Chaplain of the Nassau County Medical Center, Nassau County Jail, and the A. Holley Paterson Nursing Home stated that before he met the Lord he was driving fast backwards on the streets of Roosevelt, but since he met the Lord he is driving forward. Rev. Willie R. Reid and Elder Dorian Joyner, and I were all licensed into the Gospel ministry thirty years ago, and thank God we are still on the forward drive for God and by His grace.

The Shunammite woman was on a forward drive on the worst day of her life. She was on a forward drive on a donkey at her life's lowest low. Her miracle son, the son that God blessed her with, is dead. She saddled an ass, and said to her servant, drive and go forward. She was on a forward drive in a backwards situation. Motivational speaker Lee Street, a staff member of Friday Night Live at I Support Roosevelt Youth Center, stated that "Backward steps are really forward steps, because they are learning steps." A child learning to walk may take a few steps forward and even a few steps backwards, but they are still learning steps. The Shunammite woman's first declaration and decree, "it shall be well," and her second declaration and decree, "it is well," in the backwards situation of the untimely death of her miracle son was a major learning step. The Shunammite woman moved forward with purpose. The Shuanmmite woman's hindsight is our foresight to move forward and actually learn with a positive and progressive mindset from the good, bad, and indifferent realities of life.

SLACK NOT

The Shunammite woman, the resourceful wife and mother, in the 2 Kings Chapter 4 text in verse 24 also said, "Slack not your riding for me, except I tell you." So the Shunammite woman went and came to the man of God at Mount Carmel. It came to pass, when the man of God saw the Shunammite woman afar off, the Prophet Elisha said to Gehazi his servant, "Behold, yonder, over there is that Shunammite."

The Shunammite woman was no slacker. She was absolutely determined to get to the man of God. She was absolutely determined to receive a miracle.

IT IS WELL

Elisha told Gehazi to run now, move forward, I pray you, to meet her, and say to her, "Is it well with you?" Is it well with your husband? Is it well with the child? And the Shunammite woman answered, "It is well." Her only son is dead. Her miracle son is dead. Yet, she said "It is well." Has anything, has anyone, has any situation ever died in your life and God placed the unction in your mouth to say, "It is well"? I am so glad that the Shunammite woman declared and decreed this while her only son was dead, because that means that this text ministers to those who face death.

When the Shunammite came to the man of God at the hill, Mount Carmel, she caught Elisha by the feet, but Gehazi came near to thrust her away. Elisha said, "Let her alone; for her soul, her mind, her will, her intellect, is vexed within her: and the Lord has hid it from me, and has not told me."

Then the Shunammite woman began to vent and process her deepest pain and she said to the Prophet Elisha, "Did I desire a son? Did I not say, Do not deceive me?" Don't pull the wool over my eyes. Don't fool me.

Then the Prophet Elisha said to Gehazi, "Gird up your loins, and take my staff in your hand, and go your way: if you meet any man, salute him not; and if any salute you, answer him not again: stay totally focused on your assignment, and lay my staff upon the face of the child."

The Shunammite woman said, "As the Lord lives, and as your soul lives, I will not leave you." And Gehazi arose, and followed her. Gehazi followed the mother who declared and decreed "it is well" in the face of death.

When peace, like a river, attendeth my way,
when sorrows like sea billows roll;
whatever my lot, thou hast taught me to say,
It is well, it is well with my soul.

Gehazi passed on before every one; he was totally focused. He laid the staff of the prophet Elisha upon the face of the child; but there was no response at all, no voice, nor hearing.

Wherefore Gehazi went again to meet Elisha, and told him, saying, "The child is not awaked." God wanted the Prophet to make a house visit.

When the Prophet Elisha was come into the Shunammite woman's house, behold, the miracle child was dead, and laid upon his bed.

Elisha went in the room and shut the door and prayed to the LORD. Prayer changes things.

Elisha went up and breathed the breath of God back into the child, and steered life back into the child. He summoned the warmth of God back into the child, and the flesh of the child waxed warm. Elisha was not being gay. Elisha was God's paramedic. Elisha wanted the life of the son of his ministry supporter and partner restored. Elisha's method need not be used today, because we have a far greater method. We have the power of attorney by declaring and decreeing the name of Jesus for miracles.

SNEEZING SEVEN TIMES

Then Elisha returned, and walked in the house back and forth, and went up, and summoned the death-defying and death-detoxifying power of God back into the child, and the child sneezed seven times.

Sneeze means to expel air forcibly and spasmodically through the nose and the mouth.

1.) Sneeze seven times and expel envy.
2.) Sneeze seven times and expel pride.
3.) Sneeze seven times and expel jealousy.
4.) Sneeze seven times and expel bitterness
5.) Sneeze seven times and expel bullying.
6.) Sneeze seven times and expel greed.
7.) Sneeze seven times and expel hatred.

Sneeze it out. Sneeze out everything that is ungodly, toxic, lethal, harmful, and hurtful. Sneeze to completion. Seven is the number of completion. Completely get the lethal toxins out of your system. Seven is the number of rest.

THE CHILD OPENED HIS EYES

The child, the Shunammite woman's child, the miracle child who died in his mother's lap, opened his eyes. Someone's child died and opened his eyes in Heaven with no more pain, no more sickness, no more sadness, no more madness, and no more tears. Open our eyes. Open our eyes, Lord. Please open the eyes of our spirit, soul, and body. Open the eyes of the whole man just as this child opened his eyes by Your power and grace.

The Prophet called Gehazi, and said, "Call this Shunammite." So Gehazi called the Shunammite woman, and when she came into the room, he said, "Take up your son." He was a statistic, but now he is a testimony, because the Shunammite declared and decreed first, "It shall be well," and secondly "It is well" when her miracle son was dead. We must also move forward, today, to boldly declare and decree that our sons and daughters will not be a statistic of the streets, but rather a testimony of the transforming truth.

- Let us open our eyes and take up our sons and daughters of today from the brutally violent gangs.
- Let us open our eyes and take up our sons and daughters of today from the brutally violent streets.
- Let us open our eyes and take up our sons and daughters of today from the brutally violent crime.
- Let us open our eyes and take up our sons and daughters of today from the brutally violent peer pressure.
- Let us open our eyes and take up our sons and daughters of today from the brutally violent drive by shootings.
- Let us open our eyes and take up our sons and daughters of today from the brutally violent rapes.
- Let us open our eyes and take up our sons and daughters of today from the brutally violent bullying.

The Shunammite woman went in the room and fell at his feet, her only son's feet, and bowed herself to the ground, and took up her son, and went out. One day God's only begotten Son, Jesus, died on the old rugged, bloody, and gory cross at Calvary for the sins of all humanity. Jesus was buried in a borrowed tomb for three legal days, and on the third day Jesus rose. Jesus got up and went up to the Heavenly Father's side to be our Advocate, our Attorney, defending us right now up in Heaven. The Holy Spirit, the Spirit of Christ, is our Advocate and our Comforter here on earth.

CHAPTER TWENTY-FIVE

THE FORWARD PROCLAMATION – MOVE FORWARD

2 Chronicles 36:22-23 (Message Bible):

In the first year of Cyrus king of Persia—this fulfilled the message of God preached by Jeremiah—God moved Cyrus king of Persia to make an official announcement throughout his kingdom; he wrote it out as follows: "From Cyrus king of Persia a proclamation: God, the God of the heavens, has given me all the kingdoms of the earth. He has also assigned me to build him a Temple of worship at Jerusalem in Judah. All who belong to God's people are urged to return—and may your God be with you! Move forward!"

To truly move forward, we need far less paranoid politicians and far more positive and progressive public servants holding public office who effectively function in the power and practice of good government. We need powerful public servants who put biblically based world view principles over politically correct preferences in public policy and practice.

GOD CAN FULFILL HIS MESSAGE

God can fulfill His message. God can fulfill His forward prophecy. Now in the first year of the reign of the Persian King Cyrus over the Chaldeans, better known today as the Babylonians, in order to fulfill the forward prophecy, the word of the Lord was declared and decreed by the weeping Prophet Jeremiah, whose name means

"Jehovah is High." Jeremiah is first mentioned in the Old Testament in 2 Chronicles 35:25 and last mentioned in the New Testament in Matthew 27:9. Jeremiah is the author of the books of Jeremiah and Lamentations. Second Chronicles 36:21 and Jeremiah 25:11 clearly refer to the weeping Prophet Jeremiah who declares and decrees Israel's seventy years of slavery, which was the result of their own sins and iniquities. This was not God's perfect will for them. The land of Jerusalem had seventy years of rest and Sabbaths from Israel's sinful disobedience to God. After seventy years, it was a new season of freedom for the enslaved Israelites.

2 Chronicles 36:21:
To fulfill the word of the Lord by the mouth of Jeremiah, until the land had enjoyed her sabbaths: for as long as she lay desolate she kept sabbath, to fulfil threescore and ten years.

Jeremiah 25:11:
And this whole land shall be a desolation, and an astonishment; and these nations shall serve the king of Babylon seventy years.

Did You Know? God had also forewarned through His Prophet Isaiah's highly accurate forward prophecy in Isaiah 44:28, more than two hundred years before King Cyrus of Persia was even born, that Jerusalem and its temple worship would be rebuilt by King Cyrus, God's anointed, God's shepherd, for God raised up King Cyrus for the purpose of delivering His chosen people, the Israelites, from the seventy years bondage of slavery.

Isaiah's God-given prophecy mentions Cyrus by name, and prophetically declares a new season, a new era, and a fresh new day of freedom for Israel. Slavery, the worst example of man's inhumanity to man, is not God's perfect will, purpose, or destiny. After seventy years, God would move on Cyrus to once again let

His people go. The very mention of King Cyrus the Great in the Bible is evidence and proof that Bible history is world history for the text books. King Cyrus' name is mentioned 22 times in the Bible in four very different Old Testament books: 2 Chronicles, Ezra, Isaiah, and Daniel. King Cyrus, whose name means, "Sun and throne," is the founder of the Persian Empire. He was first mentioned in 2 Chronicles 36:22 and last mentioned in Daniel 10:1, but King Cyrus will be best remembered for laying the foundation to free the Israelites from seventy years of slavery to return to Jerusalem and rebuild the temple in Jerusalem, thereby fulfilling forward prophecies of both the prophets Isaiah and Jeremiah.

Isaiah 44:28:
That saith of Cyrus, He is my shepherd, and shall perform all my pleasure: even saying to Jerusalem, Thou shalt be built; and to the temple, Thy foundation shall be laid.

GOD CAN MOVE

The Lord moved. He stirred up the spirit, moved the heart, moved the innermost being of King Cyrus of Persia so that he prepared, declared, and decreed a forward proclamation throughout his entire kingdom which he also put in writing. God moved the Persian king and founder, Cyrus, to write the God-given vision of victory for the Jews and made it plain for every reader in his kingdom, so they would clearly understand that the Jews were free to leave the Babylonian bondage of slavery and return to Jerusalem to rebuild the temple of worship. God stirred the spirit of the king to move forward and do the right thing even if it was not politically correct.

God moved on King Cyrus to let the surviving remnant return to rebuild, revive, and renew their temple and their faith with the instruments and vessels of temple worship that King

Nebuchadnezzar took from the Temple of Solomon. God moved on Cyrus to get the people of Sidon and Tyre to assist the Israelites in rebuilding their second temple of worship in Jerusalem. God moved on Cyrus to place a powerful politician who became an even better public servant, by the name of Zerubbabel (Sheshbazzer), to lead, guide, and move forward, the returning remnant of Israel to Jerusalem.

Bishop Hezekiah Walker and the Azusa—Next Generation Choir minister a song entitled "I Feel Your Spirit" that says:

> *I feel your presence*
> > *all over me*
> *It's in my hands*
> > *in my soul*
> > *and down in my feet*
> *I feel your presence*
> > *all over me*
> *Moving, moving, moving*
> > *down in my soul*

King Cyrus had the God-given backbone to move forward and do the right thing, at the right time, and for the right reason. Everyone in his kingdom could read this decree for themselves. The Spirit of the Lord moved the soul, mind, will, and intellect of one the most politically astute politicians of that time for the plans and purposes of God.

Readers are leaders. And always remember Bible readers are awesome leaders. I strongly encourage daily Bible reading because the devil wants to kill, steal, and destroy believers with natural and spiritual dementia. Let us move forward and keep our spirit, brain, and body sharp and active with daily Bible reading, healthy diet, and daily exercise.

THE FORWARD PROCLAMATION— MOVE FORWARD

The forward prophecy is the launching pad to the forward proclamation. Jeremiah, and even Isaiah, declared and decreed the forward prophecy, but God used the Persian King Cyrus to declare and decree the forward proclamation. The forward proclamation declared and decreed from Cyrus king of Persia that all the kingdoms of the earth the Lord, the God of Heaven, had given to him, and that the God of Heaven had charged him, Cyrus, king of Persia, to build the God of Heaven a house of worship in Jerusalem, which is in Judah. Whoever there is among the enslaved Israelites, of all His people, may the Lord God be with you as you move forward up from slavery in Babylon to the sanctuary in Jerusalem.

The Prophet Ezra confirms this as a historical fact that the Levites from age 20 and upward moved forward in the rebuilding of the temple under the funding and direction of King Cyrus.

Ezra 3:7-9:
They gave money also unto the masons, and to the carpenters; and meat, and drink, and oil, unto them of Zidon, and to them of Tyre, to bring cedar trees from Lebanon to the sea of Joppa, according to the grant that they had of <u>Cyrus king of Persia</u>.

Now in the second year of their coming unto the house of God at Jerusalem, in the second month, began Zerubbabel the son of Shealtiel, and Jeshua the son of Jozadak, and the remnant of their brethren the priests and the Levites, and all they that were come out of the captivity unto Jerusalem; and appointed

the Levites, from twenty years old and <u>upward</u>, to <u>set forward</u> the work of the house of the Lord.

Then stood Jeshua with his sons and his brethren, Kadmiel and his sons, the sons of Judah, together, to <u>set forward</u> the workmen in the house of God: the sons of Henadad, with their sons and their brethren the Levites.

THE GOD OF THE HEAVENS

Our God is an awesome God. He is not only the God of the whole earth; our God is the God of the heavens. Our God is the God of all the universe. The God of the heavens moved on King Cyrus and made him an astute politician and an astute public servant.

GOD GIVES KINGDOMS

Every time the Persian Empire founder and king conquered a kingdom, he freed its enslaved people and worshiped its god. Historically, this was known as the Persian King's policy of acceptance or tolerance of the conquered people's customs, traditions, and religious practices. The God of the heavens moved on and used a powerful and politically astute government leader to fulfill His plans and purposes. The now freed people would be forever loyal to King Cyrus and his kingdom because of its tolerance policy, and the Persian Empire would continue to expand greatly throughout the known world. Thus, the Persians had territorial control all the way from Asia Minor to India, which included what is known today as Afghanistan, Egypt, Iran, Pakistan, and Turkey.

During this time, Cyrus the Great worshiped the God of the heavens who gave him the kingdoms of the earth. Cyrus was raised and trained as a shepherd by his grandfather, the King of Media, Astyages. Cyrus clearly also had extremely deep issues for he set up the Persians as an army in his adulthood and conquered his own grandfather's throne and his own father, CambysesI's, throne. Cyrus was a ruthless politician, but the God of the heavens dealt with his deep issues, for God had a greater plan for Cyrus. In spite of King Cyrus' deeply spotted past, God saw the shepherd in him, and moved on him. Blood-washed believers in the Lord and Savior Jesus Christ must move forward and expand and advance the Kingdom of God, and set the captives free from the devil's kingdom with the life-changing love of Jesus. Seek the Kingdom of God first and His righteousness. You will be blown away with the kingdoms that can be positively and progressively impacted by the Kingdom of God:

- Business Kingdom
- Economic Kingdom
- Entertainment Kingdom
- Music Kingdom
- Political Kingdom
- Social Kingdom
- Sports Kingdom

Matthew 6:33:
But seek ye first the kingdom of God, and his righteousness; and all these things shall be added unto you.

GOD GIVES ASSIGNMENTS

The God of the heavens, the true and living God, moved and stirred King Cyrus to free the Israelites from seventy years of captivity in order to rebuild the temple. Yes, God can give assignments. God gives assignments to ordinary people to do extraordinary things every single day. The God of the heavens can use whomever or whatever He desires, because history is His story. Cyrus, king and founder of the Persian Empire, was a very unlikely candidate for God to use, yet, God used him for His glory none-the-less. God can make a rock cry out if He desires. I don't want any rock crying out for me. Yes, God can give specific assignments to unlikely people so His plans, precepts, and purposes can be fulfilled.

MOVE FORWARD

God's perfect will, plan, and purpose was to move the remnant forward from slavery in Babylon to the sanctuary in Jerusalem. We must also move forward and embrace God's plan for our lives in our spirit, soul, and body. Jeremiah 29:11 in the New International Version (NIV) states, "For I know the plans I have for you," declares the Lord, "plans to prosper you and not to harm you, plans to give you hope and a future." God's perfect purpose and plan are the catalyst of change that leads us by the Holy Spirit to embrace the shift from the slavery of sin to the sanctuary of the Savior and into the refuge of the Redeemer, Jesus Christ.

Today, in our communities, there is one major thing that has led to destruction, chaos, and corruption—sin. The enemy comes at full force to do three things to our young men, our young women, our little boys and girls. Those three things are to kill our community, to steal from our community, and most of all to destroy our community. Jesus came so we would have life and have it more abundantly. Our mission is to go forth, to move forward, and to be totally committed to reaping a harvest of souls that is now ready for harvest. Mark 16:15 says, "And he said unto them, go ye into the entire world, and preach the gospel to every creature."

Let us go forth and move forward in the community. God wants our attention for His assignment and His forward proclamation.

"Here I am" simply states that something important like, making our whole spirit, soul and body available to God, is going on. Go forth in the community. Can we tell people how to find Jesus? Go forth in the community. Do we encourage or discourage their faith? Go forth in the community. Sin is extremely deceitful. Sin is destructive. The problem with our society is, it has become so sophisticated that we have made sin socially acceptable. Now is the time for true worshipers to go forth, to move forward, and to be true warriors and worshipers proclaiming God's love in our community and through the entire earth.

The Word of the Lord declares and decrees in Jeremiah 1:5, "Before I formed thee in the belly I knew thee; and before thou camest forth out of the womb I sanctified thee, and I ordained thee a prophet unto the nations." God truly desires a relationship with you, but even deeper, He desires to use you for His glory. If God could move on King Cyrus and use him, then God can move on and in you and use you for His glory.

MURRAY ON THE MOVE

Under the dynamic leadership of Supervisor Kate Murray, the Town of Hempstead, America's largest township, stands tall amidst economic uncertainties facing our entire nation and the state of New York. At the same time, America's largest township continues to move forward and make a major difference by offering the essential services, programs, and facilities that enhance the quality of life for residents. Kate Murray moved forward with purpose.

As chief executive of the Town of Hempstead, America's largest township, Supervisor Kate Murray leads a fiscally sound administration that is respected on Wall Street and trusted on Main Street. Despite the fiscal turmoil facing federal and state governments, Murray's 2012 budget held the line on taxes, kept all services intact, and maintained the town's financial vitality. Kate Murray moved forward with purpose. Supervisor Murray's hindsight is our foresight to move forward and actually learn with a positive and progressive mindset from the good, bad, and indifferent realities of life.

Supervisor Kate Murray has accomplished more than earning the respect of independent credit rating agencies. She has dedicated herself to gimmick-free transparent budgeting. This approach has won the Murray administration eight consecutive "excellence in financial reporting awards" from the non-partisan Government Finance Officers Association. What's more, Murray's government represents the first county or town on Long Island to have posted its budget online for all residents to view. Murray has moved forward and made a major difference.

Vibrant parks, pristine beaches, and stunning nature preserves symbolize the town's drive to provide residents with first-class facilities. An ongoing $40 million parks improvement project led to significant upgrades in many areas, including pools, play structures, tennis and basketball courts, golf courses, new playing fields and refurbished fishing piers and marinas. Kate Murray moved forward with purpose.

Within those parks, beaches, and nature preserves is a plethora of recreational, educational, and life-enhancing options for residents of all ages. Free summer concerts, swimming lessons, athletic clinics and leagues, and cultural art classes are among the diverse offering of quality-of-life services and activities for residents.

Sixteen senior centers across the town provide recreation, nutrition, and social activities for the town's mature citizens. Over the summer, those centers unite by the sea at Lido Beach for the popular senior summer beach program. Throughout the year, senior citizens partake in a variety of enriching activities, including a health fair and free income tax preparation assistance. Kate Murray moved forward with purpose.

The ANCHOR program provides an outlet for town residents with special needs, offering year-round services and a popular children's summer camp. The camp includes aquatic, athletic, and cultural offerings. The kids, staff, and town are eagerly anticipating the opening of the new ANCHOR recreation center in Lido Beach. Kate Murray moved forward with purpose.

Supervisor Kate Murray has embraced the environment, molding the town into a municipal role model for the incorporation of green and renewable energy concepts. The seaside community of Point Lookout is rapidly becoming a hub for clean and renewable energy. Most recently, the town opened Long Island's first hydrogen fueling station at the Point Lookout Renewable Energy Park. Hempstead town's fleet now includes three pollution-free vehicles that utilize clean hydrogen fuels. Solar and wind supply power to three town buildings, including the showcase Solar House, located at the Energy Park. Geothermal energy is currently being added to town facilities to provide efficient cooling and heating. Murray has moved forward and made a major difference.

Murray and the town take a proactive approach to the future of the shoreline and marine wildlife. In May 2011, the town unveiled a marine dredge that restored beach at Point Lookout Community

Park that was ravaged by erosion. A groin was installed to combat ongoing erosion at the site. The town's Shellfish Nursery, powered by solar and wind, benefits the ecosystem and the local shellfish industry. Millions of clams are raised at the nursery each year and placed in local bays.

Murray realizes the importance of affordable housing in the future of the town. The development of affordable single-family homes has accelerated throughout the township. Six lucky residents are prepared to move into new affordable single-family homes in Roosevelt, scheduled for completion in 2012. The town also celebrated the opening of new Golden Age housing in East Meadow and Elmont, offering residents age 55 and over more opportunities to live a comfortable, economical lifestyle in the communities they love.

Protecting the suburban character that defines our cherished way of life in the Town of Hempstead is a main objective for Kate, who has stood strong in the face of threats to neighborhoods. In line with that priority, Murray and the Town Board crafted an unprecedented mixed-use development zone at Mitchel Field. The zone was created as a means to provide a blueprint for reasonable growth to potential developers on the land surrounding the Nassau Veterans Memorial Coliseum.

West Hempstead residents celebrated the demolition of the seedy Courtesy Hotel, which plagued the neighborhood for years. In its place will be a train commuter-friendly residential community situated next to the Long Island Rail Road station. This development will cater to young professionals and has been heralded by planning advocates as Long Island's first transit oriented building zone. The zone designation provides for greater development density to developers who encourage mass transportation usage.

The former Avis headquarters on Old Country Road in Westbury, New York, is also experiencing revitalization. That long-vacated property was transformed into a 330,000 square-foot commercial center that will help stimulate the economy and create jobs. The project promises a $100 million direct investment into the economy and the creation of over 600 permanent jobs.

The first woman to be elected supervisor in Hempstead Town's 369-year history, Kate Murray, is no stranger to shattering the glass ceiling and accomplishing a host of impressive "firsts" in her career. Before becoming Supervisor of America's largest township in 2003, she was the first woman and first attorney to be elected Hempstead Town Clerk. Elected in 2001, she established the town's One Stop Passport Shop, a location where visitors can take care of all their passport needs. On February 3, 1998, Kate Murray became the first woman and first Levittown elected to the New York State Assembly from the 19th District. Murray has moved forward and made a major difference.

Before serving as an elected official, Kate Murray worked as an Assistant Attorney General in the Criminal Justice Section handling prisoner litigation. Prior to her work with the Attorney General, Kate served as advocate for the Suffolk University Battered Women's Advocacy Project representing victims of domestic violence.

Supervisor Murray has long been active in community organizations and politics. She is a member of the Nassau County Bar Association, the Women's Bar Association, the Levittown Historical Society, Levittown Kiwanis, Levittown Community Council, Levittown Property Owners Association, Friends of the Hofstra Arboretum, Irish-Americans in Government, the Sierra Club and the Board of Directors of the Bellmore-Merrick Wellness Council. Ms. Murray is a sponsor of the Irish Repertory Theatre. Murray has moved forward and made a major difference.

A graduate of Boston College and Suffolk University Law School, Supervisor Murray is a lifelong resident of Levittown. Like her father, the late, Norman Murray, who was also a legendary mover and shaker. The supervisor serves as the chief executive officer of town government. She presides over all town board meetings and directs the legislative and administrative functions of that body. The supervisor also oversees the day-to-day operations of a municipal government of 24 departments, employing just under 2,000 people, and providing services to some 765,234 residents. As the chief financial officer of the township, the supervisor is responsible for the creation and the implementation of a 2013 town budget of $419.4 million.

If God could move on King Cyrus and use him, then God can move on and in you and use you for His glory. If God could move on Supervisor Kate Murray and use her to lead America's largest township, then God can move on and in you and use you for His glory with His forward mission.

CHAPTER TWENTY-FIVE

THE FORWARD MISSION—THE STRUGGLE CONTINUES

Galatians 2:10:
Only they would that we should remember the poor; the same which I also was <u>forward</u> to do.

Fourteen long years after the Apostle Paul went up to Jerusalem to meet with church leaders at the headquarters of the early church, he goes back this time with his partners, Barnabas and Titus. It is important to remember that the Apostle Paul, his name of Roman citizenship, was formerly known as the premiere persecutor of the church; Saul was his Jewish name of birth. Quite naturally, early Christians realized that Saul, who was now known as Paul, had played a major role in destroying the lives of the early believers, the people of the way, but was now known as a Christian. Many years later, Saul is no longer known as the premiere persecutor of the church; he is saved, sanctified, and filled with the Holy Ghost and is now known as the Apostle Paul who is on a forward mission for Christ.

The Apostle Paul went up to Jerusalem by revelation, and communicated to the leaders of the early church in Jerusalem the Gospel which he preached among the Gentiles, the shut-outs. Paul declared this Gospel for the Gentiles privately to the powerful church leaders who were of great reputation lest his trip to Jerusalem be in vain. Titus, who was with the Apostle Paul and who was a Greek, was compelled and required by the church leaders in Jerusalem to be circumcised, that is, to have the foreskin of his private part cut back, even though he was a full grown man. Clearly, the practice of circumcision was the established mark of distinction for the Jew, and the step of completion in the conversion experience of the Gentile into Judaism. Many influential Jewish Christian believers deeply felt that Gentiles also had to be circumcised and be Jewish first before becoming a Christian. The Apostle Paul correctly declared and decreed that this doctrine was false and totally contradicted the grace of God. The Apostle Paul moved forward with purpose.

Taking A Stand Against False Brothers and False Doctrine

False brothers got in the church to spy out the freedom, that is, the Christ-centered liberty which the early church possessed, so that they might bring the believers into bondage.

The Apostle Paul gave no place by subjection to these false brothers and their false doctrine, not for even an hour, so that the truth of the Gospel might continue to move forward and make a difference. The Apostle Paul was on a forward mission to remember the poor, but it was extremely clear to him that forces had crept in who were discriminating against the poor and covering it up with religious language. These false brothers, who really were spiritual snobs, added nothing to the Apostle Paul's forward mission to reach the Gentiles. Yet, the Apostle Paul moved forward with purpose.

The gospel of the uncircumcision was committed unto the Apostle Paul, as the gospel of the circumcision was committed unto the Apostle Peter. As God, Himself, wrought effectually in Peter the apostleship of the circumcision, the same was mightily birthed in Paul toward the Gentiles, the shut-outs. Paul was sold out for the shut-outs—all for the cause of Christ.

Addressing Discrimination In The Church Head on

When the bishop of Jerusalem, James—the half brother of Jesus, Cephas—better known as the Apostle Peter, and Apostle John—the disciple who stayed with Jesus at the cross, who all seemed to be pillars of the early church, perceived the grace that was given unto Paul, they gave Paul and Barnabas the right hand of fellowship so that they could go on the forward mission unto the Gentiles, the heathen, the shut-outs, and James, Peter, and John could go on to the circumcision.

James, Peter, and John would only require that Paul and Barnabas should remember the poor on this forward mission to the Gentiles; the same which Paul also was eager, ready, willing, and quite able to do. The Apostle Paul moved forward with purpose.

But when the Apostle Peter was come to Antioch, a church with Black African leadership and a congregation that was quite clearly ethnically mixed in a way that portrayed God's true heartfelt intention for the church, the Apostle Paul withstood the Apostle Peter to his face, because he was clearly to be blamed for causing confusion by acting one way when the leaders were present and another way when they were not there.

Certain church representatives were sent from James. Bishop James did eat with the Gentiles at Antioch, which included Black Africans, Greeks, and other ethnic groups, but when the religious power players from headquarters in Jerusalem were come, Bishop James, the Apostle Peter, and their group withdrew and separated themselves, fearing them which were of the circumcision, the religious powers that be. This is not speculation; this is scripturally documented truth.

The other Jews dissembled, segregated themselves from the Gentiles following the actions of their Bishop, insomuch that even Barnabas was carried away with their dissimulation.

But when the Apostle Paul saw that the leadership from headquarters walked not uprightly, moving forward according to the truth of the Gospel, as established by Jesus Christ Himself, Paul said unto Peter before them all, "If you, being a Jew, live after the manner of Gentiles, and not as do the Jews, why do you compel the Gentiles to live as do the Jews?" The Apostle Paul hit the hypocrisy head on with those who are Jews by nature, and not sinners as the Gentiles, who were clearly being discriminated against by early Christian leaders high up on the chain. Have you ever thought that the only reason why heroes of the faith like Peter, James, and John are still considered heroes of the faith today, is partially because Paul boldly rebuked them in their error and deep insensitivity that certainly was not Christ-like? This rebuke made it into the canon of Scripture. So clearly, God and the Apostles wanted to take a clear stand on the issue even if it stepped on the feet of some well-known and mighty men.

Elder Dora Smith of Widows Mite Ministries stated: "Remember that your MOVEMENTS create your MOMENTS." Peter, James, and John's movements of discrimination brought about moments of discrimination that totally contradicted the life, death, and resurrection of Jesus Christ. Therefore, the Apostle Paul made major movements of speaking truth to power so Peter, James, John and others would experience the major moments of truthful transformation and total elimination of discrimination in their souls, minds, wills, and intellects.

Paul showed the Apostle Peter, Bishop James, and all the other powerful early Christian leaders from Jerusalem the poverty of their own soul—how they clearly forget where they came from, and clearly forget Jesus' mandate to go, to move forward, and reach all nations. The Apostle Paul stated, "Knowing that a man is not justified by the works of the law, but by the faith of Jesus Christ, even we have believed in Jesus Christ, that we might be justified by the faith of Christ, and not by the works of the law: for by the works of the law shall no flesh be justified." Justify simply means just as if I never sinned. In its proper context, this is wonderful—justification by faith in the finished work of Jesus Christ on the cross of Calvary. Our sins are washed away by the precious blood of Jesus, but when this teaching is used to justify treating people wrong, then that is extremely dangerous and dead wrong.

The Apostle clearly remembered when the spiritual elite in Jerusalem rejected him because of his past. Black African preachers laid hands on Paul and sent him out on his first forward mission. Paul's rebuke paid off because John became a minister to the church at Antioch, a racially mixed congregation. The Holy Spirit and the Black preachers at the church at Antioch forgave Paul of his past persecution of the early church. Please notice that the Holy Spirit called Paul by the name Saul, the name associated with his worst actions, when he confronted Paul on the road to Damascus on his way to persecute the Christians. It was then that Paul met the Saviour and experienced God's forgiveness. Simeon, who was called Niger (as in Africa's great lands of Niger and Nigeria), better known as Simeon the Black, and Lucius of Cyrene which is located in Africa, and Manaen laid their hands on the former persecutor of the church; they laid their hands on the most despised and rejected man in the Christian church, because they firmly believed that your past does not determine your future.

Acts 13:1-5:
Now there were in the church that was at Antioch certain prophets and teachers; as Barnabas, and Simeon that was called

Niger, and Lucius of Cyrene, and Manaen, which had been brought up with Herod the tetrarch, and Saul.

As they ministered to the Lord, and fasted, the Holy Ghost said, Separate me Barnabas and Saul for the work whereunto I have called them.

And when they had fasted and prayed, and laid their hands on them, they sent them away.

So they, being sent forth by the Holy Ghost, departed unto Seleucia; and from thence they sailed to Cyprus.

And when they were at Salamis, they preached the word of God in the synagogues of the Jews: and they had also John to their minister.

PRESS FORWARD AT ALL TIMES

Adam Clayton Powell Jr., the former Pastor of the historic Abyssinian Baptist Church in New York City, who represented the community of Harlem in the United States Congress from 1945 to 1970, said, "Press forward at all times, climbing forward toward that higher ground of the harmonious society that shapes the laws of man to the laws of God."

The Apostle Paul moved forward and took a firm stand against justifying wrong behavior and cruel treatment toward the church at Antioch where believers in Jesus Christ were first called and known as Christians. This experience did not happen in Jerusalem, but in the racially mixed congregation and atmosphere of Antioch. Antioch was the capital of the Roman province of Syria. Antioch was the largest city of the Roman province of Syria. Antioch had a huge Jewish community. Antioch is the very first location where Jewish Christian believers, early messianic Jews, proclaimed the Gospel of Jesus Christ to the Gentiles (Acts 11:19, 20). The multi-racial church at Antioch was the first church to send out missionaries on a forward mission to proclaim the Gospel of Jesus Christ to the shut-outs, the Gentiles (Acts 13:1–3).

Paul realized how dangerous it was to build again the things which were destroyed, and made himself a transgressor. Paul knew what it was to watch Deacon Stephen stoned to death. Paul knew what it was to have Christians murdered. The Apostle Paul was declaring that Peter and the others were just as guilty and in gross error, for they were murdering the heart and soul of the racially mixed congregation at Antioch. This displaced anger and outright discrimination was totally wrong and not the will of God. And Paul addressed it head on.

Paul went on with his God-given forward mission to let all know that I am "dead to the law, that I might live unto God."

The Apostle Paul stated, "I am crucified with Christ: nevertheless I live; yet not I, but Christ liveth in me: and the life which I now live in the flesh I live by the faith of the Son of God, who loved me, and gave himself for me."

Paul did not frustrate the grace of God, God's unmerited favor, God's supernatural empowerment to get the job done; for if righteousness comes by the law, then Christ is dead in vain. True righteousness is not self righteousness, but rather a right standing relationship with God. When one has true righteousness, a right standing relationship with God, you are crucified with Christ and discrimination must be crucified for it is not the will of God, but rather the demonic enemy of God's positive and progressive forward mission to transform the lives of the broken, the battered, and the bruised.

THE OVERCOMING TESTIMONY OF REV. DR. MARTIN LUTHER KING JR.

Like the Apostle Paul, Rev. Dr. Martin Luther King, Jr. was also on a forward mission against discrimination and segregation. I cannot listen to or sing the song "We Shall Over Come" without thinking of the life and legacy of Rev. Dr. Martin Luther King Jr. The thing I loved the most about Dr. King is that he boldly challenged racial hate. His strength to move forward with the message of love in the midst of hate made a major difference. Rev. Dr. Martin Luther King, Jr. moved forward with purpose. Dr. King's hindsight is our foresight to move forward and actually learn with a positive and progressive mindset from the good, bad, and indifferent realities of life.

The Rev Dr. Martin Luther King Jr.'s sunrise was on January 15, 1929, and his sunset was on April 4, 1968. His grandfather began his family's long tenure as pastors of the famous Ebenezer Baptist Church in Atlanta, Georgia, serving from 1914 to 1931, succeeded by "Daddy" King, the Rev. Dr. Martin Luther King Sr., who served until he died of a heart attack on November 11, 1984, at the age 84. From 1960 until his death in 1968, the Rev. Dr. Martin Luther King Jr. served as co–pastor.

I attended "Daddy" King's funeral on November 14, 1984, along with my father, the late Rev. Arthur L. Mackey Sr., my mother, the Rev. Dr. Frances Mackey–Hull, and my cousin, Bishop J. Raymond Mackey. "Daddy" King was the man who prophesied that I would become the pastor of Mount Sinai Baptist Church in Roosevelt, New York.

From the beginning, Martin Luther King, Jr. was an overcomer who moved forward and made a difference. After attending racially segregated public schools in Georgia, he graduated with extremely great honors from high school at the ripe young age of fifteen. He then proceeded to Morehouse College, a distinguished Negro institution of learning in Atlanta, Georgia. Both his father, "Daddy" King, and his grandfather were graduates of Morehouse College as well. After three long years of intense theological training at Crozer Theological Seminary in Pennsylvania, where he was elected president of a predominantly white senior class, Martin, the young overcomer, was awarded his B.D. in 1951. After the training he received while at Crozer, he enrolled in graduate studies at Boston University, completing his residence for the doctorate in 1953, and obtaining his degree in 1955. While in Boston, Martin met and married Coretta Scott, a highly regarded Christian young woman of great purpose, destiny, and uncommon intellectual and artistic attainments. Four children were born out of the union of Rev. Dr. and Mrs. King. Rev. Dr. Martin Luther King, Jr. moved forward with purpose.

In 1954, Dr. King accepted the pastorate of his historic Dexter Avenue Baptist Church in Montgomery, Alabama. Always a strong soldier and hard worker for civil rights for members of his race, Dr. King was, by this time, a member of the executive committee of the National Association for the Advancement of Colored People (NAACP), the leading organization of its kind in the nation. He was ready, then, early in December 1955, to accept the visionary leadership of the first great Negro nonviolent demonstration of contemporary times in the United States, the Montgomery bus boycott described by Gunnar Jahn in his heart-moving presentation speech in honor of the Nobel Prize laureate.

The boycott lasted as long as 382 days. On December 21, 1956, after the United States Supreme Court had actually declared unconstitutional the laws requiring segregation on buses, Negros and whites rode the buses as equals. During these difficult days of the Montgomery Bus Boycott, Dr. King, a brave overcomer, was arrested many times, his family's life was endangered, his very own home was bombed by local racists, and he was literally subjected to personal abuse, but at the same time he clearly emerged as an overcomer, a Negro Christian leader of the first class rank, order and file. Like the Apostle Paul who was an Apostle to the Gentiles, the shut-outs, Dr King was also on a God-given forward mission for the despised, disinherited, and disenfranchised, and King stated that "Courage is an inner resolution to go forward despite obstacles; Cowardice is submissive surrender to circumstances. Courage breeds creativity; Cowardice represses fear and is mastered by it. On some positions, cowardice asks the question, is it expedient? And then expedience comes along and asks the question, is it politic? Vanity asks the question, is it popular? Conscience asks the question, is it right? There comes a time when one must take the position that is neither safe nor politic nor popular, but he must do it because conscience tells him it is right." Rev. Dr. Martin Luther King, Jr. moved forward with purpose.

In 1957, Dr. King was elected as the first president of the Southern Christian Leadership Conference (SCLC), an organization formed to promote dynamic new leadership for the now burgeoning civil rights movement. He took the ideals for this organization from the principles of Christianity, the principles of the Ultimate

Overcomer—Jesus Christ, and its operational techniques from Mahatma Gandi. In the eleven year period 1957 to 1968, Dr. King traveled over six million miles and spoke over twenty-five hundred times, appearing wherever there was injustice, protest, and action. Meanwhile, he wrote five books, as well as numerous articles.

The heart and soul of the overcomer was clearly exemplified through the social justice outreach ministry of Dr. King. In these years, he boldly and bravely moved forward and led a massive protest in Birmingham, Alabama, that literally caught the attention of the entire world, providing what he called a "coalition of conscience" in his inspiring and historic "Letter from a Birmingham Jail, " a clear manifesto of the Negro revolution. Following this, Dr. King planned the now historic voter's rights drives in Alabama, the seat of deep southern racism, for the registration of Negros as voters. He also directed the peaceful and historic March on Washington, D.C. for Jobs and Freedom, 250,000 people—overcomers of all races nationwide—to whom he delivered his classic address, "I Have a Dream."

He conferred with U.S. President, John F. Kennedy, and campaigned for his successor, President Lyndon B. Johnson. He was actually arrested while fighting for civil and human rights in a racially segregated America upwards of twenty times and literally assaulted at least four times to his murder. He was awarded five honorary degrees, was named Man of the Year by *Time* magazine in 1963, and became not only the symbolic visionary leader of American blacks, but also a highly regarded world figure who spoke to the very heart and soul of the nation as a twentieth century prophet. Rev. Dr. Martin Luther King, Jr. moved forward with purpose.

At the age of thirty-five, the Rev. Dr. King, a true overcomer, was the youngest man to have received the highly prestigious Nobel Peace

Prize. When Dr. King was notified of his historic selection, he immediately announced that he would turn over the highly coveted prize money of $54,123 to the overall furtherance of the civil rights movement in a racially segregated America. Dr. King moved forward and made a difference; he gave his very life in service for others. King once said, "Everybody can be great, because everyone can serve. You don't have to have a college degree to serve. You don't have to make your subject and your verb agree to serve. You don't have to know about Plato and Aristotle to serve. You don't have to know about Einstein's 'Theory of Relativity' to serve. You don't have to know the Second Theory of Thermal Dynamics in Physics to serve. You only need a heart full of grace, a soul generated by love, and you can be that servant." Rev. Dr. Martin Luther King, Jr. moved forward with purpose.

On the evening of April 4, 1968, while standing on the balcony of his motel in Memphis, Tennessee, while he was in town to lead a protest march in support of and sympathy with striking garbage workers of that city, Rev. Dr. MLK Jr. was viciously assassinated. King was a Christian martyr as were the apostles of Christ. Like the Lutheran Pastor and theologian, Dietrich Bonhoeffer of Germany whom Hitler lynched, King was only 39 years old. My father, Rev. Arthur L. Mackey Sr. and Deacon Eddie Bryant attended the funeral of Dr. King, as civil rights representatives of New York. Times Square Department (TSS) in Hempstead, which my father worked for and Abraham & Straus Department Store (A & S), also in Hempstead at the time, paid their airfare and hotel in Atlanta, Georgia. Many years earlier in a speech in Detroit, Michigan, Dr. King stated, "If a man hasn't discovered something he will die for, he isn't fit to live." They killed the dreamer, but the dream lives on and the spirit of the overcomer is still alive. The life of Dr. King taught us that the revelation of Jesus Christ, the Ultimate Overcomer, is still relevant to the issues of everyday life. Dr. King's hindsight is our foresight to move forward and actually learn with a positive and progressive mindset from the good, bad, and indifferent jagged edged realities of life.

THE STRUGGLE CONTINUES

Frederick Douglass, who was born in 1818 and died on February 20, 1895, the legendary world renown African-American statesman, social reformer, powerful orator, anti-slavery writer, abolitionist movement leader who escaped from the brutal chains of slavery was completely right when he said, "If there is no struggle there is no progress." Frederick Douglass moved forward with purpose.

In April of 1883, Frederick Douglass also stated in a speech on the twenty-first anniversary of the emancipation in Washington, D.C., that "If we succeed in the race of life, it must be by our own energies, and our own exertions. Others may clear the road, but we must go forward, or be left behind in the race of life." Frederick Douglass' words still ring true now more than ever.

In fact, the word victory actually means "to succeed in the midst of the struggle." Therefore, as long as one more person needs to receive salvation, the struggle continues. *Aluta Continua*, meaning the struggle continues.

As long as one more person needs to receive divine healing, the struggle continues.

As long as some poor child has no food to eat, the struggle continues.

Now is the time to work side by side with parents, preachers, educators, youth leaders, and constructive community activists as they come together in a joint effort to save our children's future.

Now is the time to move forward to fast and pray for the deliverance of gang members.

Now is the time to move forward and make a difference, roll up our sleeves, let down our hair, and actually go into the hedges and highways to compel them to come to Christ (Matthew 22:9). This is the first generation in modern history that will live below the socio–economic standard set by their parents. All the statistics show that, in spite of past victories, there will be a permanent underclass in America if we do not move forward and make a difference, and if this issue of our children's future is not properly addressed in a positive and progressive manner. We must take action now. Now is the time to move forward and make a difference in the lives of the broken, battered, and bruised brothers and sisters of humanity.

Yes, it is important to remember hard-won victories of the past and to analyze present progress, but most of all we must begin to move forward and make a difference to prepare for the future with a God-given forward mission.

Part 7
MOVING FORWARD THROUGH THE IMPOSSIBILITIES OF LIFE

CHAPTER TWENTY-SEVEN

THE FORWARD FIGHT— FIGHTING TO WIN

Deuteronomy 20:1-4 (Message Bible):
When you go to war against your enemy and see horses and chariots and soldiers far outnumbering you, do not recoil in fear of them; God, your God, who brought you up out of Egypt is with you. When the battle is about to begin, let the priest come <u>forward</u> and speak to the troops. He'll say, "Attention, Israel. In a few minutes you're going to do battle with your enemies. Don't waver in resolve. Don't fear. Don't hesitate. Don't panic. God, your God, is right there with you, fighting with you against your enemies, fighting to win."

THE CLARION CALL

This message is a clarion call to the church locally, statewide, nationally, and internationally to join in the forward fight. Too many blood-washed believers are so sadly engaged and entangled in a brutally bitter backwards fight fatally wounding their own despised and deeply depressed brothers and sisters in Christ. Now is the time to join the ranks of the army of the Lord in the just and righteous forward fight. The forward fight is to war against the true enemies of the blood-washed believer's purpose and divine destiny.

- The forward fight is to war day by day, and even in the night season, against the deepest depression of the weary, wounded, and suicidal soul.

- The forward fight is to war day by day, and even in the night season, against the demoralizing pains of poverty established by plans, policies, and practices designed to keep the poor even poorer.

- The forward fight is to war day by day, and even in the night season, for the broken, battered, and bruised brother and sister of hurting humanity whose hunger pains is a daily plight that plagues the spirit, soul, and body, with real pictures of empty refrigerators, shelves with no food, and food stamps that have been cut off by the powers that be.

- The forward fight is the clear, clarion call to war day by day, and even in the night season, for the very lives of our own children of precious purpose and divine destiny who are being systematically slaughtered in demonic black-on-black and brown-on-brown gangster style shootings daily at younger and younger ages every single day.

- The forward fight is the clear, clarion call to war day by day, and even in the night season, against the rising demonic racist spirit of murder where white murderers go free for killing unarmed Black and Brown lives.

- The forward fight is the clear, clarion call to war day by day, and even in the night season, to war for effective public policy concerning the mentally ill with guns and the monthly mass shootings that occur by ignoring it after a few days.

- The forward fight is to war day by day, and even in the night season, against the overwhelming injustice of racial hatred and daily systematic demonic discrimination that demoralizes the soul of any nation as business as usual for the good ole boys system of just us and never true justice for the masses of hurting humanity.

- The forward fight is to war day by day, and even in the night season, against the ever rising tide of joblessness that shows an overwhelming lack of total commitment to cutting edge creativity, ideas, ingenuity, and imagination, and also shows a spirit of utter unwillingness to cross the isles of political party lines to come together in a spirit of true bipartisanship to push forward for the prosperity of the masses of people, and not further promote the poverty of the masses as is the case all over the nation and world.

- The forward fight is to war day by day, and even in the night season, against modern day oppression, slavery and sex trafficking, and every single demonic expression of man's inhumanity to man such as all abuse, verbal abuse, mental abuse, sexual abuse, rape, robbery, and all forms of misuse.

1.) The forward fight is a positive and progressive war against depression.
2.) The forward fight is a positive and progressive war against poverty.
3.) The forward fight is a positive and progressive war against hunger.
4.) The forward fight is a positive and progressive war against murder on many levels.
5.) The forward fight is a positive and progressive war against discrimination.
6.) The forward fight is a positive and progressive war against joblessness.
7.) The forward fight is a positive and progressive war against all forms of abuse, oppression, and slavery.

8.) The forward fight is a positive and progressive war against all of the evil manifestations of sin and Satan.
9.) The forward fight is a positive and progressive war that empowers blood-washed believers in Jesus Christ to move forward through the impossibilities of life.

THE FORWARD FIGHT AGAINST INTIMIDATION

The forward fight teaches the blood-washed believer to never be intimidated when outnumbered. You may be outnumbered in the natural, but God knows how to level the playing field. You may be outnumbered in the natural, but God functions and operates in the realm of the supernatural and is not limited by the mere schemes and abusive themes of folk. God empowers us to move forward through the impossibilities of life.

THE FORWARD FIGHT AGAINST FEAR

The forward fight teaches the blood-washed believer to not recoil or roll back in fear. Fear is the exact opposite of faith. Fear comes to shut progress down. "God has not given us the spirit of fear, but of power, and of love, and of a sound mind." The forward fight destroys the fear of the enemy, and replaces it with the fear of God.

THE FORWARD FIGHT REMINDS US TO REMEMBER

The forward fight reminds us to remember God, your God, our God, who delivered the children of Israel out of hundreds of years of brutally oppressive slavery in the land of Egypt. The forward fight reminds us to remember God, your God, our God, who brought and delivered us out of the most brutally painful lows of life's journey.

THE FORWARD FIGHT TEACHES US TO SPEAK TO THE TROOPS

The forward fight teaches that the priests must speak to the troops. The forward fight teaches that the troops must clearly hear the marching orders given by God Himself via the priest. The forward fight teaches us that effective communication is the key to lasting success. The forward fight teaches us to talk to one another and not about one another.

THE FORWARD FIGHT TEACHES THAT GOD IS WITH US

The forward fight teaches blood-washed believers that God, our God, your God, the true and living God, is with us. The forward fight teaches that God will never leave us nor forsake us. The forward fight teaches that God is an ever present help even in the time of trouble.

THE FORWARD FIGHT TEACHES THAT GOD FIGHTS FOR YOU

The forward fight teaches that God fights for you, with you, and even through you, against all your enemies.

The forward fight teaches that God fights for you against deep depression.

The forward fight teaches that God fights for you against paralyzing poverty.

The forward fight teaches that God fights for you, with you, and through you, against hunger.

The forward fight teaches that God fights for you, with you, and through you, against murder.

The forward fight teaches that God fights for you, with you, and through you, against discrimination.

The forward fight teaches that God fights for you, with you, and through you, against joblessness.

The forward fight teaches that God fights for you, with you, and through you, against abuse, oppression, and slavery, so we can move forward through the impossibilities of life.

The forward fight teaches that God fights for you, with you, and through you, against sin and Satan.

THE FORWARD FIGHT IS A FIGHT TO WIN

The forward fight against deep depression is a fight that must be won.

The forward fight against paralyzing poverty is a fight that must be won.

The forward fight against homelessness and hunger is a fight that must be won.

The forward fight against massive murders is a fight that must be won.

The forward fight against deep discrimination is a fight that must be won.

The forward fight against joblessness is a fight that must be won.

The forward fight against abuse, misuse, oppression, modern day slavery, sex trafficking is a fight that must be won.

1 Timothy 6:12:
Fight the good fight of faith, lay hold on eternal life, whereunto thou art also called, and hast professed a good profession before many witnesses.

- Win the forward fight with positive and progressive praying instead of negative straying.
- Win the forward fight with positive and progressive fasting instead of negative blasting.
- Win the forward fight by ministering healing, hope, and essential wholeness to the broken, battered, and bruised brothers and sisters of hurting humanity.
- Win the forward fight with a positive and progressive effort to actually move forward and make a difference by feeding the hungry.
- Win the forward fight with a positive and progressive effort to actually move forward and make a difference by clothing the naked.
- Win the forward fight with a positive and progressive effort to actually move forward and make a difference by rescuing the perishing.
- Win the forward fight with a positive and progressive effort to actually move forward and make a difference by caring for the dying.

THE FORWARD FIGHT AGAINST DISCRIMINATION OF THE DISABLED

I recently conducted a civil rights press conference concerning experienced five and a half year veteran Bus Driver, Don J. Roberts of Roosevelt, New York, and eight year veteran Bus Driver, Oscar Romero of Rockville Centre, who were both recently discriminated against by Baumann and Sons Bus Company of Oceanside, New York. Clearly, there is a dire need today in our communities throughout the entire nation for a godly forward fight, a powerful word of true prophetic destiny that sets the captive free from the brutal bondage of modern-day slavery where the poor are the last to be hired and the first to be fired. Even in the midst of the valley of apparent hopelessness, we must not give up, we must move forward and make a difference, because there is divine hope from above. We can be the visionaries of victory who move forward and make a difference rather than the everlasting victims of the vicious system.

Mr. Roberts stated to the press that, "My name is Don J Roberts I was a driver for Courtesy Bus Co Atlantic Express Transportation. I held this position from 11/08/08 until 12/31/13. When Atlantic Express closed down Baumann and Sons took over my route In Freeport. I drove a special education route in Freeport. I drove bus number fifteen for five years prior to the Baumann acquisition. After working for Baumann for a week they conducted a random 19a dot physical at the main office located at 70 Lawson Blvd Oceanside, New York, on this Monday. When it was my turn to get tested I was administered a whisper test. I wear a hearing aid in my left ear. A Supervisor took me off my route and told me that I am not hearing good enough. I held this route prior to this incident for five and a half years with an unblemished record. She discriminated against me and judged my hearing without a board certified audiologist approval. I felt so violated that I asked for my file to transfer to another job and she told me in verbatim that she didn't have a file for me. How can it be possible if I took a physical not more than thirty minutes ago that my file no longer exists? So I went to Logan Bus Company and took all my dot test hearing test over and passed.

I got the job. My audiologist tested me, JFK medical tested me, and I was certified to operate a bus by myself with no restrictions whatsoever. I have my audiologist charts and my medical examiner card. I was already in full compliance with DOT from Dr. Glenn MacDonald. I obtained documents to substantiate the validity of whisper testing also I have my hearing charts, my medical cards, and driving records. Also the parents of the disabled children that I drove for stated that I provided exceptional service as a driver. Baumann and Sons violated the Employee with Disabilities Act my Human Rights and so did her physician that conducted the physical based on her own judgment. I have contacted the EEOC of Nassau County; today I filed a human rights complaint, and have contacted a civil rights attorney. Discrimination is very alive today and it will not be tolerated. Eight year veteran Bus Driver, Oscar Romero of Rockville Centre got laid off and discriminated against by Baumann and Sons this week, because he has a prosthetic leg. Discrimination against the disabled seems like common practice at Baumann and Son. I am going to bring this to everyone's attention because my route was with children with disabilities and that makes this incident so very sad."

News12 Long Island reported that "Roberts and Romero say they were discriminated against because of their disabilities. Both men say their family doctors gave them physicals and say they are healthy enough and certified to drive a school bus." News 12 also confirmed that both Roberts and Romero moved forward and got new bus driver jobs.

I am proud of Don Roberts, who is a faithful member of Mount Sinai Baptist Church Cathedral in Roosevelt, where I serve as Senior Pastor, because he took the word he heard every week in Bible Study and Sunday morning service concerning "Moving Forward and Making A Difference" and literally applied it to his personal situation.

After being unjustly fired by Baumann and Sons he moved forward and got all of his highly detailed official medical proof, documentations and certifications that clearly affirmed that he can drive a bus, and he and Oscar Romero quickly moved forward and found new jobs with another bus company that appreciated and celebrated their many years of driving experience and good driving records. Pastor Joel Osteen was correct when he stated that, "You have to come to your closed doors before you get to your open doors... What if you knew you had to go through 32 closed doors before you got to your open door? Well, then you'd come to closed door number eight and you'd think, 'Great, I got another one out of the way'... Keep moving forward."

I will also support Don Roberts and Oscar Romero in their forward fight as they bring a major civil rights discrimination case against Baumann and Sons Bus Company regarding its unjust and unfair treatment of the disabled who are well able and experienced bus drivers in this case. We must have corresponding action. Faith without works is dead being alone. Even knowing that Don Roberts and Oscar Romero moved forward and found new bus driving jobs. I wholeheartedly agree with them that this case must move forward in order to make a difference and prevent this vicious type of discrimination against the disabled from happening to anyone else. Attorney Lester Wayne Mackey and Attorney Tuere T. Rodriguez will lead the legal team in this major civil rights discrimination case. Discrimination against the disabled cannot and will not be tolerated. When we hit rockbottom that is an awesome place to start our foundation to rebuild again by moving forward and making a difference.

2 Timothy 4:6-8: "For I am now ready to be offered, and the time of my departure is at hand. I have fought a good fight, I have finished my course, I have kept the faith: Henceforth there is laid up for me a crown of righteousness, which the Lord, the righteous judge, shall give me at that day: and not to me only, but unto all them also that love his appearing."

CHAPTER TWENTY-EIGHT

THE FORWARD FLIGHT— THE STRENGTH TO MOVE STRAIGHT FORWARD

Ezekiel 1:4-14

Did You Know? Ezekiel's name means "God strengthens." Ezekiel's name means "God is strong." God can and God will strengthen the true believer for our God is strong. God spoke to Ezekiel 90 times as recorded in the biblical book that bears his name. During those distinct 90 times that God Himself spoke directly to Ezekiel, God called Ezekiel "son of man" each and every time. Each of those 90 specific times that God spoke to Ezekiel, God's Word gave Ezekiel the strength to move straight forward in service. God spoke directly to Ezekiel more than He did to any other author of the 66 books of the Bible.

Ezekiel was a powerful priest and prophet. Ezekiel came from a priestly family. Ezekiel was in training at the ripe young age of 17 in the temple in Jerusalem as a priest when he was taken captive into slavery in Babylon by King Nebuchadnezzar. As a Priest in Training, a Minister in Training this laid a solid foundation for Ezekiel's future. Young Ezekiel was among the 10,000 Jews from Jerusalem who were exiled and enslaved in Babylon by King Nebuchadnezzar. Ezekiel had to receive tremendous strength to move straight forward on his forward flight for God in the midst of sudden captivity. Ezekiel knew of and wrote of the wise Prophet Daniel who was also exiled and enslaved in Babylon.

Ezekiel served faithfully as a powerful priest and prophet during one of the worst periods in biblical history. Ezekiel was the son of Buzi, and was a married man according to Ezekiel 24:18. Ezekiel is first mentioned in Ezekiel 1:3 and last mentioned in Ezekiel 24:24. Ezekiel's name, which means "God strengthens," Ezekiel's name which means "God is strong," is mentioned 93 times in the book that bears his name. Ezekiel was born in freedom in Judah and died in captivity in Babylon. God gave Ezekiel the strength to move straight forward right in the face of the unfairness of life, in captivity in Babylon. Ezekiel, whose name means "God strengthens," moved forward through the impossibilities of life. God gave Ezekiel the strength to move straight forward to prophesy to the rebellious house of Israel.

THE WHIRLWIND, THE CLOUD, AND THE FIRE

In a God-given vision, Ezekiel looked, and that priest and prophet beheld, a whirlwind that came out of the north, a great cloud, and a fire unfolding itself, and a great brightness was about it, and out of the midst thereof as the color of amber, out of the midst of the fire.

On our forward flight in backwards circumstances, God can and God will give us strength to move forward even through the very worst whirlwinds of life. Whirlwinds of dangerous cancer. Whirlwinds of deep debt. Whirlwinds of homelessness and hunger. Nothing is too hard for our God. God is faithful even in the worst whirlwinds of life's journey.

God can and God will give us strength to move straight forward even through the great storm clouds of our lives. Great storm clouds of depression. Great storm clouds of oppression. Great storm clouds of recession. These great storm clouds are no match for our great God. God is great and greatly to be praised. God is the source of our strength.

God can and God will give us strength to move straight forward even through the fire: the fire of life's most bitter losses; the fire of life's most overwhelming failures; the fire of life's hardest falls. Jesus will show up in the fire of life. Jesus will walk right with us, side by side, in the fire, in the break up, and in the shake up.

In the worst devastations of the jagged edged journey known as life, Jesus is a faithful friend even in the fire, and not a fair weather friend. Jesus will bring us out of the fire like he did Daniel's three friends, the three Hebrew boys, Shadrach, Meshach, and Abed-nego, who were also exiled from Jerusalem and enslaved in Babylon. They never compromised their faith in God by bowing down in worship to King Nebuchadnezzar's golden image. As a result, they were thrown into King Nebuchadnezzar's fiery furnace, but Jesus met them in the fire, and delivered them straight forward out of the fire. They were on a forward flight for God in spite of opposition, oppression, and occultist behavior.

LIVING CREATURES OUT OF THE MIDST OF THE FIRE

Ezekiel 1:5-8:
Also out of the midst thereof came the likeness of four living creatures. And this was their appearance; they had the likeness of a man. And every one had four faces, and every one had four wings. And their feet were straight feet; and the sole of their feet was like the sole of a calf's foot: and they sparkled like the colour of burnished brass. And they had the hands of a man

under their wings on their four sides; and they four had their faces and their wings.

According to our text, out of the midst of the fire came living creatures. Out of the midst of the fire come thankful survivors on a forward flight for truth. Out of the midst of the fire only come those survivors who flew and grew through the fire on a forward flight for what is just and right. Out of the midst of the fire only come those who served God in the midst of the fire and through the fire on a forward flight for our God. Out the midst of the fire only come those who were faithful in the fire. Out of the midst of the fire only come those with straight feet who will not stumble when things get difficult, and real heavy, hot, and overheated. Out of the midst of the fire only come those with soles like calf's feet small enough to precisely navigate through the most tight and fiery situations.

EVERY ONE WENT STRAIGHT FORWARD

Ezekiel 1:9-10:
Their wings were joined one to another; they turned not when they went; they went every one straight forward. As for the likeness of their faces, they four had the face of a man, and the face of a lion, on the right side: and they four had the face of an ox on the left side; they four also had the face of an eagle.

The power of unity is a tremendous experience. The power of being joined together in unity produces survivors and thrivers who have the inner strength to move straight forward through life's most difficult challenges. Being joined together in unity with the strength to move straight forward keeps things from turning in the wrong direction. Being joined together in unity keeps everyone who is serious about their service to God and hurting humanity strong so they can move straight forward.

The four faces of the living creatures that moved straight forward were also symbolic of "the four descriptions of Jesus" as portrayed in the four Gospels, Matthew, Mark, Luke, and John. Matthew described our Lord Jesus Christ as the King (the lion); Mark described Jesus as the Suffering Servant (the ox); Luke painted the picture of humanity of Jesus (man); and John declared and decreed the deity of Jesus (the eagle).

STRAIGHT FORWARD FOLLOWING THE SPIRIT

Ezekiel 1:11-12:
Thus were their faces: and their wings were stretched upward; two wings of every one were joined one to another, and two covered their bodies. And they went every one straight forward: whither the spirit was to go, they went; and they turned not when they went.

The legendary old Negro Spiritual declared and decreed,

Two wings to veil my face.
Two wings to veil my feet.
Two wings to fly away,
and the world can't do me no harm.

It is extremely important to stretch upward to God, and not downward to the devil, in order to have the strength to move straight forward. It is extremely important to stretch upward to God, and not side-ward to Satan, in order to have the strength to move straight forward. It is extremely important to stretch upward to God, and not backwards to Beelzebub, in order to have the strength to move straight forward and to make a difference in the lives of the broken, the battered, and the bruised.

I love the hymn which states:

> *Father, I stretch my hands to thee,*
> *No other help I know;*
> *If thou withdraw thyself from me,*
> *Ah! whither shall I go?*

Everyone who truly follows the leading of the Holy Spirit will receive the strength to move straight forward through the fire in powerful praise and worship to the true and living God even through the jagged edges of life. Everyone who truly follows the leading of the Holy Spirit will receive the strength to move straight forward in faith through the fire, and not downward to the devil. Everyone who truly follows the leading of the Holy Spirit will receive the strength to move straight forward through the fire and not sideward to Satan. Everyone who truly follows the leading of the Holy Spirit will receive the strength to move straight forward through the fire, and not backwards to Beelzebub.

- The Spirit of God can give us the strength to move straight forward and truly love that person who truly hates your guts.
- The Spirit of God can give us the strength to move straight forward through the impossibilities of life.
- The Spirit of God can give us the strength to move straight forward to care, share, and bear the burdens of the worst wounded warriors who were wounded in the house of their own friends.
- The Spirit of God can give us the strength to move straight forward and truly love one another not only in word, but

also in deed.
- The Spirit of God can give us the strength to move straight forward and reach out to the shut-outs, outcasts, disinherited, despised, and disenfranchised brothers and sisters of hurting humanity.
- The Spirit of God can give us the strength to move straight forward and empower those in deadly captivity, depression, oppression, and suppression.
- The Spirit of God can give us the strength to move straight forward and help the homeless and hungry brothers and sisters of hurting humanity.
- The Spirit of God can give us the strength to move straight forward and live a life that makes a difference.

Where He leads me I will follow,
Where He leads me I will follow,
Where He leads me I will follow;
I'll go with Him, with Him, all the way.

I'll go with Him through the garden,
I'll go with Him through the garden,
I'll go with Him through the garden,
I'll go with Him, with Him, all the way.

OUT OF THE FIRE COMES THE NEXT DIMENSION

Ezekiel 1:13-14:
As for the likeness of the living creatures, their appearance was like burning coals of fire, and like the appearance of lamps: it went up and down among the living creatures; and the fire was bright, and out of the fire went forth lightning. And the living

creatures ran and returned as the appearance of a flash of lightning.

- Out of the fire comes the next dimension of being a burning coal of fire for Jesus Christ.
- Out of the fire comes the next dimension of letting your light, letting your life, be a shining lamp for the cause of Christ.
- Out of the fire comes the next dimension where our lamp of light shines bright in both the ups and downs of life's journey.
- Out of the fire comes the next dimension of lightning that shows us Jesus moving as the wheel in the middle of a wheel.
- Out of the fire comes the next dimension that leads us to Jesus seated upon the Throne.
- Out of the fire comes the next dimension that leads us to the glory of God.

Now a days, everyone claims to be moving forward. Atheists say they are moving forward by opening so-called Atheist churches where they preach, teach, dance, and shout their total rejection of the existence of God. Modern day murderers are moving forward killing unarmed people and gloating that they got away with murder.

But God the Father, our Heavenly Father, the Source of our strength, gives the Christian the inner strength to move straight forward and speak to the social ills that impact our community and culture every single day.

God the Son, Jesus Christ, our Lord and Savior, the Source of our strength, gives the Christian the strength to move straight forward and speak a word in season to the people's pain.

God the Holy Spirit, the Comforter, the Source of our strength, gives the Christian the strength to move straight forward and speak a word of inner healing and essential wholeness to the spirit, soul, and body of hurting humanity all over the world.

LEARNING FORWARD FLIGHT FROM THE LEGENDARY FORWARD GUARD

I really cannot talk about moving forward and making a difference; I really cannot talk about the strength to move straight forward without mentioning the legendary forward/guard, Julius "Dr. J." Erving, from my beloved home town of Roosevelt, New York, who made the world jump, shout, and dance when he played the game of basketball with a spirit of excellence, second to none. I have never seen angels fly, but I have seen Dr. J. in forward flight that ended always with his classic signature slam dunk. This may not sound too spiritual, but sometimes you have to use natural examples to grasp spiritual messages.

Dr. J. gave little black boys like me growing up in Roosevelt, New York, a village one mile long, but millions of miles strong, hope that we too could move forward and make a difference. I remember like yesterday, in the 1970's, joining my sister, Vivian, and my Uncle Alfred, down in the basement of the church parsonage where we lived in Roosevelt, New York, with my father, mother, and her sister, Frances, to watch our hometown basketball hero, Dr. J., on a small black & white television set with a metal hanger as the antenna. Dr. J. used to live next to our Chairman of the Deacon Board, Deacon Aaron Scott. He was and still is our Roosevelt hometown hero, who moved forward and made a major difference with a worldwide platform of athletic excellence.

Julius Erving was born on February 22, 1950. Julius Erving attended my beloved alma mater, Roosevelt High School. Dr. J. moved forward and attended College at the University of Massachusetts from 1968–1971. In 1972, all of Roosevelt was glued to the radio and television sets as Dr. J., our hometown hero, was selected by the Milwaukee Bucks as a first round pick and twelfth overall in the NBA draft. Dr. J. moved straight forward in his basketball career from 1971–1973 as he played for the Virginia Squires in the ABA.

The forward/guard, Dr. J. moved straight forward in his basketball career from 1973–1976 and played for the New York Nets in the ABA. Dr. J. moved straight forward in his basketball career from 1976–1987 for the Philadelphia 76ers in the ABA. The forward/guard, Dr. J. moved forward and made a difference as a two time ABA champion in 1974 and 1976. Dr. J. moved forward and made a difference as a two time ABA Playoffs MVP in 1974 and 1976. The forward/guard, Dr. J. moved forward and made a difference as the NBA's Most Valuable Player in 1981. The forward/guard, Dr. J. moved forward and made a difference as an NBA champion in 1983. Dr. J.'s hindsight is our foresight to move forward and actually learn with a positive and progressive mindset from the good, bad, and indifferent jagged edged realities of life.

As I prepared to go to college in 1984 at Virginia Union University in Richmond, Virginia, Dr. J. was numbered among my hometown heroes that touched my heart and changed my life. Dr. J.'s old home on Pleasant Avenue in Roosevelt, New York, now houses the Sister

JoAnne Bell Richards' Harvest for the World Feeding Program. Nassau Road in Roosevelt has now been renamed by Nassau County executive, Ed Mangano, and legislator, Kevan Abrahams, and the County Legislature after the living legend, the forward/guard, Julius "Dr. J." Erving.

CHAPTER TWENTY-NINE

THE FORWARD FALL — THE SUICIDE OF SAUL

One Sunday morning around 2:00 a.m., I received an urgent phone call from a person who was about to commit suicide. The individual had many forward falls in life and wanted to just give up. The individual was crying out from the very depth of the soul. I reminded the person that their child needed their parent, the person's family needed their loved one, and my wife, Brenda, and I, needed this precious individual. This dear person's life still had great value and worth, because God never gave up on the person. I began to speak God's Word over the individual's life. "You're the head and not the tail. Above and not beneath. You are more than a conqueror. Greater is He that is in you. Your past does not determine your future."

Then I began to pray with the person. The prayer lasted for nearly an hour. Thank God the heavy spirit of suicide lifted, and completely moved out of the individual's deeply wounded heart and soul, and the person made it through their night season. The sermon that I had prepared over the last week went right out the window, and the Spirit of God spoke these words to my heart: "The Suicide of Saul." The suicide of Saul is the result of not moving forward in total obedience to the voice of the Lord. The jagged edges of real life causes many forward falls, <u>but God does not want it to end up in suicide</u>. Therefore, we must be sensitive to the Holy Spirit in addressing this issue.

BE ANOINTED FOR THE PAST, PRESENT, AND FUTURE

Did You Know? It is extremely important to move forward and make a difference for a godly cause and purpose. King Saul, whose name means "asked for," was the first king of Israel. Saul was anointed as king by the Prophet Samuel, but his life tragically ended in a forward fall, because he failed to move forward for righteousness every day. Six very different books of the Bible mention King Saul by name 388 times. Those books are 1 Samuel, 2 Samuel, 1 Chronicles, Psalms, Isaiah, and Acts. King Saul is first mentioned in 1 Samuel 9:2 and last mentioned in Acts 13:21. King Saul began moving forward positively and progressively with God, but sadly ended falling forward in disobedience to the voice of the Lord. Saul was moving forward for God only when he did that which was right in the eyes of the Lord, but when he chose the route of disobedience, this started his forward fall to his destruction. I say, "forward fall" because God's plan is going to go forward even if it means our destruction brought about by our disobedience. God desires leaders whose anointing will positively and progressively impact the past, present, and future. It is extremely important not only to start strong, but to also finish strong.

1 Samuel 10:1:
Then Samuel took a vial of oil, and poured it upon his head, and kissed him, and said, Is it not because the Lord hath anointed thee to be captain over his inheritance?

KEEP GOING FORWARD

It is extremely important to go forward, and to learn how to go up to God every day. It is extremely important to commune with God every day. It is important to climb the hill of God, and get in the presence of God every day because seeking God only on special occasions always leads to a forward fall. King Saul moved forward; King Saul communed with God; King Saul went up to the hill of

God; but he did all these things on his special day, not every day.

1 Samuel 10:3-5:
Then shalt thou <u>go on forward</u> from thence, and thou shalt come to the plain of Tabor, and there shall meet thee three men <u>going up to God</u> to Bethel, one carrying three kids, and another carrying three loaves of bread, and another carrying a bottle of wine:

And they will salute thee, and give thee two loaves of bread; which thou shalt receive of their hands.

After that thou shalt <u>come to the hill of God</u>, where is the garrison of the Philistines: and it shall come to pass, when thou art come thither to the city, that thou shalt meet a company of prophets coming down from the high place with a psaltery, and a tabret, and a pipe, and a harp, before them; and they shall prophesy.

KEEP ON PROPHESYING

The Spirit of the Lord not only deeply desired to come on King Saul on his special day; the Spirit of the Lord truly desired to be within King Saul. King Saul would prophesy on his special day, but the Spirit of the Lord wanted that experience of the power of prophecy for King Saul every day. King Saul turned into another man when he prophesied that special day, but the Spirit of the Lord truly yearned for King Saul to be a new man who could prophesy truth every single day. King Saul was on his way to a forward fall. The Spirit of the Lord needs more than another man. The Spirit of the Lord needs a new man because old things are passed away. Behold all things are new.

1 Samuel 10: 6
And the Spirit of the Lord will come upon thee, and thou shalt prophesy with them, and shalt be turned into another man.

SIGNS AND SACRIFICE

God sent signs to King Saul, but yet, his life ended with a forward fall. God was with King Saul, but yet, King Saul's life ended with a forward fall. King Saul witnessed sacrifices and tarried seven days, but yet, King Saul's life ended with a forward fall for whoever only moves forward for God on their special day is on their way to a forward fall. Even with the knowledge that God is with you, still watch out for the forward fall. Is God in you?

1 Samuel 10:7-8:
And let it be, when these signs are come unto thee, that thou do as occasion serve thee; for God is with thee. And thou shalt go down before me to Gilgal; and, behold, I will come down unto thee, to offer burnt offerings, and to sacrifice sacrifices of peace offerings: seven days shalt thou tarry, till I come to thee, and shew thee what thou shalt do.

REMEMBER

Remember to hear and heed the voice of the Lord speaking words of wisdom to your heart every day, and not just on our special day like King Saul. Remember our anointing empowers us to destroy the enemy of destiny.

The Prophet Samuel speaks of his act of anointing King Saul, as the very first King of Israel, to set the tone for his ongoing role as the point man of God's directives to King Saul.

1 Samuel 15:1-2:
Samuel also said unto Saul, The Lord sent me to anoint thee to be king over his people, over Israel: now therefore hearken thou unto the voice of the words of the Lord.

Thus saith the Lord of hosts, I remember that which Amalek did to Israel, how he laid wait for him in the way, when he came up from Egypt.

GO AND SMITE AMALEK

The Amalekites, who were enemies of the Israelites, were descendants of Esau. The Amalekites were a nomadic desert people who stayed in the area of the south part of Judah and even further towards Egypt. God required King Saul's total obedience. King Saul's assignment was to utterly destroy all in Amalek. His God-given assignment was made clear. King Saul had to take the test of total obedience. Go and smite the enemy of your future, purpose, and destiny.

1 Samuel 15:3-7:
Now go and smite Amalek, and utterly destroy all that they have, and spare them not; but slay both man and woman, infant and suckling, ox and sheep, camel and ass.

And Saul gathered the people together, and numbered them in Telaim, two hundred thousand footmen, and ten thousand men of Judah.

And Saul came to a city of Amalek, and laid wait in the valley.

And Saul said unto the Kenites, Go, depart, get you down from among the Amalekites, lest I destroy you with them: for ye shewed kindness to all the children of Israel, when they came up out of Egypt. So the Kenites departed from among the Amalekites.

And Saul smote the Amalekites from Havilah until thou comest to Shur, that is over against Egypt.

THE SIN YOU SPARE WILL KILL YOU

The liquor you keep on drinking will kill you. The poison you keep on taking will kill you. The sexually transmitted diseases you continually are exposed to will kill you.

King Saul killed the Amalekites but spared the life of their King, Agag, and their best animals. King Saul committed spiritual suicide with a forward fall of disobedience. He disobeyed the God who made him king of Israel by keeping the Amalekite King, Agag, alive. King Agag would have descendents. One of King Agag's descendents was the Persian Prime Minister Haman the Agagite of Amalekite lineage. Hateful Haman was Prime Minister to the Persian King Ahasuerus. Hateful Haman schemed up a plot to have the Jews slaughtered, and God had to use a woman with backbone named Esther to turn the situation around, because King Saul many years before was disobedient to God's command and had no backbone to do God's will. King Saul committed spiritual suicide with a forward fall of deep disobedience.

1 Samuel 15:8-9:
And he took Agag the king of the Amalekites alive, and utterly destroyed all the people with the edge of the sword.

But Saul and the people spared Agag, and the best of the sheep, and of the oxen, and of the fatlings, and the lambs, and all that

was good, and would not utterly destroy them: but everything that was vile and refuse, that they destroyed utterly.

WHEN YOU WERE LITTLE IN YOUR OWN SIGHT

Saul got too puffed up with pride. Saul got too blown up with being Mr. Big. Saul allowed arrogance to alter his anointing to disobedience. Saul became a bold face liar. Saul claimed that he obeyed God when he clearly disobeyed the voice of the Lord. When Saul was little in his own eyes he operated in the fullness of his anointing as the first king of Israel, but pride pulled him to peril. Arrogance aligned him with the witch's assignment of rebellion. Disobedience got Saul out of God's divine destiny and into the devil's demonic destiny. Knowledge is power when applied. So, in order to truly move forward and make a difference, we must know not only what to do, but also what not to do. We must clearly understand the grave and great danger of not moving forward with God, and following Satan's system instead.

1 Samuel 15:16-21:
Then Samuel said unto Saul, Stay, and I will tell thee what the LORD hath said to me this night. And he said unto him, Say on.

And Samuel said, When thou wast little in thine own sight, wast thou not made the head of the tribes of Israel, and the LORD anointed thee king over Israel?

And the LORD sent thee on a journey, and said, Go and utterly destroy the sinners the Amalekites, and fight against them until they be consumed.

Wherefore then didst thou not obey the voice of the Lord, but didst fly upon the spoil, and didst evil in the sight of the Lord?

And Saul said unto Samuel, Yea, I have obeyed the voice of the Lord, and have gone the way which the Lord sent me, and have brought Agag the king of Amalek, and have utterly destroyed the Amalekites.

But the people took of the spoil, sheep and oxen, the chief of the things which should have been utterly destroyed, to sacrifice unto the Lord thy God in Gilgal.

OBEY THE VOICE OF THE LORD

Obedience to the voice of the Lord is the key to moving forward in the plans and purposes of God. Disobedience to the voice of the Lord is the key factor that leads to a forward fall. Offerings and sacrifices are wonderful, but obedience to the voice of the Lord is better. Constant and consistent disobedience to the voice of the Lord is spiritual suicide. King Saul's disobedience to God's assignment was spiritual suicide and outright rebellion.

The classic hymn, "Trust and Obey" with words by John H. Sammis penned in 1887 and music by Daniel B. Towner states:

> *Trust and obey, for there's no other way*
> *To be happy in Jesus, but to trust and obey.*

1 Samuel 15:22:
And Samuel said, Hath the Lord as great delight in burnt offerings and sacrifices, as in obeying the voice of the Lord? Behold, to obey is better than sacrifice, and to hearken than the fat of rams.

REBELLION LEADS TO THE REJECTION OF THE LORD

Rebellion is synonymous to the sin of witchcraft. King Saul, the first king of Israel, was already in rebellion, meaning, he was practicing witchcraft long before he consulted the witch of Endor as recorded in 1 Samuel 28:3-25. The devil and his demons were pulling the strings in King Saul's soul. King Saul's stubbornness amounted to idol worship and a daily lifestyle of sin known as iniquity.

1 Samuel 15:23:
For rebellion is as the sin of witchcraft, and stubbornness is as iniquity and idolatry. Because thou hast rejected the word of the Lord, he hath also rejected thee from being king.

FEAR GOD and OBEY GOD—DON'T BE CONTROLLED BY THE PEOPLE

King Saul's forward fall of disobedience to the voice of the Lord happened because he feared the people and obeyed their voice instead of God's voice. The Lord totally rejected Saul from being Israel's king because of this direct disobedience. As Saul turned away he stepped on and tore the bottom of his mantle just as God had torn His kingdom.

It is extremely important to move forward and fear God. It is extremely important to move forward and obey God. It is extremely important to move forward and heed the words of the voice of God. It is extremely important not to be controlled by the people. This forward fall of disobedience was spiritual suicide for Saul. This forward fall of disobedience, this spiritual suicide, foreshadowed something far worse that never should have happened, and could have been prevented if Saul would have feared God instead of fearing the people, and obeyed God instead of obeying the people. **GOD REQUIRES TRUE REPENTANCE.** Saul wanted no parts of true repentance or real revival.

God, the strength of Israel, would not repent of His rejection of Saul as king because Saul did not truly worship Him in Spirit and truth. Saul did not care about getting the Ark of the Covenant back in Jerusalem like David, a man after God's own heart, did. Saul just wanted to merely mouth words of repentance and still have rebellion in his heart. God looks on the heart, and Saul's heart was corrupt. He only wanted to verbally ask for his sins to be pardoned so he would be honored by the elders of the people. Saul's priorities were all in the wrong place, and God, therefore, rejected him as king. God repented that He ever choose Saul to be the first king of Israel. The Prophet Samuel had to cut King Agag in pieces, because Saul ignored the voice of the Lord, and did not think or care that future descendents of Agag would unjustly desire to exterminate the Jews.

Know that Jesus died on the cross for the remission of our sins, so don't be crazy and claim that cutting someone in pieces is right, because you read it in the Old Testament. That piece of history is there to show us our dire need for the salvation that comes only through our Lord and Savior Jesus Christ. The Prophet was dealing with matters in the Old Testament times before Christ physically died on the cross for the sins of humanity. In other words, since Jesus died on the cross, we have no right to take matters into our own hands and take a life. There are many mass murderers who try to use Old Testament passages to justify their killings, and this is utterly irresponsible behavior that is dead wrong. They completely misuse and misinterpret the historical information contained in the Bible that shows how matters were dealt with before the Savior of the world, Jesus Christ, lived, died, and rose again.

1 Samuel 15:25-35:
Now therefore, I pray thee, pardon my sin, and turn again with me, that I may worship the Lord.

And Samuel said unto Saul, I will not return with thee: for thou hast rejected the word of the Lord, and the Lord hath rejected thee from being king over Israel.

And as Samuel turned about to go away, he laid hold upon the skirt of his mantle, and it rent.

And Samuel said unto him, The Lord hath rent the kingdom of Israel from thee this day, and hath given it to a neighbour of thine, that is better than thou.

And also the Strength of Israel will not lie nor repent: for he is not a man, that he should repent.

Then he said, I have sinned: yet honour me now, I pray thee, before the elders of my people, and before Israel, and turn again with me, that I may worship the Lord thy God.

So Samuel turned again after Saul; and Saul worshipped the Lord.

Then said Samuel, Bring ye hither to me Agag the king of the Amalekites. And Agag came unto him delicately. And Agag said, Surely the bitterness of death is past.

And Samuel said, As thy sword hath made women childless, so shall thy mother be childless among women. And Samuel hewed Agag in pieces before the Lord in Gilgal.

Then Samuel went to Ramah; and Saul went up to his house to Gibeah of Saul.

And Samuel came no more to see Saul until the day of his death: nevertheless Samuel mourned for Saul: and the Lord repented that he had made Saul king over Israel.

FIGHTING, FLEEING, AND FALLING

In life, we must learn from the good, the bad, and the indifferent, in order to realistically move forward. King Saul's forward fall of disobedience foreshadowed a far worse forward fall that never should have happened. It is extremely important that we don't just learn from King Saul's wonderful early days, but also from his bad and indifferent days in terms of God's perfect will. At the end of his life's journey, King Saul with his Israelite soldiers were in a battle against the Philistines. The men of Israel fought the Philistines. The men of Israel fled from the Philistines. The men of Israel fell and were slain by the Philistines at Mount Gilboa. Yes, we must learn from the good, the bad, and the indifferent, in order to move forward and make a difference.

1 Samuel 31:1:
Now the Philistines fought against Israel: and the men of Israel fled from before the Philistines, and fell down slain in mount Gilboa.

THE FATALITY OF THE FAMILY

The fatality of the family is not the perfect plan of God. The fatality of the family is the plan of Satan and his demons. The enemy desires to kill, to steal, and to destroy the family. Jesus came to give life more abundantly to the family and anyone who believes on Him. King Saul's forward fall of disobedience led to the fall of his army, and then to the fatal fall of his family line, and the slaying of his three sons, Jonathan, Abinadab, and Melchishua, by the Philistines. God's focus is healing and helping the family. The enemy is after you because the enemy wants to destroy your family. Let's learn from the good, the bad, and the indifferent, and fight the forward fight of faith for our families in order to prevent the fatal forward falls of our families. Arch enemies don't stop. Arch enemies follow hard, for arch enemies are satanic assassins that yearn for a forward fall to be fatal and not end up faith filled. The archers, the assassins hit their target, Saul, and wounded Saul badly, but Saul was still alive.

1 Samuel 31:2-3:
And the Philistines followed hard upon Saul and upon his sons; and the Philistines slew Jonathan, and Abinadab, and Melchishua, Saul's sons.

And the battle went sore against Saul, and the archers hit him; and he was sore wounded of the archers.

THE SUICIDE OF SAUL— SUICIDE IS NOT THE ANSWER

Saul was so very deeply far out of the perfect will of God for his life that he would rather have his armour-bearer kill him with his sword than to be taken hostage and tortured by the Philistines. When King Saul's armour-bearer would not kill Saul, Saul took a sword and fell on it. Instead of turning to God in his darkest hour, Saul committed suicide. Suicide is not the answer. Hold on to your life, survive and move forward through the impossibilities of life.

1 Samuel 31:4:

Then said Saul unto his armor bearer, Draw thy sword, and thrust me through therewith; lest these uncircumcised come and thrust me through, and abuse me. But his armor bearer would not; for he was sore afraid. Therefore Saul took a sword, and fell upon it.

Many troubled veterans of war and civilians, overwhelmed by the cares of life, even today, seriously suffer from high anxiety, devastating brain damage, deep depression, and extreme emotional trauma, that can lead to dangerous suicidal leanings. Supportive services such as professional counseling, effective support groups, holistic therapy, and powerful prayer for troubled veterans of war and civilians overwhelmed by the cares of life can assist in saving lives from suicide. Hold on to your life, survive and move forward through the impossibilities of life.

In the stress blog article entitled, "Learning from the past helps us move forward" Edward T. Creagan, M.D. of the world renown Mayo Clinic states that "If the stress in your life is more than you can cope with, get help right away."

National Suicide Prevention Lifeline
1-800-273-TALK (8255)
Go to the nearest hospital or emergency room
Call your physician, health provider or clergy

National Alliance on Mental Illness
www.nami.org
1-800-950-NAMI (6264)

Our life is part of HIStory despite overwhelming debt, cheaters, heart breakers, failures, falls, and faults of our own deeply public and private pain. Suicide is not answer, because God created you and I in HIS image to move forward and make a difference in spite and despite of the tremendously overwhelming stresses and messes of the jagged edged realities of life.

Suicide is not the answer, because life is an extremely precious and priceless gift from God, the Creator and Sustainer of all life, even life on the edge of suicide, and God still loves us and His Son, Jesus, died for us despite our many sinful and sinfilled failures, falls, and faults. World renown singer and song writer, Bill Gaither, was right when wrote the classic words of his legendary Hymn entitled, "Because He Lives", that "Life is worth the living just because He lives."

Jesus Christ lived, died, and rose again. So we can move forward and rise above our failures, falls, and faults. Your life is needed on this earth for the plan and purpose of the Prince of Peace.

Suicide is not the answer, because you and I have a God given predestined purpose to develop, implement, and spread a positive and progressive mindset for change despite every single failure, fall, and fault that tick us off from time to time.

My wife, Elder Brenda Jackson Mackey, a licensed Mental Health Worker and Social Worker, states that "There is always hope. Things will not always remain the way they are. Find professional help. Don't keep it to yourself find spiritual, medical, and mental health help immediately right away. Check medications and side effects. Some medications bring about suicidal thoughts. Change the medications. Get into professional group therapy with professionals who won't judge them or minimize what they are going through."

We must constantly be in tune to the cries for help. Tearful and crying alot. Saying "I wish would die". Remarks like "I am tired of living". Isolation and no life in their eyes. Using belts and ties, etc. to hang themselves. It is extremely important to be in tune with the many cry for help. Storing up and hiding pills and drugs to over medicate. That comes from deep desperation and we must move forward and make the difference by constantly being in tune to brutally bone chilling cry of the suicidal.

THE SUICIDE OF SAUL'S ARMOR BEARER – SUICIDE IS NOT THE ANSWER

Saul's forward fall on his sword, the suicide of Saul, led his armor bearer in the wrong direction of following Saul's example. Saul's disobedience to the voice of the Lord ended in devastating loss of life that never should have occurred. The man who assisted Saul takes his own life, because this is the example that he was exposed to. Saul's influence was used in an extremely negative manner. Two wrongs don't make a right. Think for yourself, and don't follow leadership that disobeys God's commands. Move forward and speak life. Move forward and declare and decree life. Hold on to your life, survive and move forward through the impossibilities of life.

John 10:10:
The thief cometh not, but for to steal, and to kill, and to destroy: <u>I am come that they might have life, and that they might have it more abundantly</u>.

Suicide is not the answer. Move forward and make a difference by living your life to the glory of God in spite of the greatest challenges and setbacks. Don't follow the horrible example of the forward fall and suicide of Saul and his armor bearer. Put down that gun and pick up your purpose. Hold on to your life, survive and move forward through the impossibilities of life.

1 Samuel 31:5:
And when his armourbearer saw that Saul was dead, he fell likewise upon his sword, and died with him.

Suicide is not the answer. Yes, there are forward falls in jagged edge experiences of real life, but suicide is not the answer. No matter how bad it is, God does not want you to kill yourself. Don't commit suicide. God knows your deepest and innermost pains of the past, present, and future. God wants you to live in spite of the overwhelming pain of now. God wants you alive to finish your course. God wants you alive to complete your journey of faith. Put down those pills and pick up your purpose. Put down that knife and continue to live your life. God wants you to live. Put that gun down. God wants you to live. Open up that garage door, roll down the windows of your car. Take that noose from around your neck. God wants you to live. Hold on to your life, survive and move forward through the impossibilities of life. **Acts 17:28** states that **"For in him we live, and move, and have our being."**

CHAPTER THIRTY

THE FORWARD WALK—
THE VALLEY WALKER

Psalm 23:
The Lord is my shepherd; I shall not want.

He maketh me to lie down in green pastures: he leadeth me beside the still waters.

He restoreth my soul: he leadeth me in the paths of righteousness for his name's sake.

<u>Yea, though I walk through the valley of the shadow of death,</u> I will fear no evil: for thou art with me; thy rod and thy staff they comfort me.

Thou preparest a table before me in the presence of mine enemies: thou anointest my head with oil; my cup runneth over.

Surely goodness and mercy shall follow me all the days of my life: and I will dwell in the house of the Lord for ever.

One of the most magnificent, meaningful, moving, legendary, and lasting literary passages of purpose in the entire Old Testament is Psalm 23. The 23rd Psalm is one of the most quoted and well known Bible passages in the entire Bible. The 23rd Psalm is a positive and progressive Psalm of David. The 23rd Psalm is a mighty melody of David. The 23rd Psalm is a prophetic praise and prayer of David. The 23rd Psalm is the nightingale song of the Holy Scriptures. It is one of the most explosive and powerful examples of moving forward and making a difference in spite of overwhelming obstacles designed to destroy the sheep, designed to destroy the valley walker, designed to destroy David, designed to destroy us all, but thank God for the Shepherd of the sheep. Valley walkers moved forward through the impossibilities of life in order to make it to the mountain top.

DID YOU KNOW? David's name means "beloved." David was first written of in the Bible in Ruth 4:17 and last written of in Revelation 22:16. David was a shepherd boy working with his father, Jesse's sheep. Not only was David a shepherd, but he was also a true worshiper of God, and king of Israel. David was also a prophet, a priest, and a king who foreshadowed Christ in that sense. David was born in Bethlehem and died at the age of 70 in Jerusalem. David's name is mentioned in 28 different Old and New Testament books, 1,118 different times.

David stated in **Psalm 23:1, "The Lord is my shepherd; I shall not want."**

The Amplified Bible breaks it down this way by declaring and decreeing that, **"The Lord is my Shepherd [to feed, guide, and shield me], I shall not lack."**

The 23rd Psalm of David moves our thinking forward in a positive and progressive manner by teaching us that:

- The Lord is my Shepherd in this present life.
- The Lord is my Shepherd before death.
- The Lord is my Shepherd during death.
- The Lord is my Shepherd after death.
- The Lord is my Shepherd forever.

THE VALLEY WALKER MOVES FORWARD THROUGH THE VALLEY EXPERIENCE
Psalm 23:4a

"Yea, though I walk through the valley of the shadow of death" The valley walker keeps it moving, because the valley walker is on a forward walk through the valley of the shadow of death while following the shepherd. The valley walker moves forward through the valley of the shadow of death, because the shepherd has a better place, a higher place, and a safer place for the sheep. The valley walker fully embraces the valley experience for it is only temporary. The shepherd will skillfully guide the sheep, the valley walkers, through the valley of the shadow of death. Valley walkers move forward through the impossibilities of life in order to make it to the mountain top.

THE VALLEY WALKER MAKES A LONG LASTING DIFFERENCE THROUGH THE VALLEY EXPERIENCE
Psalm 23:4a

"Yea, though I walk through the valley of the shadow of death" This life journey is a forward walk challenging us to be valley walkers, who are called, chosen, and created to minister a word of inner healing and essential wholeness to the broken, the battered, and the bruised brothers and sisters of our deeply hurting humanity. David, whose name means "Beloved," was a valley walker whose life made a lasting difference as a shepherd of the sheep, a prophet, a priest, and a king. Valley walkers move forward through the impossibilities of life in order to make it to the mountain top.

WALKING THROUGH THE VALLEY OF THE SHADOW OF DEATH
Psalm 23:4a

"**Yea, though I walk through the valley of the shadow of death**" A valley is a long depression in the low surface of the land that usually contains a river. A valley formed by flowing water, or river valley, is usually V shaped. The exact shape will depend on the characteristics of the stream flowing through it. Rivers with steep gradients, as in mountain ranges, produce steep walls and a bottom. The Valley of the Shadow of Death that David wrote of in Psalm 23 is located in Israel. The Valley of the Shadow of Death is a place where experienced shepherds would walk their sheep in order to move their sheep forward, onward, and upward to higher ground and to far greater and greener pastures. Valley walkers move forward through the impossibilities of life in order to make it to the mountain top.

I love the song entitled *I'm Going Through* by Danniebelle Hall.

> *I'm going through, I'm going through*
> *I don't care what the rest of the world decides to do*
> *Made up my mind and I ain't gonna turn around, no*
> *Walkin' with my Jesus and I gotta go through*
>
> *I started running this Christian race*
> *Counted up the cost to see if I could stand the pace*
> *Turned my back on the world with Heaven in my view*
> *Made up my mind one day and I gotta go through*

THE VALLEY WALKER LEARNS TO BE FEARLESS OF EVIL THROUGH THE VALLEY EXPERIENCE
Psalm 23:4b

"I will fear no evil"
The valley walker learns to be fearless right in the face of evil even though there is danger in the valley.
The valley walker learns to be fearless right in the face of evil even though there is darkness in the valley.
The valley walker learns to be fearless right in the face of evil even though there is depression in the valley.

THE VALLEY WALKER WALKS WITH THE SHEPHERD THROUGH THE VALLEY EXPERIENCE
Psalm 23:4c

"for thou art with me"
The valley walker is safe, sound, and secure on this dark, dangerous, and depressing forward walk, because the Shepherd is right there leading, guiding, and providing. The Shepherd's presence makes the major difference.

The valley walker is safe, sound, and secure on this dark, dangerous, and depressing forward walk through the valley of the shadow of death, because the Shepherd's presence brings deliverance in the very lowest valleys of real life.

The valley walker is safe, sound, and secure on this dark, dangerous, and depressing forward walk through the valley of the shadow of death, from slippery sloped mountainside edges of the deepest danger, darkness, and depression in order to find divine deliverance and destiny through the guidance of the Shepherd of the Soul. Valley walkers move forward through the impossibilities of life in order to make it to the mountain top.

THE VALLEY WALKER IS COMFORTED THROUGH THE VALLEY EXPERIENCE
Psalm 23:4d

"thy rod and thy staff they comfort me"
The Valley of the Shadow of Death has a side which is a wall of the mountain while the other side of The Valley of the Shadow of Death is an extremely steep and dangerous drop off off the edge.

The shepherd's staff was skillfully utilized to scrape along the very edge of the cliff on The Valley of the Shadow of Death, while the shepherd's rod was strategically utilized to beat the wall of the mountain on The Valley of the Shadow of Death. This would allow the sheep to feel safe, sound, and secure between the sounds of the rod and staff as they travel along the steep cliff's edge. Likewise, we remain safe, sound, and secure through hearing the Word of God through preaching and singing.

Jefferson Hazel Scott, was the second son of the late Deacon Aaron Scott, Sr. and the late Mother Barbara Lee Scott. Jefferson Hazel Scott was born on May 3, 1940, in Clearwater, South Carolina. He departed this life on November 6, 2013, at Good Samaritan Hospital in West Islip, New York. Jefferson Hazel Scott was a graduate of Hempstead High School in

Hempstead, New York and furthered his studies at New York University. Jefferson Hazel Scott accepted Jesus Christ at an early age at the Mount Sinai Baptist Church in Roosevelt, New York, under the leadership of my grandfather, the late Rev. Walter R. Mackey, Sr. He served on the junior usher board and was a member of the junior choir. Jefferson Hazel Scott was a diligent worker who helped with the building of Mount Sinai Baptist Church. Jefferson Hazel Scott was a valley walker.

Upon his graduation from college, Jefferson Hazel Scott began a successful thirty-three year career as a probation officer with the Nassau County Department of Probation. He retired from this position as a supervisor. In the 1960's and 1970's he was an active member of the NAACP and worked diligently to recruit members. Jeff was totally devoted to his family, and was always ready to lend a helping hand both financially and physically. After the death of his father he became a loving and major caregiver of his mother. Valley walkers like Jeff Scott move forward through the impossibilities of life in order to make it to the mountain top. Jeff enjoyed participating in sports, particular, basketball, swimming, and cycling. He touched the lives of many people teaching them to trust God in the valley experience of life knowing that their mountain top experience in on the way. Jefferson Hazel Scott was a valley walker. Brother Scott's hindsight is our foresight to move forward and actually learn with a positive and progressive mindset from the good, bad, and indifferent jagged edged realities of life.

THE VALLEY WALKER HAS A LIFE AFTER THE VALLEY EXPERIENCE

Psalm 23:6

"Surely goodness and mercy shall follow me all the days of my life"

The valley walker is on the forward walk with the Shepherd of the sheep through the valley of the shadow of death and up the mountains of mercy, missions, and ministry to make a major difference by caring, sharing, and bearing the burdens of broken, battered and bruised valley survivors. The valley walker has a real life, a forward walk with the Shepherd of the soul even after the valley experience that will help prepare the valley walker for any future valley experiences. The valley walker keeps it moving with the forward walk with the Shepherd of the sheep, because there is life after the valley. The valley walker keeps it moving with the forward walk with the Shepherd of the soul, because there is life after deep depression. The valley walker keeps it moving with the forward walk with the Shepherd of the sheep, because there is life after devastation. The valley walker keeps it moving with the forward walk with the Shepherd of the soul declaring and decreeing that, "For the rest of my life I'll serve the Lord."

THE VALLEY WALKER HAS ETERNAL LIFE DURING AND AFTER THE VALLEY EXPERIENCE
Psalm 23:6b

"and I will dwell in the house of the Lord for ever"
Jesus Christ is my Lily in the Valley of life. Jesus Christ is my Bright and the Morning Star. Only valley walkers make it fair and square to the mountain top. Only those valley walkers who trust in the Lord in the valley of life dwell in the house of the Lord for ever. It is not too late, valley walker; keep it moving, and trust in the Lord, today. You will never regret it for eternity.

CHAPTER THIRTY-ONE

WHEN FORGIVENESS MAKES THE DIFFERENCE—FORGIVENESS SETS THE SPIRIT, SOUL, AND BODY FREE

Luke 23:33-35:
And when they were come to the place, which is called Calvary, there they crucified him, and the malefactors, one on the right hand, and the other on the left.

Then said Jesus, Father, forgive them; for they know not what they do. And they parted his raiment, and cast lots.

And the people stood beholding. And the rulers also with them derided him, saying, He saved others; let him save himself, if he be Christ, the chosen of God.

Condition of Existence - We all have a common condition of existence. We all need to forgive ignorant people who have done us brutally wrong.

- Moving forward in forgiveness sets the spirit, soul, and body free to do the will of God.
- Moving forward in forgiveness sets the spirit, soul, and body free to fulfill our divine destiny despite the deepest depressions of life.
- Moving forward in forgiveness sets the spirit, soul, and body free to finish our course with joy in spite of constant obstacles and setbacks.
- Moving forward in forgiveness sets the spirit, soul, and body

free to teach, touch, and transform the Holy Spirit to hurting humanity even when we are going through the worst of times ourselves.
- Moving forward in forgiveness sets the spirit, soul, and body free to minister with fresh new meaning, the Master's mission, to the broken, battered, and bruised.
- Moving forward in forgiveness sets the spirit, soul, and body free to care, share, and bear the burdens of the brutalized, demoralized, and stigmatized members of modern day society.
- Moving forward in forgiveness sets the spirit, soul, and body free to deeply love again, deliberately learn again, and desperately laugh again, and again, and again.

1.) **Come To The Place** – Come to the place of your divine destiny. Come to the place of your powerful purpose. Come to the place of your supreme sacrifice. Come to the place of your giving that will pave the way for others better living. Come to the place of your total surrender. Come to the place of the skull. Come to the place— The Cross of Calvary—where Jesus Christ died for the sins of all of hurting humanity past, present, and future. Jesus moved forward through the impossibilities of life.

2.) **Called Calvary** - The Greek word for Calvary is *kranion*, which means a skull. The place of the skull was called Calvary for it was there that Jesus Christ shed His precious blood so that our minds and mindsets could be renewed, revived, and revolutionized. The place of the skull was called Calvary for it was there that Jesus Christ shed His precious blood so that our imperfect wills could line up with His perfect will. The place of the skull was called Calvary for it was there that Jesus Christ shed His precious blood so that our intellects would be wondrously enlightened and empowered by the Eternal Savior of our souls.

3.) **Crucified Christ** – Jesus is the crucified Christ; Jesus moved forward in the power of forgiveness and took our place. Jesus is the crucified Christ; Jesus moved forward in the power of forgiveness and paid our penalty. Jesus is the crucified Christ; Jesus moved forward in the power of forgiveness and took our punishment at the place called Calvary, at the cross of Calvary. The crucified Christ made the difference. Jesus moved forward through the impossibilities of life.

4.) **Cast Lots** – The Roman soldiers cast lots for Jesus' garments, but Jesus forgave them; He wanted His Heavenly Father to forgive them of their ignorance. The Roman soldiers, who whipped an innocent Savior named Jesus, 39 times, cast lots for Jesus' garments, but Jesus forgave them; He clearly asked His Heavenly Father to forgive them of their ignorance. The Roman soldiers, who cruelly put a crown of thorns on Jesus' head, cast lots for Jesus' garments, but Jesus forgave them; He wanted His Heavenly Father to forgive them of their ignorance. The Roman soldiers, who brutally and viciously nailed Jesus' innocent hands to the old rugged cross of Calvary, cast lots for Jesus' garments, but Jesus forgave them; He wanted His Heavenly Father to forgive them of their ignorance. The Roman soldiers, who brutally and viciously nailed the innocent feet of Jesus to the cross of Calvary, cast lots for Jesus' garments, but Jesus forgave them; He wanted His Heavenly Father to forgive them of their ignorance. The Roman soldier, who pierced Jesus in the side, was among those who cast lots for Jesus' garments, but Jesus forgave them; He wanted His Heavenly Father to forgive them of their ignorance. Jesus Christ moved forward and sought forgiveness for those who committed the most unforgivable acts of hatred, pre-planned torture, and powerfully brutal punishment while nailed to an old rugged cross at the place of the skull—Calvary.

- Forgiveness makes the difference when forgiveness is the

order of the day. Dr. Anthony T. Evans, Pastor of Oak Cliff Bible Fellowship in Dallas, Texas, stated the following about forgiveness: "Why do you grant someone forgiveness who doesn't want it, ask for it or even know that you are giving it? Because you need to give it to move forward. It's for you. Let it go."

- Forgiveness makes the difference when forgiveness grows and flows through our very own spirit, soul, and body. Nelson Mandela who said after 27 long years of unjust imprisonment in South Africa that, "As I walked out the door toward the gate that would lead to my freedom, I knew if I didn't leave my bitterness and hatred behind, I'd still be in prison."

- Forgiveness makes the difference when forgiveness grows and flows through our own life in spite of current strife and we can declare and decree with the classic song made famous by the Imperials which simply says,

I'm forgiven
Now I have a reason for living
Jesus keeps giving and giving
Giving till my heart overflows

- Forgiveness makes the difference when forgiveness grows and flows through our own life in spite of current strife as it did in the soul of former South African President Nelson Mandela who remarkably declared and decreed that, "If there are dreams about a beautiful South Africa, there are also roads that lead to their goal. Two of these roads could be named Goodness and Forgiveness."

- Forgiveness makes the difference when we embrace

forgiveness as we move forward and declare and decree the words of Jesus as recorded in **Matthew 6:13-15:**

And lead us not into temptation, but deliver us from evil: For thine is the kingdom, and the power, and the glory, for ever. Amen. For if ye forgive men their trespasses, your heavenly Father will also forgive you: But if ye forgive not men their trespasses, neither will your Father forgive your trespasses.

- Forgiveness makes the difference when we embrace forgiveness as we move forward and declare and decree the words of Jesus as recorded in **Mark 11:24-26:**

Therefore I say unto you, What things soever ye desire, when ye pray, believe that ye receive them, and ye shall have them. And when ye stand praying, forgive, if ye have ought against any: that your Father also which is in heaven may forgive you your trespasses. But if ye do not forgive, neither will your Father which is in heaven forgive your trespasses.

- Forgiveness makes the difference when we embrace forgiveness as we move forward through the impossibilities of life and declare and decree the words of Jesus as recorded in **Luke 6:37:**

Judge not, and ye shall not be judged: condemn not, and ye shall not be condemned: forgive, and ye shall be forgiven:

- Forgiveness makes the difference when we embrace forgiveness as we move forward and declare and decree the words of **Ephesians 4:32:**

And be ye kind one to another, tenderhearted, forgiving one another, even as God for Christ's sake hath forgiven you.

DO YOU KNOW JESUS CHRIST AS YOUR SAVIOR?

If you are reading this book and do not know the Lord Jesus Christ as your personal Savior, please read the following to find out how you can begin a real, personal relationship with Jesus Christ today:

1. **Accept the fact that you are a sinner, and that you have broken God's law.** The Bible says in Ecclesiastes 7:20, "For there is not a just man upon earth that doeth good, and sinneth not." Romans 3:23 says, "For all have sinned and come short of the glory of God."

2. **Accept the fact that there is a penalty for sin.** The Bible states in Romans 6:23, "For the wages of sin is death..."

3. **Accept the fact that you are on the road to hell.** Jesus Christ said in Matthew 10:28, "And fear not them which kill the body, but are not able to kill the soul: but rather fear him which is able to destroy both soul and body in hell."

The Bible says in Revelation 21:8: "But the fearful, and unbelieving, and the abominable, and murderers, and whoremongers and sorcerers, and idolaters, and all liars, shall have their part in the lake which burneth with fire and brimstone: which is the second death."

4. **Accept the fact that you cannot do anything to save yourself!** The Bible states in Ephesians 2:8, 9: "For by grace are ye saved through faith: and that not of yourselves: it is a gift of God. Not of works, lest any man should boast."

5. **Accept the fact that God loves you more than you love yourself, and that He wants to save you from hell.** John 3:16 says, "For God so loved the world, that He gave His only begotten Son, that

whosoever believeth in Him should not perish, but have everlasting life."

6. With these facts in mind, please repent of your sins, believe on the Lord Jesus Christ and pray and ask Him to come into your heart and save you this very moment.

The Bible states in Romans 10:9 and 13: "That if thou shalt confess with thy mouth the Lord Jesus, and shalt believe in thine heart that God hath raised Him from the dead, thou shalt be saved." "For whosoever shall call upon the name of the Lord shall be saved."

7. If you are willing to trust Christ as your Saviour please pray with me the following prayer:

> Heavenly Father, I realize that I am a sinner and that I have sinned against you. For Jesus Christ's sake, please forgive me of all of my sins. I now believe with all of my heart that Jesus Christ died, was buried, and rose again for me. Lord Jesus, please come into my heart, save my soul, change my life, and fill me with your Holy Spirit today and forever. Amen.

If you just trusted Jesus Christ as your Saviour, and you prayed that prayer and meant it from your heart, based upon the Word of God, you are now saved from Hell and you are on your way to Heaven. Welcome to the family of God! Congratulations on doing the most important thing in life and that is trusting Jesus Christ as your Lord and Saviour.

ABOUT THE AUTHOR

ARTHUR L. MACKEY, JR., is the senior pastor of the historic Mount Sinai Baptist Church Cathedral in Roosevelt, New York, owner of I Support Roosevelt Youth Center, and the upcoming Mother Barbie Lee Scott Senior Housing and Mount Sinai Workforce Housing. He is also president of Vision of Victory Ministries and Arthur Mackey Ministries, and Chairman of the Mount Sinai Development Corporation and I Support Roosevelt Youth Center of Long Island. He is a graduate of Virginia Union University in Richmond, Virginia, where he majored in religion and philosophy. He is also a community research assistant in the Office of Communications and Public Affairs for the Town of Hempstead, America's largest township. Pastor Mackey is the noted author of the *Biblical Principles of Success, Walking Through the Doorways of Destiny, Inner Healing for Men, Inner Healing for Women, Real Revival, Revival in the Valley of Dry Bones,* and *Seven Levels of Promise for the Overcomer.* Pastor Mackey has ministered throughout America, Europe, and Africa. He is married to Elder Brenda J. Mackey, a Social Worker and Mental Health Counselor. They have three children: Yolanda, Jordan, and Faith.

www.ingramcontent.com/pod-product-compliance
Lightning Source LLC
Chambersburg PA
CBHW070548100426
42744CB00006B/244